Not Just on S~~undays~~

Seeking God's Purpose in Each New Day

Bonnie Lyn Smith

GROUND TRUTH PRESS

NASHUA, NEW HAMPSHIRE

Not Just on Sundays: Seeking God's Purpose in Each New Day

Published by GROUND TRUTH PRESS
     P. O. Box 7313
     Nashua, NH 03060-7313

Editors: Maryrose Gaymon and Janet Guenther

Cover art: Traci Carmichael, www.tracicarmichael.wix.com/portfolio

Photography: Mandi Dinsmore

First printing 2014

Printed in the United States of America

Some of the anecdotal illustrations in this book are true to life and are included with the permission of the persons involved. All other illustrations are composites of real situations, and any resemblance to people living or dead is coincidental.

Unless otherwise indicated, Scripture quotations are from *The Holy Bible, English Standard Version*® (ESV®). Copyright © 2001 by Crossway, a publishing ministry of Good News Publishers. Used by permission. All rights reserved.

Scripture references marked KJV are from the *King James Version* of the Bible.

All emphases in Scripture quotations have been added by the author.

Trade paperback ISBN-13: 978-0-9908303-0-6

Trade paperback ISBN-10: 0990830306

Publisher's Cataloging-In-Publication Data
(Prepared by The Donohue Group, Inc.)

Smith, Bonnie Lyn.
  Not just on Sundays : seeking God's purpose in each new day / Bonnie Lyn Smith.

  pages ; cm

  Issued also as an ebook.
  Includes bibliographical references.
  ISBN-13: 978-0-9908303-0-6 (trade paperback)
  ISBN-10: 0-9908303-0-6 (trade paperback)

  1. Christian life--Anecdotes. 2. God (Christianity)--Anecdotes. 3. Anecdotes. I. Title.

BV4501.3 .S65 2014
248.4/02   2014916817

Dedication

I dedicate this book first and foremost to my Lord Jesus Christ, the God Who informs my every breath and brings me fresh hope in His finished work of the cross on my behalf—on behalf of us all. It's Your story, breathing through daily life, that I want to tell. It's Your unending love that gives me purpose.

I also dedicate this book to anyone seeking to know Him or know Him better. This book was written for you. I used to think I was just sucking in air, using up oxygen, occupying space on this planet. How I know better now! I have found His purpose through prayer, the reading of His Word, the fellowship and interaction with others, and the daily discipline of asking Him to show me Himself. I hope you find part of your story in these pages. Or maybe you can return to a story you left sitting on a shelf when life smacked you around or you became complacent. That was me—I had shelved my story for a while. But the good news is that even when we're not faithful, He is. He was there for me all along, and He is there for you too. It really is best to read the Bible directly. This book merely skims the surface as to how it relates to daily life. His words are what give life. My goal is simply to illuminate that.

Finally, I dedicate every single page to my wonderful husband and three amazing children. You have dealt with my writing mania days and my disappearing acts for writing retreats. You have informed so much of what I have to say. You have been both my teachers and my muses. Your grace reflects that of the Father, and I thank you for it. Our lives together are sweet blessings dripping down from the honeypot of heaven. I thank God for you.

Proverbs 16:24

Gracious words are like a honeycomb, sweetness to the soul and health to the body.

Acknowledgments

What a precious gift it is to work with such skilled editors. Maryrose Gaymon, over the many years, you have been a rock, both mentor and oasis, never judging, always checking in: the absolute sweetest of unconditional friends. Janet Guenther, dedicated prayer warrior and dear friend, I was so blessed to join you at a Lutheran Bible study years ago; I knew you would review the Scripture in this book and hold me accountable for interpretation.

Pastor Ed, your valuable suggestions gave this book both direction and clarity. It's hard to mention you without using the word "grace." Thank you for your wise counsel and your everyday ministering heart. Your deliberate thoughtfulness and inclusive pastoring encourage us all to seek God's purposes in our lives, bring honor to Him, and hopefully bless others along the way.

I would like to acknowledge my mother, Eleanor, for instilling in me a love of words and teaching me how to write, and my father, Fitz, who has stared three unrelated cancers in the face five times and come out the victor; God has used that as a powerful testimony in your life. To my sister, Heather, every cup of good espresso I raise to you; I'm grateful for the opportunity to grow in the ways of God with you.

I must thank my husband, Mark, and our three blessings from God: Christopher, Caroline, and David. Thank you for letting me be transparent and share all we have learned together as a family so far. We do so well when we remember that Jesus is our center.

Time spent with the following groups of amazing people brought me much personal growth: Moms' Prayer, Women's Book Club, Mom-to-Mom, the (Prayer) Warrior Princesses, Junior High Sunday School class, Calvary Chapel, His Presence Christian Fellowship, New Life Community Church, Island Memorial Chapel, Great Valley Presbyterian Church, and the parents and staff at our local dance studio.

To my writing community—whether it's a blog, medical articles, poetry, or a novel—thanks so much. Keep going; don't ever stop. Your voices have given me great courage. I'm honored to be in your company. Jim Pickett, Mollie Lyon, and Darlene McKenna: Thank you for sharing your publishing journey with me.

Thank you to those friends who have spoken directly and boldly into my life and were willing to walk through valleys as well as scale mountains together. Some of you have journeyed decades with me, shaped who I am, and helped me see the Father in the everyday: Angi Bailey, Micaela Razo, and Denise Reeves, to name a few.

I am so appreciative of, and strengthened by, the prayer support I received for this endeavor. I'm grateful for dear ones prayerfully offering feedback and instruction, or even challenging me when necessary. It makes me a better person and this book stronger.

There would not have been a story to tell without the many people whose lives either appear in or inspired many of these pages. Thank you for letting me share the gift of you: Jennifer Alberghene, Steve and Suzy Allen, Abbigayle Bailey, Kerri Baysinger, Ruth Bendig, Tricia Blaszak, Janine Botha, Rhonda Calvert, Mindy Cantrell, Betsey Chandler, Rebecca Chiasson, Angela Christoffel, Michelle Colasante, Chris and Jolene

DelSanto, Mandi and Madisyn Dinsmore, Juliet Donnell, Paula Fluhrer, Brandi Grebe Fox, the Karl Grindley-Christie Bliss Team, Robyn Hamel, Alma Healey, Amy Lynne Helwig, Amanda Ilg, Robyn Iversen, Micah Johnson, Naomi Jones, RuthMarie Lewis, Hilde Loosigian, Alison Macko, Krista Marcello, Suad Mohamed, Kay Monroe, Ashley Narankevicius, Melissa Ortiz, Cynthia Overman, Merrilynn Peirce, Leslie Phillips, Melanie Plesko, Jennifer Reeves, Jennifer Robb, Lori Robertson, Rianne Rome, Kathy Rowe, Carolyn Veirup, Jean Veseskis, Rose Wanyoike, Garth Wiebe, Tammie Wommack, and Lauren York.

A special thank-you goes to the very kind innkeepers at the Lantana House in Rockport, Massachusetts, where I finished my final draft while you delighted me with selections from the Westminster Choir every morning.

Finally, to Salvatore Brunsvold, "Sam," who married Mark and me in 1993: Your life was snuffed out way too soon, but your works for the Kingdom of God continue in the many student lives you touched. And to my sweet Grandmom Genevieve Hanna: You taught me so much about loving people, staying positive, and cheerleading others toward good. Your investment in my life has informed my understanding of a loving Father in heaven and a Jesus Who loved in the flesh. You have been, and forever will be, the pearl inside my heart.

Contents

Introduction

Being a stay-at-home mom in this season of life when the children are all launched into school, I've spent some time re-evaluating: "Okay, what's next?" I'm still working that out and looking for editing/writing gigs to log a certain number of hours (and ministry opportunities). Stay-at-home mom hours—plotted carefully around three different school bus departures and arrivals—can feel frustrating and pointless at times. But last night, when I was telling my husband (otherwise known as Salad Boy because he's on a fitness kick, eating salads while I shove in pasta by the platefuls) that even dinner didn't turn out right and that I feel like I accomplished nothing all week, he said the wisest words ever said to a mom in that moment, I'm convinced. They were something to the effect of: "You solved a bully problem this week. Our children know they are worth advocating for." Oh yeah, that's right. I did. Not that I should be idle and shouldn't still be productive, but yes, yes I did. And no, I wasn't a fancy engineer solving military communication issues, and nobody offered me a paycheck, but what I did today *mattered*. I am *not*, apparently, *just sucking in air*. Amazing how we can be so critical of ourselves. Truly amazing!

So, I put together this book of anecdotal moments, not only for the stay-at-home mom but for anyone, with or without kids, wondering where purpose might be found. I was raised to focus on academic excellence and achievement, endlessly driven toward all these goals, which, in and of themselves, weren't bad ideals. But what I didn't know was that fulfillment is really spiritual in nature. It's doing what God has purposed for your life each day. If that is folding the laundry and getting one child's character realigned one day, then that is my purpose. On another day, it might be the frenzy of caring for kids, getting them ready for school, listening to and praying for several friends, managing a play date, driving kids to activities, sending an encouraging letter to a different friend or stranger, and packing lunches for the next day.

I used to think that each day had to be measured in how *many* things I checked off my list. Some days are like that, but many days are about just doing a few things *really well*. So, I stopped comparing my days with the productivity of others and started saying: "Lord, please order my steps today." You know what? At times, He directed me toward ministry, but sometimes, He directed me toward rest. Rest was often physical rest, but it also could be going to see a movie or enjoying some coffee time with a friend. Truly "resting" in Him should be easy. We shouldn't be striving. His *yoke is easy*, His *burden is light*, and He never, ever fails. Not ever. For all of these reasons and more, I simply can't stop praising His name!

Matthew 11:28-30, Jesus speaking

"Come to me, all who labor and are heavy laden, and I will give you rest. Take my yoke upon you, and learn from me, for I am gentle and lowly in heart, and you will find rest for your souls. For my yoke is easy, and my burden is light."

Jeremiah 33:3, the Lord speaking through Jeremiah the Prophet

"Call to me and I will answer you, and will tell you great and hidden things that you have not known."

Jeremiah 29:11-13, Jeremiah the Prophet narrating

"For I know the plans I have for you," declares the Lord, "plans for wholeness and not for evil, to give you a future and a hope. Then you will call upon me and come and pray to me, and I will hear you. You will seek me and find me, when you seek me with all your heart."

Part 1
Reflecting the Little Ones

I've worked with children in one way or another since I was a preteen. Like many girls that age, I pretty much babysat my way through junior high and high school (including several vacations here and abroad as a mother's helper). For a brief time, I served as the Children's Ministry Director, which essentially meant running the summer Vacation Bible School Program and coordinating Sunday School and Children's Church teacher volunteers at a church of 250 in Central California, at the ripe ole age of 23. Even though I had none of my own yet, I needed to communicate to others how exciting it was to give of one's time and volunteer teaching other people's children every Sunday for a year at a time. During that time, I also ran a few homeschool seminars about Japan, trying to cater to ages 4 through 12 that were all in the same room at the same time. We would attempt Japanese calligraphy, practice properly holding chopsticks, sing "If You're Happy and You Know It" in Japanese, and discuss cultural differences and similarities. It was mind-blowing how much the children of all ages could absorb in a short time because of their amazing hunger to experience new things and their eagerness to learn.

To our great delight, Salad Boy and I have taught preschool or toddler Sunday School for many of our 21 years together, only very recently having moved on to junior high students. Before moving up to the teenage crowd, I can't tell you how many times we sprayed water to mimic storms at sea while preschool disciples rocked the boat (our row of chairs) before Jesus calmed it; or finger-painted rainbow promises of no more catastrophic, world-altering floods; or built a biblical-times home with LEGO®s to demonstrate the Shunammite woman's hospitality toward Elisha (a lesser known but fascinating story in 2 Kings 4:8) or Paul and Silas breaking out of prison. I am a parent of only 14 years so far, and I remain completely inspired by how children respond to specific people and the community God has placed into their lives. As my own three children grow, I'm constantly refreshed by the way the world enfolds before them, from their vantage point. They always see things that I miss.

Not surprisingly, this section came from encounters with my own children as well as other people's. Adults can learn so much from the simplicity of a child's world, but only if we're willing to stop and take note. My best days are the days when I think like a child. When I hear my kids approach a problem, so simply, so purely, I can recapture that innocence for a few minutes, even as an adult. I can be calmer, stop to admire more, and drink more deeply from the cup of life. And, oh my goodness, guess what else I can do when I respond like a child? I can *slow way down*. I think if we really stop to listen, most days, children make wonderful muses, even when they struggle to right the unfair things of the world, twist in frustration over not feeling big enough to have a voice, and are disappointed or scared.

I learn so much about God when I look at His wee ones. In that place of humility, I realize how much more I still have to learn. Through their lenses, I can see more clearly the Father Who has all the patience in the world to teach me, one of His little ones, as I try to find my own appropriate voice. This developing voice of mine may squeak at times and boom at others, working out my temper tantrums with intermittent bursts of faith, but like a trusting, love-hungry, eager-to-please child, I want to dialogue with Him, and about Him, as honestly as I can.

At the end of the day, walking with an Almighty God is entirely about relationship, and that's what children grasp so beautifully but so many of us adults fall short of understanding. They don't stand in the place of failure for endless seasons of regret like we do. Instead, they eagerly capture grace and forgiveness and get right back up again because that's what He intended. Anyone who works closely with children knows how much grace weaves itself into each tender heart and soul and how much children respond to it. They are closer to hearing His holy whisper, most days, than those of us believing the lie that we are tainted and weighed down by the darker, heavier things of life forever. We think we are permanently stuck, but they know they can still climb onto His lap and find unconditional, infinite affection. A loving teacher or coach models this. So does a good parent. And in healthy interactions, children live this way with their whole hearts, out loud and bouncy with hope. Jesus valued them deeply, enough to set them as a model for how we adults should approach Him. I'm very happy to go back to that place and find Him there. That's a place I like to cuddle up to and heal my heart wounds, a place where He speaks deep truth to my soul. Won't you join me in traveling there?

Matthew 18:10, Jesus speaking

"See that you do not despise one of these little ones. For I tell you that in heaven their angels always see the face of my Father who is in heaven."

Mark 9:36-37, Apostle[1] John-Mark narrating

And he [Jesus] took a child and put him in the midst of them, and taking him in his arms, he said to them,

"Whoever receives one such child in my name receives me, and whoever receives me, receives not me but him who sent me."

What Preschool Bonnie Learned Today in Sunday School

Matthew 19:13-15, Apostle Matthew narrating

Then children were brought to him that he might lay his hands on them and pray.
The disciples rebuked the people,
but Jesus said, "Let the little children come to me and do not hinder them, for to such belongs the kingdom of heaven."
And he laid his hands on them and went away.

This was my Sunday School lesson with the preschoolers one day: Jesus always has time for you. We made clocks with a cross that went around marking the time, reminding us that He is with us each hour of the day. There is no time when He is too busy for us. To see how excited they were helped me reflect more on this truth. Jesus was likely weary and tired but would not let the disciples turn away the children, even though the disciples, perhaps a little protectively of Jesus as well as a bit selfishly, wanted to turn them away. How often do we, acting as the disciples in this case, push people away from God because we ourselves are so stingy with our time? We have limits to what we want to give. His arms are always open wide. Ours need to be as well. We can't do this on our own, but He enables us.

According to tradition at the time, parents brought their children to the rabbis to be blessed. That is essentially what these parents were doing, and Jesus did not turn them away, weary as He was. How often do we as parents remember to bring our children to the Rabbi for a blessing? Are we too busy? Because the Rabbi isn't.

I learned two things from this lesson in my "preschool mind," which is frequently where I need to meet Jesus. With my childlike heart. With my full vulnerability. With full and not-withholding trust. Adult

Bonnie is often jaded, pessimistic, withholding, loaded with trust issues, guarded, insecure, conditional. Preschool Bonnie loved with her whole heart, and her whole heart was open to what Jesus would do. So, in these moments of teaching, Preschool Bonnie woke up again and learned:

1) **Jesus is not only for adults and not only in churches.** He was and is very much for the children. Did I know this intellectually already? Yes. Did I grasp the many incredible nuances of that before today? Not really. Not until I saw twinkly, bright-eyed children hear in Preschool-ese that Jesus goes around the whole clock with them. He isn't in the kitchen too busy making dinner. He isn't too busy doing homework. He isn't too busy at all. Not for anyone. Not for the persecuted, the widow, the sick, the addicted. Not anyone.

I remember this hitting home a bit when I went to Japan as a college student at age 19. In a country so very pantheistic with less than 2 percent (at the time) of its population claiming belief in Christ, I think I expected God not to show up. (This notion is ridiculous from a theological perspective since He always indwells a Christian believer with His Holy Spirit; technically, He always comes with those of us who profess our faith in Christ.) Boy, was I in for a shock!

He was very real and very much with me when I greeted my new parents for the next four months, trusting all over to folks who barely could communicate with me besides the sweet, yet misspelled (in English) sign they held up for me. God was all over Japan. Because most of the people in Japan don't know Him, they don't see Him in the everyday. But my Rabbi was definitely there and was not too busy to make sure I figured out which wrong bus I took in the middle of the night to get back to my host family's home. To help me speak fluently when I had no choice. To know when my American presence was not welcomed in certain places, and to know which gentle words to use when World War II was still on the older generation's mind, and they wanted me to know that. He gave me healing words for them. I had none of my own at 19. But the Rabbi wasn't too busy. He filled my mouth with words that united, not divided. Jesus does indeed travel the clock with us. He crosses the international dateline as well. I found that out many years later in my move to the Marshall Islands.[2] And He doesn't discriminate based on what age we are or how long we have trusted in Him. Again, I knew this with my intellect. But in practice, I had to find out if my Rabbi really was everywhere at all times to offer a blessing. I can assure you that He is.

2) **Jesus was likely weary when He made sure the disciples didn't turn the parents and children away.** While it doesn't state it directly in this passage, we know from the Apostle John-Mark's account of Jesus and the Samaritan woman at the well in John 4:6[3] that Jesus grew tired. He was God-man walking the earth at that time, very much human experientially, and dealing with crowds was exhausting. He could have drawn a boundary: "No more today. Tell them to come back tomorrow." After all, isn't that what I do all of the time, with my kids, with needy folks, with many other things pulling on me? Don't get me wrong: We can't, as humans, say yes to everything, but I thank my Rabbi that He doesn't turn *me* away. When I needed to learn some hard lessons in the Marshall Islands, He could have easily rolled His eyes at me and said: "Haven't we done this lesson a thousand times?" but instead He still taught me gently all over again. He does not turn away. Only we do that. Only we

put limits on Him, as in "Surely this time I've done it! He is definitely going to give up on me now." That is not at all what He says in His Word.

And those disciples...they were being protective and controlling, perhaps. They didn't get it. They thought there were limits too. They learned, in time, each at his own pace, that He doesn't have our limits. He loves with arms open wide enough to hold a whole sinful world on His shoulders and bear our iniquities. Imagine those children when Jesus's voice called out gently, welcoming, drowning out the nay-saying, negative disciples.

In class, as we talked about how the children ran to Jesus, I asked the kids: "Do we run too?" At times I think we only walk or stumble to Jesus. Personally, I'd rather have my running feet on to catch a blessing. Personally, I'd rather leap to my Lord. Adult Bonnie hangs her head in shame and slowly m-e-a-n-d-e-r-s her way to the Rabbi, often taking the long path, often procrastinating, self-justifying. Preschool Bonnie has her old black Mary Janes on, and while she may slip and slide with little tread, stockings half at her ankles trying to hold her back in that twirly skirt, she somehow makes it to the Rabbi quickly. She trusts completely. She knows her Rabbi and the blessing He offers. She knows He won't turn away.

Adult Bonnie, let me introduce you to Preschool Bonnie. She has such a pure heart. She sits at the feet of Jesus, and there is no clock or frantic schedule there—only my sweet, sweet Rabbi.

Dreams of Splendor

This particular entry was written after starting the book *Captivating: Unveiling the Mystery of a Woman's Soul*, by John and Stasi Eldredge.[4] If you are a woman and haven't read it, it's a must. With my only daughter's waking-up, delicate arms wrapped tightly around my neck, yawn-stretching her sweet little face against mine one morning, I (Bonnie) thought to myself:

> You are so precious, my daughter. Oh, that you would know what a treasure you are and save your heart for a deserving gentleman someday, that you wouldn't settle, and that you would know your incredible worth and purpose as an individual, created to show God's compassion to others. That you would shine for Him and be God's girl in all that you do. That others would encounter you and never be the same for the amazing beauty of your soul that reflects a little bit of heaven here on earth. That's what I want for you, my sweet child. You don't have to take anything less: not the negativity nor cynicism around you. You can be truly beautiful, inside and out.

And then, a few days later, I saw that same little girl skipping into the house after school, and her first thought was giving her older brother the smart-phone-design eraser she bought him at the book fair. Chickie, I love how you love *big*! Also sweet, Older Brother, not annoyed by her vigorous knock on the door, let her in and made an appropriately kind response, which was him stretching outside his comfort zone and usual flat tone. I knew they very well could start a shouting match over something dumb within the hour, so I chose to soak in the beauty of that moment. Yeah, pretty much sucked it down with a straw, like the caramel at the bottom of an iced caramel swirl latte. It's only there for a minute, but while it is, it is *beyond awesome*!

But what I see in that moment, as tender as their brief after-school interaction was, is the skipping. Why is that the part I focus on? Because when my daughter flits and flutters around the house, I see carefree childhood. I see love and joy and hope. I see delight in things big and small. And I see that today is a day when heaviness doesn't weigh down her heart and her biggest thought is to give her brother an eraser she bought especially for him. In her skipping, I see her innocence preserved, her childhood held sacred, her femininity speaking loudly, and her dreams of splendor. She dances around with big dreams in her heart—and something inside me heals. Something that was broken starts to fuse, and I can rest in the fact that whatever words of correction I offered her this morning did not tear her apart. I can know that she weathered it, and other than her temporary "sting" in my discipline, she moved on and looked up, her dreams intact.

I want to dream like Chickie does. It makes me wonder, and think more deeply on, which dreams have been planted in each of our hearts? I might see her as a certain profession or giftedness one day, but she may see herself as another. We each need to listen to what God tells us. We need to see where He is leading our children instead of telling Him where to lead them. One child looks like he has great potential to be an engineer, but he definitely wants composing music to remain a part of his life. What if I told him to pursue engineering and missed that Chickie was my engineer? Or what if a great composer could arise out of our family, but I was too stuck on what I could see, and I missed his dreams, the ones God gave him?[5]

And what about me? Most days I want to write. Like crazy. Often at the expense of almost every other priority. But even though I believe that is the passion He has put into my heart, there are days I hear a different instruction. When I remember to start my day off prayerfully, He frequently tells me to do something else: call this person, go visit that person, bring a gift to this one. I love ministry, but I also adore my writing cave. He knows this, and He also knows that I whine because I get edgy when I can't write, but when He gives me something outside today's dream to do, I am much more peaceful and joyful following His direction for that day, or even a season. I'm not suggesting we take off work all of the time to meet endless needs (and there will always be more to meet). But I am saying that the dreams we hold onto need to be kept on a loose tether where He still gets to lead. Even in our chosen career, job, or other pursuit, there must be room for Him to flex us. It's so easy to resist this, but my dreams of splendor, or yours, are only going to rock this world for the better when He is behind and ahead of us, His glory being the "splendor." So, as King David says in Psalm 139, "You hem me in, behind and before, and lay your hand upon me," "You have searched me and known me," and "You...are acquainted with all my ways."

Dear God: Please breathe Your purposes, hopes, and dreams where You want them to be. Order them in my life, my spouse's life, my children's lives.

Psalm 139:1-6, King David speaking to God when he was made king over Israel

O LORD, you have searched me and known me!
You know when I sit down and when I rise up;
you discern my thoughts from afar.
You search out my path and my lying down
and are acquainted with all my ways.

Even before a word is on my tongue,
behold, O LORD, you know it altogether.
You hem me in, behind and before,
and lay your hand upon me.
Such knowledge is too wonderful for me;
it is high; I cannot attain it.

Also, take the reins away from my greedy, little controlling paws, and show me the good works that I was created to do. If You've prepared the good works beforehand, who am I to argue or fight it? I want to live where Your assigned good works, Your purposes, and the dreams You have given me all converge. I'm pretty sure that's where Your splendor and glory are as well, because at the end of the day, if I'm doing what You've purposed for me, I'm fulfilling the dream, and others should be pointed toward You. Amen.

Ephesians 2:10, Apostle Paul speaking

For we are his workmanship, created in Christ Jesus for good works, which God prepared beforehand, that we should walk in them.

Lessons From Frogger-oggy

Here begins a story about a stuffed (very unattractive) frog that we brought home from Australia when we enjoyed living in that part of the world. The only reasons it hasn't made it to a trash can or donation bin by now are because it is a memory from Australia and my sons won it together at one of those carnival stands at an amusement park in Sydney. That makes two hoarders in my house imploring me to never let go of it. But Frogger-oggy has some major issues. For one, he keeps tearing his cheap "epidermis," and his stuffing keeps leaking out. So, yesterday I set aside time to poke a needle and thread through him a few times to close these holes and then publicly congratulated myself on social media that I had fixed all of his issues (and there were many). I reveled in that the rest of the day, eagerly anticipating the fuzzy redhead finding him on his bunk bed ladder all fixed. I pictured squeals of delight, maybe even a spider-monkey hug of gratefulness. But when he saw the frog, instead of my beautiful scenario of a stuffed animal welcomed back into the club after being properly "doctored," Little Man declared: "His heel is still ripped." *What*?! I had seen a lovely assortment of other ailments to fix, but I apparently missed the very one I had been directly commissioned to repair.

And so it is with us. We walk around thinking we see the obvious "repairs" needed in someone, but we can't see them all. We miss the big picture. Maybe this one disappointment issue here, this past regret there, and that heartache there can be patched up, but we fail to see the leak springing up in someone in a completely different place. Well-intentioned and big-hearted though we may be, we can't sew a patch fast enough to get to the next place where healing is needed. But our heavenly Father can. He sees where we are coming undone, where we are thread-bare and soul-hungry, tired and spent. He sees each Frogger-oggy with eyes that know the holes and then also with eyes that see the redeemed, whole, sanctified version after we receive what He has already offered us.

When His Son hung on the cross, it was for those holes in us. He became like Frogger-oggy, riddled with our holes that He himself did not deserve in any way, so He could emerge from the grave victorious and present us with the gift of eternal life and restored holes. This side of heaven, I still need to be patched up, but when I take each hole to Him, it is truly repaired. Supernaturally healed! The stuffing can no longer pop out in that place. Unlike me, the amateur sewing mom with blurred vision for all of Frogger-oggy's issues, He sees me just as I am and knows exactly how and when I will finally submit each rip and tear to His Holy Stitching, and He stitches me with a glorious golden thread that says: "I made you. You are beautiful. You are accepted, and you are greatly loved."

Psalm 139:13-18, King David speaking to God when he was made king over Israel

For you formed my inward parts;
you knitted me together in my mother's womb.

I praise you, for I am fearfully and wonderfully made.
Wonderful are your works;
my soul knows it very well.

My frame was not hidden from you,
when I was being made in secret,
intricately woven in the depths of the earth.

Your eyes saw my unformed substance;
in your book were written, every one of them,
the days that were formed for me,
when as yet there was none of them.

How precious to me are your thoughts, O God!
How vast is the sum of them!

If I would count them, they are more than the sand.
I awake, and I am still with you.

Snakes at Our Feet

There it was: on the floor of a child's room, that wooden snake from a long ago something-or-other that we went to where we bought this souvenir. A snake that actually bends and twists. So cool. It had been a favorite of my children for years. The snake isn't scary; it's subtle. Hmmm. But as I got some folded clothes out of that room, I also saw the paper-and-popsicle-stick cross on his dresser from some Vacation Bible School event.

And then I got to thinking: I am going to put the cross over the snake, symbolically, and see if my son picks up on the symbolism when he returns home from school. Because the snake isn't scary when we think it's at a distance from us, but the problem is, it's at our feet before we know it, slinking around. But the cross! And that wonderful Savior Who hung on that cross! That snake is destined to be under our heel because of what Jesus did at the cross. We don't have to fear it if we know Jesus. There is such power in the name of Jesus. I want the truth of the cross daily reminding me that the snake has been conquered; the truth sends it slithering away into the shadows where it belongs. The snake likes to come in and lisp out lies, wrong suggestions, and temptations. But we mustn't forget that the heel of Christ crushed his head already. It was foretold in Genesis long before Christ was born, and it is now finished! Cross trumps snake!

Genesis 3:13-15, Moses speaking

Then the LORD God said to the woman, "What is this that you have done?" The woman said, "The serpent deceived me, and I ate."

The LORD God said to the serpent,

"Because you have done this,
cursed are you above all livestock
and above all beasts of the field;
on your belly you shall go,
and dust you shall eat
all the days of your life.
I will put enmity between you and the woman,
and between your offspring and her offspring;
he shall bruise your head,
and you shall bruise his heel."

Keeping the Dreads Because That's Just How I Roll

> Grateful for friend time this morning and part of the afternoon. Could have chatted our way into next year, and she didn't mind the fact I have partial dreads on one side of my head out in public. Now, that's a good friend!

Okay, so that was my Facebook post that day. Seems like it requires a bit of a rewind....

Some of the things I completely delight in are the little surprises of parenting. Midlife has hit me, and sometimes I find myself catching little catnaps on the couch. One day I woke up to find my hair broken out into about seven tiny braids. I looked a bit Rastafarian—well, for me anyway. The fact my daughter took the time to do that made me smile and not want to undo the moment. It's a bit more dignified than the days of wearing baby spit-up on my shoulder, for sure, but it's still intimidating to show up to a local sandwich shop with the dreads still in, especially when that's not my usual look, nor did the rest of my head match. I was meeting up with a classy friend who would be amused at my hairdo but perhaps a bit confused why I wore it "out" that day. And that made me laugh even harder, thinking of that, so I had to do it. I can be pure ornery that way.

It made me think of John the Baptist.[6] He didn't care at all what folks thought of his camel-skin get-up and locust diet. He was as wild as they come, if you think about it, but he was God-wild. He had a purpose. He knew he was calling out in the desert the name of someone coming Who was so much greater. He went out as he was assigned, not adding anything or taking anything away. God didn't tell him to cloak himself in fine robes or even a multicolor coat like Joseph's. In some ways, John was a "Dreads for Jesus" kind of guy.

I want to be more like that. I want to care less about what my outward appearance conveys or how together I seem, and I want to wear whatever Jesus wants to dress me in that day, so to speak. Some days my best conversations come from the pajama-bottom mornings as I drop the missed-the-bus-kid off again and run into another mom. (Since said child for the longest time did not have the upper arm strength to shut the van door, "this girl" had the immense pleasure of getting out of the van in front of the very sophisticated principal and multiple parents behind me and shut it for him—on the other side of the vehicle no less. I hadn't thought about what I was wearing when I boarded my vehicle that morning. Not at all.) Sometimes the no-makeup, messy-bun, holes-in-my-shoes outings are the ones in which I am used by God the most frequently. Now, I'm not saying God can't be evident in the interactions of folks dressed to the nines. He knows no socioeconomic boundary. But He does want us to drop everything and follow Him. Every day. I think, at times, that means dropping the cell phone, the iPad, the trendy yoga pants, and just follow Him out the door. Because those things are wrong to have? No. Because they distract us.

I am often most approachable and "real" to the person sitting next to me at the library when I am rocking the real and raw Bonnie. Somehow it tears walls down, or perhaps it merely prevents them from going up in the first place. People often need to feel graced by us in our simplest form, to know that we, too, might have had a "keeping it real" morning, and that, along with no cosmetic face paint that day, was a backstory a mile long. This backstory might have included (but this is hypothetical, of course) any or all (trust me, *all*) of the following: 20 minutes to wake up the middle schooler, finding the husband ate the last of the only bagel flavor the kid whose lunch I was packing would eat, an argument upstairs between the younger two who shouldn't even be awake yet, the garbage truck going by right when the thought occurred to me that the trash hadn't been taken out, and seeing a mouse in the trap of the potholder drawer. Yeah, something like that. Well, that's just one example.

But I bet the woman next to me in the grocery checkout line has a similar story, a need to be heard, a desire to have some love or hope—or both. She might need to know that I'm rocking the kid-designed dreads so she can see if I am safe, if she can vent, if I will listen. She needs to know Jesus; she doesn't necessarily need to know me. But she needs to feel His cloak close enough to touch. She needs to see the bare sandals, the basin to wash her feet, the humble carpenter-turned-Rabbi. I am none of those things, but I can be humble. I can be safe. I can be this way only through Christ Who strengthens me.

Philippians 4:11-13, Apostle Paul speaking

Not that I am speaking of being in need, for I have learned in whatever situation I am to be content. I know how to be brought low, and I know how to abound. In any and every circumstance, I have learned the secret of facing plenty and hunger, abundance and need. I can do all things through him who strengthens me.

The other lesson the dreads morning taught me was that what our kids do is beautiful and creative. I can wear "inconvenient" for a few moments if it means the message of love they are sending me can get through, felt, heard, acknowledged. Following Jesus can be inconvenient, but I propose that wearing the plaits He puts on us, in obedience, not only shows Him how much we love and trust Him, but it also shows a frightened world Who He is and that He's safe. I think that's what all followers of Christ ultimately want to do: let Him mold us and help us to reach a frightened and lost world.

Isaiah 64:8, Isaiah the Prophet[7] speaking

But now, O LORD, you are our Father; we are the clay, and you are our potter; we are all the work of your hand.

John 3:17, Apostle John speaking

For God did not send his Son into the world to condemn the world, but in order that the world might be saved through him.

Dave, Jr.: I Once Was Lost but Now Am Found

We celebrate small moments in our house. Yesterday, after renewing our prayers for "the search," calling it back on after thinking we left Dave, Jr. (yes, we name our stuffed toys after ourselves) in Canada this past summer, our missing toy was found. After a long separation, our Dave, Jr., has finally come home, and we broke out a feast of hot chocolate (and coffee) to celebrate. Oh, the joy at seeing our prodigal blue fuzzy thingie come home. We danced, we laughed, we cried, and we welcomed him back into our bunk bed. There is much celebration afoot in our home. It's never too late, Dave, Jr., to set things right. As the Father loves us, so we love you. The door is always open.

My kids thought I was a bit crazy using this analogy for a stuffed toy. I even went so far as to take his picture with a sign propped up against him that said: "I once was lost but now am found" and posted it on Facebook. I admit I was trying to amuse folks because even those among my friends and family who don't follow Jesus are familiar enough with that story. But my main point in posting it was to generate thought and discussion. I want people to consider whether they feel "lost" or not. In my everyday interactions in my community, I find that some feel completely lost and without hope, but more often than not, a few, when forced to think about it, are willing to admit that they feel this way in one or more areas of their lives. This is an inroad to deeper exploration. Part of why my son's stuffed toy made his Facebook debut was because people need to hear the message that they can be found again, that it's not over, that the rest of the script is not written, that it's not all a cruel joke.

To back up, our friend Dave, Jr., went with us to Canada to see Niagara Falls, where we stayed in a KOA cabin that made for a great adventure but one that most of us would rather not remember. Dave, Jr., had found his piggyback spot on Little Man's backpack, along with several other clip-on stuffies the size of a Valencia orange. Somewhere along the line (and I have his "there" and "no longer there" moments documented in photos), Dave, Jr., jumped off the beloved backpack and went AWOL. I remember that at the time we dismissed it as more than likely that he was packed somewhere else for the ride home—until we got home and unpacked. At that point, Dave, Jr., was notably absent. This caused all kinds of distress among all three kids because if there's one thing my kids aren't, it's able to let things go. Yeah, we're all pretty intense people. We mourned the loss of Dave, Jr., while I tried to keep a little flame alive that someday he would resurface. Maybe I can't let go either.

Fast-forward to about six months later when one of the kids revisited the subject. I think it was my daughter because I vaguely remember giving her the stink-eye for bringing the topic up again to the sensitive, deeply feeling younger brother. At that point, I privately discussed with my daughter the possibility of finding a new Dave, Jr. (he was still "on the market") and rolling him around a bit in dirt and spit until he matched the original, resurrecting himself one fine day very soon. Just as I had shamefully resorted to one of the oldest parent tricks in the book, I decided to do my due diligence of dusting under Little Man's bed. It was my way of shaking the guilt of not fighting the forces of dust more faithfully on a weekly basis for my asthmatic son. But I gave up too soon, and Oldest took over. And behind one gigantic dust bunny, tucked around the corner from a plastic clothing bin under the bed, was, to our great surprise, our little blue friend. He looked as spit-soaked and dirty as I had remembered, with a pinch of spiderweb and dash of hair and dust. Out he came, where all three children rejoiced as if we had told them school was out four months early this year. And that was where this story really began...

Upon the return of our sweet friend, I thought about how lost I would feel in every part of my life without Jesus. How do I know this? Because there are times I give him 75 percent of the areas in my life that need surrender but not the other 25 percent. The truth is that when I don't give Him the relational difficulty, the bully issue one of my children is dealing with at school, an ongoing insecurity that I need put to rest, etc., it's like something is gnawing away at me from the inside out. I can't imagine letting all 100 percent of me fly solo. That's a very scary thought. So, I not only want to give more of myself to Him every day so that I can truly live it and be even healthier, but also so others can see how we "take every thought captive" one thought at a time.

2 Corinthians 10:5, Apostle Paul speaking

We destroy arguments and every lofty opinion raised against the knowledge of God, and take every thought captive to obey Christ.

Often folks aren't ready to dive 100 percent into a life that acknowledges Jesus. Like any relationship, they need to test the waters, giving Him only one piece at a time, to see if He is trustworthy, especially if they have been hurt somehow in the church by the understandable imperfections of believers. So, I saw Dave, Jr., as a perfect illustration of not only the prodigal son returning home, but also the idea that we can start that relationship with Jesus no matter where we are on that spectrum of "lost" or disillusioned. I have no idea how Dave, Jr., went from being presumably lost in a tiny cabin on the outskirts of Toronto to landing under the bed of the child who cherished him, but the point was: He could be found again. And thank You, Jesus, so can we. So can we indeed—one dust bunny moved out of the way at a time.[8]

Can We Bless Those Who Curse Us?

Tonight my oldest showed me a paper he had written for school. Impressed, I mentioned how amazed I was that he knew how to organize and prove something in a five-paragraph paper, and asked was that because of his Massachusetts standardized test, long composition training? He replied that he credits a former language arts teacher for his ability to do this well now.

At this point, my heart kind of skipped a beat as I remembered a teacher who never seemed to "get him" or even be very kind at times. And while that was a struggle for him and a huge disappointment to have to face her every day (for two subjects) for an entire school year, he credits her in full humility for this awesome skill.

These are the small moments in life I celebrate. Each and every one. Because a kid who can weather a year of being really misunderstood now rises up to call her blessed (at least in this one area) and give credit where credit is due. And you know what? I'm going to email her one simple sentence telling her that he credits her with progress he had made in that area. Because, while we had some hard conversations last year about her perceived lack of grace, I want to let her know where she hit a home run. She may not have chosen to encourage him that particular year for whatever reason, but that doesn't excuse us from blessing her. It's our own behavior we need to tend, as James and Jesus state in the verses that follow. I learned a huge lesson from my middle schooler tonight. May I always remain as teachable as this one small moment in time.

James 3:9-12, James, brother of Jesus, speaking

With it [tongue] we bless our Lord and Father, and with it we curse people who are made in the likeness of God.

From the same mouth come blessing and cursing. My brothers, these things ought not to be so.

Does a spring pour forth from the same opening both fresh and salt water?

Can a fig tree, my brothers, bear olives, or a grapevine produce figs? Neither can a salt pond yield fresh water.

Luke 6:27-36, Jesus speaking

"But I say to you who hear, Love your enemies, do good to those who hate you, bless those who curse you, pray for those who abuse you. To one who strikes you on the cheek, offer the other also, and from one who takes away your cloak do not withhold your tunic either. Give to everyone who begs from you, and from one who takes away your goods do not demand them back. And as you wish that others would do to you, do so to them.

"If you love those who love you, what benefit is that to you? For even sinners love those who love them. And if you do good to those who do good to you, what benefit is that to you? For even sinners do the same. And if you lend to those from whom you expect to receive, what credit is that to you? Even sinners lend to sinners, to get back the same amount. But love your enemies, and do good, and lend, expecting nothing in return, and your reward will be great, and you will be sons of the Most High, for he is kind to the ungrateful and the evil. Be merciful, even as your Father is merciful."

Ninja Marshmallow and Other Brave Warriors

My youngest guy is a collector. Frequently, that manifests itself in small gumball machine toys, superhero toys, and obscure art materials. When I say obscure, what I really mean is fluffy, squishy, marshmallow-looking, white, cylindrical puffs. In fact, I'm pretty sure they were intended to make s'more crafts somewhere along the way but got lost in the wrong section of the craft store. Regardless, one of his most favorite passions, recently, is to make faces on them, turning them into models of members of our family —red hair and all—superheroes, animals, you name it. Just this week, I came downstairs at o'dark-thirty to start the lunch-making process for my middle school child, and without clearing the sleep from my eyes or even starting that comforting whir of the coffee machine, I faced a small, yet fierce, character on the countertop straight on, looking me in the face, daring me to contest his prowess. This intimidating character was none other than a little dude I have affectionately named "Ninja Marshmallow."

Besides the more obvious amusement I experienced at seeing the latest marshmallow creation and reflecting on my son's creativity and the fascinating, vast tundra that must be his mind, I was struck by how, oftentimes, the fiercest warriors come from the unlikeliest of places. I'm sure on some level, for those of us with Sunday School backgrounds, our minds automatically go to the little shepherd boy David, youngest of a clan of brothers, who all had greater strength, more years on this planet, and bigger muscles, and yet it was David who defeated the giant Goliath. But I'm thinking of something much more subtle: um, *us*! When I speak to my kids about what their hopes and dreams are, I encourage them to call in the impossible. On a micro level, when I speak to them about that mountain right in front of them, I try to remind them we have a big God. He takes us lightweight, fluffy, barely-flexed-our-pathetic-muscles followers and makes God's ninjas out of us. It doesn't matter if it's a difficult authority figure, an unrelentingly unkind peer, seemingly insurmountable academic or athletic challenges, or even family problems within the house. He shows Himself strong in our weakness.

So as the kids go out the door, I remind them we are really strong where we think we are weak. A case of mind over matter? No. A case of a mighty God taking marshmallow people like us, cloaking them with His power and grace, and putting them on the countertop in front of significant problems to battle and partner with Him against forces of darkness. Why? To set the captives free, to speak encouragement and hope in hopeless situations, to breathe the fresh life that comes from His Word. The question isn't so much whether we are marshmallows with ninja potential. The question is really: Are we willing to let Him dress us up any way He wants in each situation to reach an individual, to deposit His amazing love, or to war against evil? The question is: Are we going to be put on any countertop anytime He wants, or are we going to try to call the shots, control the opportunities, only respond when our plan lines up with the request to be in a certain time and place?

When I walked down to the kitchen that morning, I didn't know an art marshmallow character would be waiting, albeit a ninja one. I bet he didn't either. That little guy, less than an inch tall, was completely controlled by the whims of my seven-year-old son, a very imaginative one no less. That's how I think of God: infinitely creative and imaginative, waiting to place us in some truly awesome scenarios. I surely hope I agree every day when I wake up, every hour when something else distracts me, that I yield to being the marshmallow in His hand: ninja, lioness, superheroine, or whatever else He calls me to—whatever markers and glue He wants to use to make me be *all things to all people* that day.

1 Corinthians 9:19-23, Apostle Paul speaking

For though I am free from all, I have made myself a servant to all, that I might win more of them. To the Jews I became as a Jew, in order to win Jews. To those under the law I became as one under the law (though not being myself under the law) that I might win those under the law. To those outside the law I became as one outside the law (not being outside the law of God but under the law of Christ) that I might win those outside the law. To the weak I became weak, that I might win the weak. I have become all things to all people, that by all means I might save some. I do it all for the sake of the gospel, that I may share with them in its blessings.

Isaiah 64:8, Isaiah the Prophet speaking

But now, O LORD, you are our Father; we are the clay, and you are our potter; we are all the work of your hand.

2 Corinthians 12:8-10, Apostle Paul speaking

Three times I pleaded with the Lord about this, that it should leave me. But he said to me, "My grace is sufficient for you, for my power is made perfect in weakness." Therefore I will boast all the more gladly of my weaknesses, so that the power of Christ may rest upon me. For the sake of Christ, then, I am content with weaknesses, insults, hardships, persecutions, and calamities. For when I am weak, then I am strong.

Swimming With Sharks

> Dreamer Little Man this morning to Skeptical Chickie: "You know, when I was little, Mom swam with sharks!"
> Chickie: "No, she didn't! Mom didn't swim with sharks."
> Little Man: "Yes, she did. She even showed me a picture."
>
> So, I think I know the confusion that came from our little jaunt to the Great Barrier Reef many years ago, although Mark was the one diving (not sure about the sharks). Either that, or Little Man remembers the nurse sharks in the lagoon in the Marshall Islands when we lived there. Either way, I'm all about the metaphor there. "Mom swims with sharks" makes him feel safe, makes me sound like some kind of a warrior parent, and I think for about five seconds, I made it onto his growing list of superheroes. I'm good with that.

This Facebook post was written a few weeks after the Boston Marathon bombings, during which this book was written, where folks from my town ended up in the hospital on a day that started with much promise and happy energy. I don't claim to be the first person to think about this, but I finally have found the words to explain what bothers me about the way our culture responds to children after bombings and school shootings.

At breakfast this morning, my smallest son told me that a well-meaning staff member at his school told another child he was wrong when that child stated he "knew how to make poison for strangers." Now, yes, that would need to be explored to make sure it wasn't something hostile or of ill intent behind it, but knowing that child and also male children in general, here's my take on it: That child was expressing, indirectly, that the world feels unsafe, and he needs to be prepared to keep himself and others safe. I heard a protector in that. I heard a young child want to restore order after chaos. To be clear, I don't fault the staff member. Her intent was good, and she was absolutely doing her job.

More than bombings and shootings, what scares me most, in the generation currently in childhood, is that the message they will hear is "correctspeak," to make all of us adults feel comfortable, and it will rip out their very identities. Little boys, especially, are being taught it's wrong to have any protective thoughts at all. Can I simply scream against our culture: It isn't! We need this generation to grow up and be enforcers of the law (some of them), whether that is military or police or what have you. Little boys, especially, are wired to protect and defend. I am weary of well-meaning folks telling children that they are wrong for thinking that way. If we were in a country that lived through daily bombings, I'm pretty sure we wouldn't want to raise a passive generation. I don't want a violent generation either. I want a generation that recognizes and discerns evil when they see it and isn't afraid to stand up to it. I fear that our society will no longer have any protectors if we keep telling little boys to stop being little boys.

How am I tying this in biblically? The answer is simple: We all swim with sharks! We all must battle a world full of evil, and for those of us who profess faith in Jesus as our Risen Savior, we have a guaranteed power dynamic to put evil in its place. Spiritual warfare[9] is real. Having our kids live in a bubble is dishonest. We need armor, which the Lord gave to us for a reason. Every day we fight some kind of evil, if our eyes are open to see it. Otherwise we are defeated regularly. Our shark tank on any given day could be the Boston Marathon bomber or the Sandy Hook Elementary School killer, but it can also be lies from our past being whispered in our ear, inappropriate content on the Internet sneaking into our Web browser on sites commonly used by our children for school-related research, the bullying personalities we encounter in various scenarios. How we see the sharks makes all the difference in the world. We need to always be mindful that we are in a shark tank, but when we tell the sharks they can only circle but not come near (boundaries!), because of Jesus, we are exercising the authority and power of the name of Jesus, which are available to all believers. Here is what the Apostle Paul says about the reality of our swimming with sharks:

Ephesians 6:10-20, Apostle Paul speaking[10]

Finally, be strong in the Lord and in the strength of his might. Put on the whole armor of God, that you may be able to stand against the schemes of the devil. For we do not wrestle against flesh and blood, but against the rulers, against the authorities, against the cosmic powers over this present darkness, against the spiritual forces of evil in the heavenly places. Therefore take up the whole armor of God, that you may be able to withstand in the evil day, and having done all, to stand firm. Stand therefore, having fastened on the belt of truth, and having put on the breastplate of righteousness, and, as shoes for your feet, having put on the readiness given by the gospel of peace. In all circumstances take up the shield of faith, with which you can extinguish all the flaming darts of the evil one; and take the helmet of salvation, and the sword of the Spirit, which is the word of God, praying at all times in the Spirit, with all prayer and supplication. To that end keep alert with all perseverance, making supplication for all the saints, and also for me, that words may be given to me in opening my mouth boldly to proclaim the mystery of the gospel, for which I am an ambassador in chains, that I may declare it boldly, as I ought to speak.

Besides the more common references to this verse about needing our gear, the armor of God, I'd like to point out the verses following that. *Pray(ing) at all times in the Spirit...* Yeah, I don't know about you, but when I see sharks headed straight for me, I automatically squeal out a "Help me, Jesus!" That part seems natural to some of us. The problem is, I am still a little slow to see some of the sharks coming right at me until their teeth are gleaming within inches of my face. The beauty of these verses in Ephesians is that we are to be prepared with the Word on our tongue and to be so in tune with the Spirit that we see what He sees. When we see what He sees, it's clear and distinctive, but we don't have fear because

1 John 4:18, Apostle John speaking

There is no fear in love, but perfect love casts out fear. For fear has to do with punishment, and whoever fears has not been perfected in love.

So, yes, at the end of the day, we need our kids to know we are indeed swimming with sharks, but we also have a fantastic power source to subdue them, and His name is Jesus. He happens to be in the tank with us, and He already took the shark bites for us, so to speak. And yes, our little boys, and children in general, need to know that protecting is biblical. We are to be ready. There is a very real battle afoot. We don't walk in fear, but we do need our gear. I'm completely okay with my children knowing that reality right now because it isn't necessarily about terrorist attacks or school shootings or nuclear risks; it's about *arguments and every lofty opinion raised against the knowledge of God.*

2 Corinthians 10:3-5, Apostle Paul speaking

For though we walk in the flesh, we are not waging war according to the flesh. For the weapons of our warfare are not of the flesh but have divine power to destroy strongholds. We destroy arguments and every lofty opinion raised against the knowledge of God, and take every thought captive to obey Christ.

"There Are No Problems That Can't Be Solved in Room 9"

My youngest child had a teacher who had the kindest, calmest, most patient demeanor on the planet. While I was helping on two different occasions in the classroom, when presented with an upset or challenge from a child, her response was: "Remember: There are no problems that can't be solved in Room 9." The second time I heard this, I posted it on a social networking site, and immediately a good friend commented: "I want to live in Room 9!" Oh my goodness! Me too! I'd pack my bags right now if I could only plant myself there and camp out for a while.

As I write this, a very dear college friend was diagnosed with triple-negative breast cancer. It was discovered late, and we are waiting to hear what the prognosis is, which stage it falls under, and which treatment plan options are available. I'm sick to my stomach. What a rough blow to the gut. At the same time, another friend gave me the news that a long-time fertility prayer has been answered, and a new baby was on its way. My friend is only 38, but it's been a long wait. And isn't that exactly how life is? Tragedy and joy all gushing in full throttle in the same week? Desperate prayers ache out of our pores for one loved one while simultaneously we offer praise and thanksgiving to Him for the answered prayers for another? I feel that way with my kids some days: One has an issue resolved after a long go of praying, trusting, re-trusting, and trusting some more, and then that very day of resolution, another one has a heart hurt. It's like playing Whac-A-Mole somedays. It can overwhelm.

At the moment, I'm sitting here an hour and a half away from my home looking out the window of a coffeehouse on the waterfront of Cape

Ann. As I type away, I see about 10 tween boys jumping off a stone wall into the waters this side of the Cape. They have absolutely no fear. They just dive in, ridiculously close to the wall, scale it, and dive again. To be honest, I don't see a parent, and that makes me anxious. I'm feeling like an off-duty parent who now has to keep an eye out for these young divers, but the greater point is: They are carefree in this moment. For a few hours, they are living in Room 9. I have spent so much of my life wanting to escape to Room 9, that I want to go out and join them. Life outside Room 9 is full of cancer, heartache, divorces, sick children, fracturing relationships, intimidating Individualized Education Programs (IEPs), bullies, death, and decay. Why can't this sweet teacher open up Room 9 to all of us? Keep it going 12 months of the year? I don't want to be seven years old to qualify. I want to barge in right now.

And then I think about the Room 9 that we do have available to us. It's under His wings, in the cleft of His trust, face down to the floor at His feet. In her book *One Thousand Gifts: A Dare to Live Fully Right Where You Are,* Ann Voskamp ties it all so beautifully to a grateful heart, to re-enacting the Eucharist in everything that we do.[11] In having a thankful heart, we must come from a place of trust, and our thankful heart then returns us there. In looking to the Scripture to find a figurative Room 9, the Psalms offer some perspective on this whole trust issue. We often want to work around that inconvenient truth of the trusting requirement on our part, but it's there. It's about rehearsing our history with God and honoring Who He is.

Notice how King David begins Psalm 25:

To you, O LORD, I lift up my soul.
O my God, in you I trust;
let me not be put to shame;
let not my enemies exult over me.
Indeed, none who wait for you shall be put to shame;
they shall be ashamed who are wantonly treacherous.

Make me to know your ways, O LORD;
teach me your paths.
Lead me in your truth and teach me,
for you are the God of my salvation;
for you I wait all the day long.

Remember your mercy, O LORD, and your steadfast love,
for they have been from of old.
Remember not the sins of my youth or my transgressions;
according to your steadfast love remember me,
for the sake of your goodness, O LORD!

Good and upright is the LORD;
therefore he instructs sinners in the way.
He leads the humble in what is right,
and teaches the humble his way.
All the paths of the LORD are steadfast love and faithfulness,
for those who keep his covenant and his testimonies.

For your name's sake, O LORD,
pardon my guilt, for it is great.
Who is the man who fears the LORD?
Him will he instruct in the way that he should choose.
His soul shall abide in well-being,
and his offspring shall inherit the land.
The friendship of the LORD is for those who fear him,
and he makes known to them his covenant.
My eyes are ever toward the LORD,
for he will pluck my feet out of the net.

Turn to me and be gracious to me,
for I am lonely and afflicted.
The troubles of my heart are enlarged;
bring me out of my distresses.
Consider my affliction and my trouble,
and forgive all my sins.

Consider how many are my foes,
and with what violent hatred they hate me.
Oh, guard my soul, and deliver me!
Let me not be put to shame, for I take refuge in you.

May integrity and uprightness preserve me,
    for I wait for you.

Redeem Israel, O God,
    out of all his troubles.

I see a recurring theme:

- *O my God, in you I trust*
- *Wait for you*
- *Lead me in your truth*
- *For you I wait all the day long*
- *For the sake of your goodness, O Lord*
- *Good and upright is the Lord*
- *My eyes are ever toward the Lord*
- *For he will pluck my feet out of the net*
- *For I take refuge in you*
- *For I wait for you*

That's a tremendous amount of affirmation about God. A lot of truth spoken. A forceful confidence. But it's also a huge declaration of trust. King David isn't saying "for he *may* pluck my feet out of the net." He says "he *will*." I don't know about you, but I think King David found Room 9. And likewise, my seven-year-old son, as well as his classmates, all trusted their amazing teacher this past year. She declared that no problem was too big, and they believed her. They functioned all year on that trust, and nothing polluted that truth.

Again, David speaks from Psalm 63, and we see a recurring theme of praise, trust, and acknowledgment:

> O God, you are my God; earnestly I seek you;
>   my soul thirsts for you;
> my flesh faints for you,
>   as in a dry and weary land where there is no water.
> So I have looked upon you in the sanctuary,
>   beholding your power and glory.
> Because your steadfast love is better than life,
>   my lips will praise you.
> So I will bless you as long as I live;
>   in your name I will lift up my hands.
>
> My soul will be satisfied as with fat and rich food,
>   and my mouth will praise you with joyful lips,
> when I remember you upon my bed,
>   and meditate on you in the watches of the night;
> for you have been my help,
>   and in the shadow of your wings I will sing for joy.
> My soul clings to you;
>   your right hand upholds me.
>
> But those who seek to destroy my life
>   shall go down into the depths of the earth;
> they shall be given over to the power of the sword;
>   they shall be a portion for jackals.
> But the king shall rejoice in God;
>   all who swear by him shall exult,
>   for the mouths of liars will be stopped.

My favorite parts of this Psalm? *For you have been my help, and in the shadow of your wings I will sing for joy. My soul clings to you; your right hand upholds me*, and *all who swear by him shall exult, for the mouths of liars will be stopped*. Can I (or, rather, King David) get an "Amen"? Many times, David is talking about running from his enemies, which was a regular reality in his life even before becoming King of Israel and Judah, but what about those mouths of liars? Know any? Besides the king of liars (the enemy of our soul), there may be many people in our lives, or even voices from the past, telling us there is no Room 9. That's a regular thought that tries to swirl around in my head. But I think David was onto something: *in the shadow of your wings I will sing for joy.* He isn't just sitting in the figurative Room 9; he's acknowledging what is praiseworthy there. How on earth could we ever sit in the shadow of His wings and not be praise-filled?

Now that doesn't mean all answers have come in yet. Sitting in Room 9 isn't an instant fix. David still needs the Lord's rescue. He still needs to be heard, but as he sits in the waiting place, expecting God to act, he clearly professes, "on my bed I remember you; I think of you through the watches of the night." Likewise, tears still flowed in Room 9 this year, but this sweet, faithful teacher simply reminded those kids of her pledge to them. I think we each need to crawl under His wings and remember His pledge as well.

Psalm 91:1-4[12] is another great reminder. Actually, the entire Psalm is awesome, but here is the direct reference to the safety and shelter of His wings:

> He who dwells in the shelter of the Most High
>   will abide in the shadow of the Almighty.
> I will say to the LORD, "My refuge and my fortress,
>   my God, in whom I trust."
>
> For he will deliver you from the snare of the fowler
>   and from the deadly pestilence.
> He will cover you with his pinions,
>   and under his wings you will find refuge;
>   his faithfulness is a shield and buckler.

So, Psalm 91 talks about how we can protect ourselves in the shadow of His wings. But what do we do when we are surrounded by the stuff of life? How do we help other people find Room 9? Not everyone is on our same page. Not all of them believe Room 9 exists in Christ, or maybe their faith is tattered and torn from the storms raging against them, and they simply can't bring themselves to walk through the door and trust. The Apostle Paul gives us a good strategy for this in Philippians.

> Philippians 4:4-9
>
> Rejoice in the Lord always; again I will say, rejoice. Let your reasonableness be known to everyone. The Lord is at hand; do not be anxious about anything, but in everything by prayer and supplication with thanksgiving let your requests be made known to God. And the peace of God, which surpasses all understanding, will guard your hearts and your minds in Christ Jesus.
>
> Finally, brothers, whatever is true, whatever is honorable, whatever is just, whatever is pure, whatever is lovely, whatever is commendable, if there is any excellence, if there is anything worthy of praise, think about these things. What you have learned and received and heard and seen in me—practice these things, and the God of peace will be with you.

The Lord is at hand. Prayer and supplication, with thanksgiving. If there is any excellence, if there is anything worthy of praise—think about these things. It sounds to me like being in Room 9 is affirming that which is good and praiseworthy while we wait for His answers. But stepping into His Room 9 requires faith and trust, a movement toward Him in such a way that presupposes He truly is there, has redeemed us, and *is* the answer, the only one.

The Apostle Paul gives further instructions in 1 Thessalonians 5:

> 1 Thessalonians 5:12-18
>
> We ask you, brothers, to respect those who labor among you and are over you in the Lord and admonish you, and to esteem them very highly in love because of their work. Be at peace among yourselves. And we urge you, brothers, admonish the idle, encourage the fainthearted, help the weak, be patient with them all. See that no one repays anyone evil for evil, but always seek to do good to one another and to everyone. Rejoice always, pray without ceasing, give thanks in all circumstances; for this is the will of God in Christ Jesus for you.

Hmmm. *Respect, be at peace, encourage, help, be patient, always seek to do good to one another.* Oh wait, and then there's: *Rejoice always; pray without ceasing; give thanks in all circumstances.* Paul doesn't waver on what it takes to live in that place of trust. We can be an open door for our figurative Room 9 when others see us remaining positive, rehearsing our history with the Lord, and being patient. Not everyone has that perspective. Without faith, it can be very difficult to walk in constant trust of anything.

Some people have understandably believed the lie, or part of it, that problems can't be solved, or they've put limits on what "solving" means. There are also those who mistakenly think Room 9 is a swift reversal of all that is wrong, a quick fix. What Room 9 really is: a sanctuary of trust, a safety zone, a place to be vulnerable and cry out, a venue for truly living while we wait for things to recalibrate in our lives. It's surrender at Christ's feet. Until those around us walking in their own turmoil and personal life struggles can see that, we are to persevere and show them the way, letting them know that the solving is God's business. Ours is simply entering His Room 9 in complete and glorious abandon. Every day my son was privileged to walk into that classroom and know the commitment and safety there to work through difficulties and stress. I find that under the wings of my sweet Savior, nestled in, beckoning others to join me. Room 9 is a real place, but we must be willing to trust enough to open the door. I want to go in and sit down. How about you?

"Mom, Why Exactly Do You Have a Sewer Dump in the Front Seat?"

It's probably time for confessions. This title more or less begs to be explained. I'm the girl who buys something for my kid when I know s/he really wants it and puts it away for an occasion, even if that occasion is four months away. I've learned the hard way that if you go back to the store four months later, that item is often not there. Now, I don't do this for everything, only for the big items they have wanted for a while. As a general rule, our kids don't just get stuff to get it. They have small ways to make a little cash, and they are encouraged to use it for a movie they want to see (beyond the ones we want to see as a family), to spend on a vacation treat, and to save, save, save. For the most part, we give items on a wish list only at birthdays and Christmas. We feel they savor the gifts better that way.

So, when Little Man was with me at the store and saw the beloved Trash Packs Sewer Dump Play Set, it was a toy I knew he'd play with a lot. I cranked out the ridiculous $40, saved the receipt, and told him that was it for his birthday. He was having a birthday party this year (my kids have to take turns each year having a birthday party), and the party was his present. He seemed content with that, so win-win.

Fast-forward to one month later and a certain toy store advertised "Door Busters" for Thanksgiving evening. Do I overall embrace Black Friday shopping? I do not, mostly because I avoid crowds. I was especially adamant about not leaving the family for a deal. Wasn't even going to open the flyer. But there it was: that Trash Packs Sewer Dump Play Set for $20.

Oh my! So, I did what I needed to do. I fed my family, enjoyed *Star Wars* Episode 2 with them, relaxed and stayed in my pjs until 4:00 PM. And then I did it: I got in my car and headed to the Door Busters, stood outside in late November New England temperatures for 20 minutes, and managed to get to the play set in time to catch one. I had told myself it didn't matter if I didn't. I wasn't going to push into anyone or rush ahead, violently crashing my cart, to have it. But I'll admit that placing it into my cart was a sweet reward.

So, I unwrapped the birthday present sewer dump (to make sure the two versions matched because I've been there and done that before: bought the wrong one!) and left it in the front seat to return to the other store, which is where we pick up on this story. Little Man got into the van the next day and saw the unwrapped $40 version on the front seat because I hadn't returned it yet. And then came the question: "Mom, why exactly do you have a sewer dump in the front seat?"

What I heard in that question went beyond the literal, the obvious. I knew he was thinking: "Did she get me two? Is she taking the other one back? Did I do something wrong?" So, I cleared up the mystery, and he let it be, knowing how sale-crazy I am. But I also heard: "Sometimes we sit with our sewer dump of life right there as a passenger, toting it around because we can't get rid of it." I started to think about what sewer dump I was foolishly keeping company with. What toxins was I letting intrude? That moment of unwrapped present in full view was one that begged confession, submission, vulnerability. It was time to take inventory, and it's never fun when we look at our own sewer dump, especially when it's right there staring back at us.

It reminded me of a recent conversation I had with one of my children about what communion really is, what it's for, how we ask God to take inventory of our hearts. Psalm 51[13] offers me one of the best ways of getting that sewer dump to stop riding shotgun.

> Have mercy on me, O God,
> > according to your steadfast love;
> according to your abundant mercy
> > blot out my transgressions.
> Wash me thoroughly from my iniquity,
> > and cleanse me from my sin!
>
> For I know my transgressions,
> > and my sin is ever before me.
> Against you, you only, have I sinned
> > and done what is evil in your sight,
> so that you may be justified in your words
> > and blameless in your judgment.
> Behold, I was brought forth in iniquity,
> > and in sin did my mother conceive me.
> Behold, you delight in truth in the inward being,
> > and you teach me wisdom in the secret heart.
>
> Purge me with hyssop, and I shall be clean;
> > wash me, and I shall be whiter than snow.
> Let me hear joy and gladness;
> > let the bones that you have broken rejoice.
> Hide your face from my sins,
> > and blot out all my iniquities.
> Create in me a clean heart, O God,
> > and renew a right spirit within me.
> Cast me not away from your presence,
> > and take not your Holy Spirit from me.
> Restore to me the joy of your salvation,
> > and uphold me with a willing spirit.
>
> Then I will teach transgressors your ways,
> > and sinners will return to you.
> Deliver me from bloodguiltiness, O God,
> > O God of my salvation,
> > and my tongue will sing aloud of your righteousness.
> O Lord, open my lips,
> > and my mouth will declare your praise.
> For you will not delight in sacrifice, or I would give it;
> > you will not be pleased with a burnt offering.
> The sacrifices of God are a broken spirit;
> > a broken and contrite heart, O God, you will not despise.

Do good to Zion in your good pleasure;
    build up the walls of Jerusalem;
then will you delight in right sacrifices,
    in burnt offerings and whole burnt offerings;
    then bulls will be offered on your altar.

I was thinking about my anger levels this week, the occasional swear word that escaped my lips, and even though the kids didn't hear it, God and I did. I was thinking of the gossip I participated in, even the gluttony of needing two lattes that day to comfort myself. It's not about self-condemning. To someone else or even to me on a different day, two lattes aren't a big deal. But my heart that day was in escaping, self-comforting, feeling entitled mode. So, in reading this, if your biggest problem is bigger than a swear word (by the way, so are some of mine), this isn't meant to belittle. This is meant for us to check our hearts. Screaming at my son in frustration the other day was a lot different from expressing frustration, disappointment, and discipline God's way. I think of the sewer dump as a collection of where I took the helm instead of letting God. Of where I responded like an unforgiven human instead of a sanctified truster in Christ.

So, when my son asked me why there was a sewer dump in the front seat, it was really God speaking to me the way He often does. He may speak to each of us differently[14] through our prayer lives, but when God speaks to me, it's often through something my child or someone else intended quite literally, but I hear it on a completely different level. I'm going to return that original sewer dump play set and get my money back, but I'm thankful for the 48 hours or so it will have served as a reminder of something greater and more meaningful.

When Children Pray and Minister: The Best Pastoral Care Team There Is

When I was a child, two years in a row my father had two unrelated forms of cancer. One of them was declared terminal. Our church rallied, a second opinion was sought, and a group of believing Christians prayed my father into better health. Yes, we had an amazing medical community, but a "terminal" diagnosis can only be fought so far without faith. In addition to the bedside visits from our pastor, elders, and other church members, I had one profound experience that has never left me.

One particular Sunday morning I came into Children's Church at the ripe old age of 9 1/2 years old. When the teachers went to pray, I think at one point they mentioned my father. I don't remember a lot about that day. I couldn't tell you which teachers or even if I cried or not. I simply recall a heavy heart. One of my very best friends, Lauren, two years *my junior*, with whom I took vacations and spent many Sundays at her home, put her hand on my back and prayed over me. Out loud. She might not even remember it, but I do. I knew we had praying community for my father, but this single moment in time is a huge part of my faith story. Ministering touch through the appropriate laying on of hands is very significant, as is the ministry of children. The Holy Spirit spoke to my heart that day through a friend who counted only seven years on this planet at that point. Obedient prayer does that. It changes everything. And children are really good at it.

*****

A prayer request came in through a phone message the other day. I couldn't get to the phone right away, but I came in to see Little Man's hands folded and eyes closed, praying for the request and the person expressing it on the answering machine. In that one moment, I needed to forgive and let go of every obsessive, perseverating, inattentive, hyper-jumpy, overly talkative behavior and thank God for opening heaven for a minute for me so I could see His Light shine down in my kitchen on a little boy who interrupted eating his favorite thing in the world, pizza, to fold his hands for a friend of mine. *Thank You, Jesus. I'm sorry for the moments I don't tend this soul as tenderly and patiently as You would. You are so faithful when I am not.*

What do I learn when my children stop to pray? That our communion with God is that simple. We talk. We tell Him everything. We hear a problem we can't solve, and we ask His help. That's what's so beautiful about childlike faith. It's interesting to me that Luke talks about humbling oneself right before an account of Jesus and the children in Luke 18. He was first comparing a Pharisee and a tax collector,[15] finding humility in the tax collector and not the self-righteous law-abiding Pharisee.

Luke 18:9-14, Luke the Physician narrating

He also told this parable to some who trusted in themselves that they were righteous, and treated others with contempt: "Two men went up into the temple to pray, one a Pharisee and the other a tax collector. The Pharisee, standing by himself, prayed thus: 'God, I thank you that I am not like other men, extortioners, unjust, adulterers, or even like this tax collector. I fast twice a week; I give tithes of all that I get.' But the tax collector, standing far off, would not even lift up his eyes to heaven, but beat his breast, saying, 'God, be merciful to me, a sinner!' I tell you, this man went down to his house justified, rather than the other. For everyone who exalts himself will be humbled, but the one who humbles himself will be exalted."

48

Then, Luke segues from a lesson in humility to another example of how very simple coming to relationship with Jesus is: in childlike faith, which follows the humility parable very well.

Luke 18:15-17

> Now they were bringing even infants to him that he might touch them. And when the disciples saw it, they rebuked them. But Jesus called them to him, saying, "Let the children come to me, and do not hinder them, for to such belongs the kingdom of God. Truly, I say to you, whoever does not receive the kingdom of God like a child shall not enter it."

I wish I were that faithful. I wish that every time a problem presented itself I didn't get so distracted by the magnitude of it that I forgot to turn immediately to my Father in heaven for help. I like to pet it, toss it around, look for answers, wrestle it, or even beat it up (or myself) a bit first. But not Little Man. Little Man simply bows his head, talks to His Father, and wraps it up in confidence with a big Amen. It really is that simple. Why can't we adults do that?

Another one of the most precious sights in the world to me is seeing children minister to other children. It can be a prayer, yes, but it can also be an "I'm going to sit right next to you until you feel better. We're going to do this together." Adults get it so very wrong sometimes. They think you have to be a Bible scholar or know the right way to say something or be a certain, allusive "age of maturity" to do the work of Christ. Not so! If Luke 18:15-17 doesn't make this clear enough for us, Matthew and Mark both express it as well.[16] Some of the most precious people to Jesus were the children. They followed Him right where they were. They didn't need a seminary or theology degree to be acknowledged or appreciated by Him. They just wanted to be like Him. One time, in church, one of my children sat next to another child during prayer time while that child was prayed for. That's it. Sat there to be by his side. In church. With all of the big people around praying. And he didn't take over, he didn't spout verses, he didn't even hug him. He simply climbed up right next to him and said something along the lines of: "I'm gonna just sit here next to you, okay?" That is ministry in its purest form, without any requirements, and it's the closest thing to the purity of the Gospel I have ever seen.

If I were to take away anything from my children teaching me how simple prayer is, it would be a play on the Fire Safety campaign of "Stop, Drop, and Roll": "Stop, Drop, and Pray." Why do we adults sputter and twitch, wondering when God is going to show up (when really He is always there ready and waiting to be consulted) when we forget to involve Him in the first place? If our children had an issue, wouldn't they come directly to us (we'd like to think so, as that's what we aim for)? Why do we forget our heavenly Parent? He wants to be involved. Look at the last verse of this section of Matthew 21.

Matthew 21:18-22, Apostle Matthew narrating

In the morning, as he [Jesus] was returning to the city, he became hungry. And seeing a fig tree by the wayside, he went to it and found nothing on it but only leaves. And he said to it, "May no fruit ever come from you again!" And the fig tree withered at once.

When the disciples saw it, they marveled, saying, "How did the fig tree wither at once?" And Jesus answered them, "Truly, I say to you, if you have faith and do not doubt, you will not only do what has been done to the fig tree, but even if you say to this mountain, 'Be taken up and thrown into the sea,' it will happen. And whatever you ask in prayer, you will receive, if you have faith."

Notice the simple if/then statement: "Whatever you ask in prayer, *you will receive, if you have faith.*" I don't want to be the fig tree or mountain in this story, but the point is: Where is our power source? Our believing children just plug themselves directly in. We may not see it right away, but faith in what God can do is our power source: belief.[17]

More and more I want to sit alongside the hurting, praying comfort, hope, peace, and a blessing. I don't want to hesitate. I want my responses to be as automatic as a child's. We adults get overwhelmed thinking it's all on us, we're responsible, and we carry the heavy load. We will know our Savior best when we come to Him like an eager child climbing on His holy lap, in humility and simple faith. I want to be part of the best pastoral care team there is, but to do that, I need to approach my Father in heaven as if I were three feet tall and short on life experience. He meets us right there in that beautiful place and uses us to move mountains and defeat unproductive fig trees. How I thank Him for the three innocent examples running around my own house. May my heart always be so teachable.

*****

As I wrote this, I received an email from one of my children's school nurses telling me some alarming news about some significant vision trouble my child was suddenly having, as well as a "bouncing eyeball." It was urgent, and an appointment needed to be made today. I felt that heart-flutter, the not-trusting-God one: the one that makes us human but can be turned around and calmed because of my trustworthy Jesus. It was no coincidence I was writing about childlike faith at the time. Where was mine? Can I even include this section if I don't walk it out? No, I can't.

So, I did what I humanly needed to do:

Prayed. Told my Father in heaven right away.

Returned contact with the school and made a medical appointment.

Then I recognized my part was done.

I needed to trust in my mighty, loving Savior that we were facing a growth issue or change in vision that did not mean something bulging from the brain against the eyeball, and if we're not, He's still my Savior. Amen?

Panic started to whisper again.

"Shut your mouth, Panic. Jesus has 'got this.'"

Did that mean everything would instantly be okay? I had no idea. I just knew my Jesus was walking this with me.

Blood pressure rising.

I then stopped and recited my beautiful history of loving my Lord, flawed and fickle as my love is, and Him loving me, faithful, tried, and true.

Blood pressure down.

One agonizing minute at a time, but this is how we do it, Folks. And if we let ourselves linger in panic, as soon as we recover our senses, we need to place our concern or stress back at the foot of the Throne again. Surrender it 100 times in an hour if we have to. No matter how much we waver in our faith, He is the same yesterday, today, and forever, as the author of Hebrews exhorts us to remember.

Hebrews 13:7-8, author unknown, but he is recording the words of God

Remember your leaders, those who spoke to you the word of God. Consider the outcome of their way of life, and imitate their faith. Jesus Christ is the same yesterday and today and forever.

He created this child's eyes. He loves every part of this child. I can trust Him. End of story.

Part 2
Dysfunction Junction, What's Your Function?[18]

This section is very important to me. I've spent the past two decades learning healthy boundaries (still learning). As I write this, I want to make sure it's understood that I am not pointing a finger at anyone but rather everyone, with one finger perpetually pointed at myself as well. We are *all* dysfunctional and broken. We are all sinful. We all have brokenness in us that rubs up against the brokenness in others. We all mess up. We all function in unhealthy ways. Hopefully, we commit ourselves to letting the Lord reshape us into the new creations He promises, and that will happen through sanctification, but until we receive perfected bodies given to us in heaven, while we sit on this side of the Garden, we all make stops at Dysfunction Junction. At times we lead ourselves there, and sometimes the train stops there because of brokenness in others. As I heal and learn to wear His grace, I choose to write about each victory, each lesson learned, each new way to choose better responses. Perhaps the Apostle Paul says it best.

Philippians 3:12-14, Apostle Paul speaking

Not that I have already obtained this or am already perfect, but I press on to make it my own, because Christ Jesus has made me his own. Brothers, I do not consider that I have made it my own. But one thing I do: forgetting what lies behind and straining forward to what lies ahead, I press on toward the goal for the prize of the upward call of God in Christ Jesus.

Let's press on together toward the goal. If I have to stop at Dysfunction Junction, I want the prize at the end. Don't you?

Between the problem and the solution is a waiting place I don't like very much. I kick and scream and shout and wail, and then when I finally lick my shut-up-sicle, my God has things to teach me there. But my tantrum has to be over first, and my listening ears have to be on. I have to be sitting criss-cross-applesauce on the listening rug to hear what my Rabbi, Abba Father, has to say. I want the solution now. No pain, no more thrashing. But He wants my attention between problem and solution. Like a patient first grade teacher, He taps me on the shoulder to remind me to have self-control and sit like a good listener, go back to my place on the rug. He tells me His story, and in it are instructions about yielding to the will of the Father, "not my will but Thy will be done." And like a headstrong seven year old, I don't like that part at all, but the adult in me knows "Thy will be done" is so much better than "my will be done" because I screw it up when I think I'm in control of everything.

So, Abba Father, I'm sitting here on the rug. See me? My listening ears are on. My tantrum is over. I am no longer in the "stop and think chair" to settle down. My eyes are on You, my Teacher—until the next distraction when I might need You to do that "tap me on the shoulder" thing again. Here I am. I'm trying so hard not to wiggle and squirm. I want to let only Your voice in. Will You teach me? I have focus issues, but Your Word always guides me back to You. Amen.

Chains No More

When I was sinking in despair,
My precious Jesus found me there.
"What lies are you believing, Child?
My yoke is light; my love is wild."
Yet I thought chains had tied me down, had weighed me to the shore,
But Jesus said: "Look down, My Child, and see the chains no more."

And when I looked, I saw that I had freedom all along
But had chosen life inside a pit to sing a death-filled song.
Whilst day had brightened all about with joy that kissed the moon,
I'd given up my hope and sold out my heart much too soon.
When Jesus sang His song to me, he wakened Truth and Life;
Right there I traded peace for all that used to cause me strife.
So, when He greets me in the morn and breathes Life's precious breath,
I know that when He comes for me, He brings not with Him death.

Bonnie Lyn Smith

My Armor Still Fits and Works in Bizarro World

Ephesians 6:11-18, Apostle Paul speaking

> Put on the whole armor of God, that you may be able to stand against the schemes of the devil. For we do not wrestle against flesh and blood, but against the rulers, against the authorities, against the cosmic powers over this present darkness, against the spiritual forces of evil in the heavenly places. Therefore take up the whole armor of God, that you may be able to withstand in the evil day, and having done all, to stand firm. Stand therefore, having fastened on the belt of truth, and having put on the breastplate of righteousness, and, as shoes for your feet, having put on the readiness given by the gospel of peace. In all circumstances take up the shield of faith, with which you can extinguish all the flaming darts of the evil one; and take the helmet of salvation, and the sword of the Spirit, which is the word of God, praying at all times in the Spirit, with all prayer and supplication. To that end keep alert with all perseverance, making supplication for all the saints.

One of the biggest battles in my life has always been lies spoken into who I am. So many folks can relate, I'm sure. We all encounter many lies, accusations, and rewritings of our personal history by others who prefer it to read differently than it actually does. Over and over again, I have found this verse to be my only survival against denials of who I really am, what I was created for, and what my personal story is. I've had to be disciplined about buckling the *belt of truth* around my waist securely. Whenever I don't, other forces come in and try to unbuckle it or put something else over it: a sash of their own fabrication. When I start thinking that manufactured version of truth is correct, I miss walking in His Truth. I miss His plan for me, His definition of who I am.

Shoes for your feet, having put on the readiness are my only way to experience the *gospel of peace*. His *breastplate of righteousness* covers over my own unrighteousness because of the work done on the cross. When I don't have my *shield of faith* on, lies can permeate and soak in. And I start believing them. The *helmet of salvation* keeps my mind sound, and having a sound mind is God's plan for us. Consider what the Apostle Paul writes to his son in the faith, Timothy, to encourage him in 2 Timothy 1:7:

> For God gave us a spirit not of fear but of power and love and self-control.

Now, I like that it refers to self-control in the English Standard Version (ESV), but the King James Version (KJV) offers us this translation: *a sound mind*.

> 2 Timothy 1:7, Apostle Paul speaking, KJV
>
> For God hath not given us the spirit of fear; but of power, and of love, and of *a sound mind* [emphasis mine].

While they essentially have the same meaning in this context, doesn't a sound mind sound good? Don't we want to sign up for one of those? Put me on the wait list! I'll prepay, for crying out loud; just give me some of that sound mind stuff! I need that helmet of salvation to protect my mind from dwelling on what man says about me, right or wrong, and to find God's Truth only. Only inside that helmet can my thoughts be more like His thoughts and my ways more like His ways—and only because I seek Him and listen only to Him there.

> Isaiah 55:8-9, Isaiah the Prophet speaking
>
> "For my thoughts are not your thoughts,
>   neither are your ways my ways," declares the LORD.
>
> "For as the heavens are higher than the earth,
>   so are my ways higher than your ways
>   and my thoughts than your thoughts."

The *sword of the Spirit* is helpful to gauge my motivations. When I have checked them with the Spirit, I have to leave the rest in God's hands. I don't need to do any battle on my own. Other people are in God's merciful hands, not mine, which is a relief on all fronts. If we keep all of this in mind and if we wear the armor and live inside of it, then peace reigns supreme. We don't have to worry about codependency trying to assault from certain directions, jabs about who we are, passive-aggressive attacks, mind games, high drama, lures to come back into a pit we long ago crawled our way out of, or petty jealousies of our own personal strength, and with whom and how often we interact. Those are orchestrations of a life outside of Christ. Even those of us who yield to Christ have behaviors to correct and make new. But the Bizarro World that defined so much of how we used to interact doesn't even have to be a place on our personal maps anymore, for the grace of God! Does any of that sound familiar to you? We all struggle with it because relationships and people aren't perfect, including ourselves.

So, if lies assault you, and you know Jesus, you have access to all of this armor in His name. Indirectly, a sweet friend reminded me of that today: getting my armor on. How can I make it through one day without it? Who else protects us in full power (and every time we ask) like Jesus? As the old song goes:

> "What can wash away my sin?
> Nothing but the blood of Jesus.
> What can make me whole again?
> Nothing but the blood of Jesus.
> Oh, precious is the flow
> That makes me white as snow.
> No other fount I know
> Nothing but the blood of Jesus."[19]

And Ephesians 6:11-18, the "armor of God" verses, end with this little nugget, which simply cannot be ignored, although many of us consider it very inconvenient at times:

"To that end keep alert with all perseverance, making supplication for all the saints."

How else can we defeat the untruths coming at us than to have our armor on, be alert, and pray for people? *Keep alert* suggests that we should expect the battles and not be discouraged or overwhelmed by them. *Making supplication (praying) for all the saints* means that we are not off the hook in responsibility. We must pray for those who speak against us, and they are sometimes those who share our faith (if we follow Christ). The beautiful thing about that little mandate is that it grows us a heart that beats more with God's. I don't know about you, but whenever I have prayed about Bizarro World, I am more peaceful and loving toward others. When we regress to Bizarro World behaviors at times ourselves, don't we want people to do the same for us? Many people have prayed me out of it. Who am I to decide someone else deserves to sit there and swirl around? If my armor is truly on because I've been obedient to wear it, that person can't really hurt me, and my arm should be extended to him or her, not in an effort to crawl in and join, but rather to help pull that person out.

Reflections on Judgment: What Side of the Whirlpool Are We Actually On?

A sweet mentor and friend e-mailed me this one simple thought today: "We should be slow to judge; we don't know what demons someone else struggles with." I wholeheartedly agree.

Unless we've done battle in another person's war, we really have no authority to pass judgment. Discernment, yes. Judgment, no. Someone battling a situation or behavior we don't approve of isn't going to get better from our critical spirits. Judgmental attitudes turn eyes away from Christ and put them on man, where they do not belong.

> 1 John 4:19, Apostle John speaking
>
> We love because he first loved us.

He loved us first and taught us how to love. It does not say "We judge because He first judged us." Judgment *does* belong to Him, but it does *not* belong to us.

> Matthew 7:1-5, Jesus speaking
>
> "Judge not, that you be not judged. For with the judgment you pronounce you will be judged, and with the measure you use it will be measured to you. Why do you see the speck that is in your brother's eye, but do not notice the log that is in your own eye? Or how can you say to your brother, 'Let me take the speck out of your eye,' when there is the log in your own eye? You hypocrite, first take the log out of your own eye, and then you will see clearly to take the speck out of your brother's eye."

Been thinking on this a *lot* lately. I often don't understand another person's perspective or reaction to something, but I do not have a right to label that person "wrong" and myself "right," tempting as that is most of the time. There are pains, anguishes, and trials out there I have thankfully never had to bear. And for those who have not borne mine, I would really appreciate receiving the benefit of the doubt from you, knowing there are wars I am still trying to win, and through His strength, I will get to the other side. Some things keep trying to hold me under water; this is true for all of us. Just because I sometimes still suck in that water, mistaking it for air, doesn't mean I'm not still learning my lessons. We all fall. Hopefully, we try to get back up. Better not to suck in the water? Yes. But better to keep trying each time, lungs filling or not? Yes.

So today, I write for those still stuck in that whirlpool that tries to suck them back in, whether it be: insecurities, addiction, toxic relationship, depression, crisis of faith, a torn wound of the past, or any other personal struggle. I want to be the one extending my hand to help lift them up. I don't want be the one piling more water on top of them, rehearsing their failures. I also want to be more aware of those reaching their hands out to me in friendship. May I remember to take those hands and not try to fight the battles on my own. He sends us tangible help. I am arrogant when I choose not to take a gift He offers me.

I wonder if our judgment of others comes from a place deep inside of us where we are afraid to admit to our own whirlpool, so pointing to someone else's is a great way to deflect our own issues. Meanwhile, we are taking a nice little spin in one we think we've kept hidden from everyone else, neat and tidy, full of enough fragrant bubbles that nobody can see us heading toward the middle. It's so easy to talk about another person's whirlpool, when in fact, we may very well be treading water in our own. I want to live life more honestly, more genuinely. If I'm in my whirlpool today, I want to be able to tell a few safe people:

Yo, I am swirling here and need your help. Not proud of it, but I'm not going to let shame or blame keep me from taking down the pride wall and asking for help to get out. Now that I'm sharing this, the next time your own whirlpool pulls you under, I will not judge; rather, I'll just nod and say: "Yup, I get it. No questions asked. Let me point you back to the Savior, and let's commit to living more days outside this whirlpool than in until we realize how set free we already are and reside outside of it permanently because of Jesus, Amen?"

Same Goal, Same God: Looking Past Differences in Parenting Styles, Even Within the Church Community

This is another look at judgment. Why? Because it's the opposite of grace, there's too much of it in our everyday lives, and it can even intrude in the church. This particular examination is of parents judging other parents. Get your seat belts on. I think we've all been on both sides of this ride. Ouch.

In a conversation with one of my kids this summer over something we don't allow but other parents do, it was a fantastic opportunity to share that although we have our reasons for not saying yes to that particular thing and it's okay to say why (when asked), we also don't stand in condemnation of others who do say yes. We aren't about condemnation or condescension. Because I'm not about raising my kids with a bunch of rules just for the sake of rules, and neither am I about raising them to enforce those rules on others. That's simply not our job, unless we are law enforcers in the literal sense of the word. I am about raising them with guidelines that are important to our family, that I would love to see passed on, but all served up with huge portions of never-ending grace toward others—not because we are overlooking their wrongs and we are so right, but because everyone is free to make their own choices.

My boundary may not be the same as another's. As our children grow into those heavily peer-influenced ages, it becomes harder in some ways, but it truly is much easier to be able to state, when asked, why we don't do this or that than to say: "You shouldn't either." Of course, there is a time and a place for speaking truth to people in unhealthy or toxic thought patterns or behaviors who are seeking help or answers, but being in someone's face about an issue isn't the way to go about it. So, instead of getting in the car and telling me: "Can you believe so and so was allowed to wear this, do that, buy that," I want to hear how my children showed grace when another child rubbed something in their face or mocked our family's choices. How did they speak a loving, but firm, response to that? Unreasonable expectation? I don't think so. I think the training in grace begins the minute toddler Sally Ann shoves toddler Katie Sue on the playground. How does each mama handle that? Because in just a few short years, that will be how Sally Ann and Katie Sue handle it. Guaranteed.

But, like any other lesson I try to offer my children, there it was, lived out toward *me*! I made a seemingly benign comment about a weed-filled lawn we saw while driving. I was merely reporting, not intending to sound judgmental, but one of my children said: "Mom, they moved in only a short while ago. It took us at least a year to start caring about the outside of our house." While that doesn't tie in directly to the fact we may answer questions differently than other people might, it did speak to me that some of that grace is grabbing hold and starting to pour out. Few things make me as happy as grace lived out. Very few things.

Okay, awesome. But what happens when we differ inside the church, the Body of Christ, in fellowship with other believers? Yikes, a sticky wicket, that one. There are parents with an even more conservative, protective stance than mine. I need to remember that we each are praying for guidance from the same God, and it's not my place to rail about them being protective. It's also not their God-given role to cast judgment on me for a different choice. Isn't this where it gets tricky, Folks? The same can be said when parents are more permissive than we are. If they seek our counsel, we can certainly share what has worked for us or even some danger zones, but there is definitely a need within the church itself to allow for differences in schooling choices, what technology we allow in and when, and when to discuss delicate, moral choices with our children, as just a few examples. We need room to grow, to make mistakes, and to get back up again. Judgment from others is a relationship-crusher, almost every time.

James 4:11-12, James, brother of Jesus, speaking

Do not speak evil against one another, brothers. The one who speaks against a brother or judges his brother, speaks evil against the law and judges the law. But if you judge the law, you are not a doer of the law but a judge. There is only one lawgiver and judge, he who is able to save and to destroy. But who are you to judge your neighbor?

I apparently felt strongly about this, recently, because I blogged on social media about it. I think I had experienced a few days in a row of feeling on the "judged" end of the spectrum, and this was the result:

I'm going to take a minute to briefly blog about something only because I have had this conversation face to face many times, and if I'm going to write it, I'm also willing to have it in person. I guess lately I have felt the need to write it in general, not to anyone in particular. But this is expressly for the faith community. We absolutely *need* to stop placing constant judgment on one another. I respect a choice whether or not to let a child play a certain video game, make Santa a small part of Christmas, trick-or-treat, school a child a certain way, or see certain movies at certain ages (whether they be Disney, *Star Wars*, or *The Lord of the Rings*) because they introduce the idea of evil. Okay then. I am not gonna judge here. We make different choices because as parents we are choosing to let our kids experience the world differently. And that's okay. At the end of their growing-up years, it all eventually gets worked out regardless of how we raise these kids. We're all doing the best we can. But please don't ever make statements directly to my children that make them feel less than or judged, question their faith, or demean us as parents. If you are going to directly question my judgment, please don't do it in front of my kids; also, please be prepared for my very different perspective. Follow whatever rules make you feel safe as a family. I'm all for it. But if mine look different, please respect I also look to God in raising my kids. We're on the same page, share the same goals, love with the same love. Let's please, please, *please* not polarize each other.

With Love, Bonnie

67

That about sums up my feelings on the subject, but at the end of the day, we should measure our interactions with and responses to people with God's words, not mine:

Hebrews 12:14-15, author unknown, but he is recording the words of God

Strive for peace with everyone, and for the holiness without which no one will see the Lord. See to it that no one fails to obtain the grace of God; that no "root of bitterness" springs up and causes trouble, and by it many become defiled.

Can I get an Amen?

Abandonment: At Times, People Walk Away From Us, but Are We Ever Called to Do the Same?

Abandonment: A big word, a huge subject, and a topic so broad that books have been written about it. Volumes, I'm sure. I don't come at it from a psychology or counseling degree. I so badly wanted to *not* write this section. I had left a placeholder for it in the middle, hoping that was good enough and that I could delete it on the final edit. But then it kept coming back as a subject in my life. It kept haunting. I had to continue to give it to Jesus. I had to tie it up, drag it kicking and screaming back to the cross, and practically weigh it down there with an anchor so it wouldn't come floating back to me. But then I started to see that it wasn't that He was making it return to me; it was that I never fully trusted He could take it. Our conversation, when it came to including the topic of abandonment in this book, went something like this:

> But I don't want to include it, Lord. This is my first book. People will run screaming from this chapter. It's too heavy.
>
> *Put it in.*
>
> But it's too painful of a subject. Who wants to read about that? Can't I pick this up in a later publication?
>
> *People need to hear My voice in it.*
>
> But I have no degree in this, no authority, no real wisdom.
>
> *You have what I impart to you. You have My authority. They need to know I am there in that place where they are alone, feeling left behind. They need to see Me there.*

And that's more or less how the conversation went for a while. I eventually gave in. It was easier. Those of us who know abandonment in one form or another wear it like a lettered jacket. Hopefully, we don't always wear a wound with neon highlights flashing whenever anyone gets too close to us, although I'm sure some of us may seem like that in the early stages of healing. But I can spot someone with an abandonment issue a mile away, even if they've mostly worked through it. How do I recognize them? They have a hole in their emotion shirt that has been mended by God. They go deep. They get it. They know how precious relationships are —but also how fleeting. They are the first to tell you that only God sticks it out to the end; only He is faithful. Only He lives in that place with you when everyone else got off the island.

Proverbs 18:10, King Solomon[20] speaking

The name of the LORD is a strong tower; the righteous man runs into it and is safe.

As one of my faraway friends recently messaged me: "I'll pray for the broken relationships in your life. I know broken. I know exactly how to pray."

I want to take a second to acknowledge here that abandonment covers the big and the small. It can be a significant relationship that leaves us disempowered because the other party wouldn't work it through. I don't want to trivialize how serious it can be by equating the end of a five-year friendship with a husband walking out after 20 years of marriage, but pain is pain. Some know parental abandonment. Some have been discarded in ways that involve extensive abuse and mistreatment. I'm not trying to cover all of that. I'm merely offering a jumping-off point: a place to see where God can work. No matter how or why we've been abandoned, in addition to the cycle of pain and anger, a lie sneaks in and becomes part of the new recordings in our head: "You are not worthy. See how people walk out on you? Nobody wants to be around you."

If relationships in several areas of our lives are fleeing for the hills, we must look inward, examine our hearts, and ask God to show us if we have hurtful behaviors that make people retreat. There could be something to pay attention to or learn from, or a reason to seek biblical wisdom or counsel. But in our lives we will likely know a steady stream of people who can't stick around to resolve, who find it easier to abandon relationships than to work on them. The goal here is to discuss how to deal with it when people give us no choice and walk away from us. But the really uncomfortable thing we feel when we look at this issue is that we have to also consider whether we are guilty of the same. Do *we* abandon? This discussion cuts both ways. It absolutely has to if we are to live truly authentic lives.

One of the biggest frustrations I have is when people, at the first sign of conflict, pick up their bags and walk completely away. I understand not being comfortable with confrontation, but I can never fully comprehend folks shutting down and stomping off as if there is no chance to work anything out or no hope for resolution. There are, of course, times to draw boundaries (in cases of abuse or toxic influence), but how do people just walk away, sometimes carrying all of that unresolved hurt with them? I've been reflecting on this lately. It's an area where I need more grace toward others, maybe because I've been the abandoned one a handful of times. A few years ago, I watched close friends toss their friendship right out the door when their children simply needed a break from each other. I can usually get past that stuff. For a while, there will be a stinging tension, for sure, but it breaks my heart that instead of just taking some space for a while, people immediately head toward a relational exit ramp. That taps into old wounds of mine, wounds that constantly remind me that I don't want to live like that. I want to give people a chance at resolution instead of choosing abandonment.

Maybe some people never learned hope or conflict resolution. But maybe they also were never taught what it means to be committed, to see something through, to stick around when it gets a little uncomfortable—and it always will at some point because that's life. Often we shove the discomfort somewhere where it still makes us twitch, and we seek out trivial, shallow distractions. We're so afraid of self-reflecting that we would rather ride on the surface. But when the magic carpet we are escaping on finally lands, all of the heartache is still waiting there for us, steaming in a pile. It makes me so sad when I see this play out over and over again in various scenarios. I want to learn to help people break through and find the hope again. It's one of my new challenges to try to get inside their hurt and figure out how to help them knock those walls down, but some folks are unwilling. Others want to but simply do not know how.

If we think about it, Hollywood (television, movies, the love lives of celebrities) teaches everyone this model of easy abandonment. Our culture has become one of "If you don't like it, you don't have to deal with it. Just walk away." I have watched friendships break up over kids having some issues with each other, only to realize that issue would not go on forever. Two minutes later, the children might be friends again, and where does that leave the parents? I've seen people shut off communication because of political disagreements on social issues they were coming at from different directions but both with the same heart. I've seen people give up on ministering to someone in a difficult place, running out of patience, sending the message that eventually, the love runs out. But does it? That's what I always ask myself. Maybe if we have to take that break from a needier person, we can try honesty: "I feel like I fail your expectations right now, but I'd like to try to meet the ones that I can. I'd like to find a way to still love you the way that I am learning to. Can we do this together?" I've seen people shut out their own family because they're "fed up" with misunderstandings, passive-aggressive dart-throwing contests, and extreme miscommunication.

Am I guilty of same? You bet. I long ago thought walking away was sending a nice, final message to people who hurt me. Once in a while that thought still crosses my mind, drags me to a place of temptation, lies in my ear, sweetening the deal by saying conflict ends when you walk off. Is that what Jesus says? The answer is: sometimes. But let's look at what "sometimes" means. So many people have advised me through the years to follow these verses over small battles and hurts. I don't think that's at all what Jesus is saying. What do you think?

Matthew 10:1-15, Apostle Matthew narrating

And he [Jesus] called to him his twelve disciples and gave them authority over unclean spirits, to cast them out, and to heal every disease and every affliction. The names of the twelve apostles are these: first, Simon, who is called Peter, and Andrew his brother; James the son of Zebedee, and John his brother; Philip and Bartholomew; Thomas and Matthew the tax collector; James the son of Alphaeus, and Thaddaeus; Simon the Zealot, and Judas Iscariot, who betrayed him.

These twelve Jesus sent out, instructing them, "Go nowhere among the Gentiles and enter no town of the Samaritans, but go rather to the lost sheep of the house of Israel. And proclaim as you go, saying, 'The kingdom of heaven is at hand.' Heal the sick, raise the dead, cleanse lepers, cast out demons. You received without paying; give without pay. Acquire no gold or silver or copper for your belts, no bag for your journey, or two tunics or sandals or a staff, for the laborer deserves his food. And whatever town or village you enter, find out who is worthy in it and stay there until you depart. *As you enter the house, greet it. And if the house is worthy, let your peace come upon it, but if it is not worthy, let your peace return to you. And if anyone will not receive you or listen to your words, shake off the dust from your feet when you leave that house or town.* Truly, I say to you, it will be more bearable on the day of judgment for the land of Sodom and Gomorrah than for that town [emphasis mine]."

Note verses 12-14: "As you enter the house, greet it. And if the house is worthy, let your peace come upon it, but if it is not worthy, let your peace return to you. And if anyone will not receive you or listen to your words, shake off the dust from your feet when you leave that house or town." Um, what? So, in moments of sharing a relational conflict, I've had well-meaning Christians dismissively tell me to "shake the dust off my feet." Now, that certainly sounds awesome and empowering, but I'm not really sure that's what is intended. I don't think it means when people don't agree with you. I think it's more when the truth of Christ is spoken, evangelically, and is not welcomed. We move on. We don't beat those people with the Truth. We can pray for them and love them, we can even stay in touch, but we move on to people who have hearts to receive Christ.

Jesus is talking to His disciples here, preparing them to carry on His work after His ministry walking the earth as flesh is over. He is telling them to go out and heal and drive out unclean spirits in His name. He calls them to freely give the Good News and grace of Christ they have received to others. In this case, He sends them specifically to the "lost sheep of the house of Israel." He also says to find a person "worthy" to stay with, and if someone isn't peaceful or receptive, to let the peace return to the disciples and leave. Nothing about this is suggesting we walk away when there is personal conflict, disappointment, or hurt. This entire passage is about

74

spreading the Good News of Jesus. He tells them what to do and expects them to move on when ears are closed to His goodness.

Getting back to my original question: Are we to abandon people who hurt us?[21] No, I don't believe so. Have I taken space from some relationships when they were becoming toxic to my soul, keeping my focus away from Christ, becoming an idol or unhealthy fixation? Yes, I have, but I try to place those relationships at the foot of the cross and ask Him to redeem them, to clean my heart and theirs, to bring them to an understanding of His saving grace (if they have refused it), and to tell me when to pick those relationships back up again. There have been moments when I haven't felt led to do that. Other times, there has been a clear prompting or "divine intervention," for lack of a better term, to re-engage. At times, amazing healing and maturity had taken place on both sides and sometimes on only one side. But He never has asked me to pick something back up again—that I've truly given to Him in full trust—without preparing me for how to go forward from there. He does incredible redeeming work in relationships. Don't give up. Take space if you need to, but have integrity and deep compassion in the process.

I've had to be honest at times: "I need a little space right now. For whatever reason, some of our struggles with each other are pressing into pain (or anger) in me that I need to explore with God. I need to examine my own heart." I wish I could say I remembered to do this step always at the right time, but it is becoming clear to me how very important it is not to skip it. It shows the other person that he or she has value and that we love him or her without aiming hurtful darts of blame.

So, what do we do when people walk away from *us*? And it seems so incredibly unjustified and painful? After seeking out what our own responsibility was, if they truly won't come back into relationship, we speak our last words for now in love and care and then: Wait. We take it to God. We turn it over to Him, multiple times if we have to, until we completely unclench our hands and let it be fully in His grip. In certain situations, this has taken me weeks, and at other times, it has literally taken me years. Control, even over relationships, is really hard for us to give up most of the time. He can do amazing things even with ugly, dark estrangement. He can put people back together again to shine like a diamond. I've seen it firsthand. But relational repair usually didn't happen until I got my grubby hands off whatever it was.

God loves to bring healing to relationships. The Bible is loaded with screwed-up relationships that He redeemed. Look at the story of Samson in Judges 13-16.[22] Samson did not keep his vow to God and betrayed the secret of his personal strength to a prostitute informant to his enemy, the Philistines. Afterward, Samson was repentant, and God gave him another chance to fight the Philistines and claim victory for God and Israel when he asked. It was a chance, while still proving ultimately fatal to himself, that allowed him back in relationship with God.

Judges[23] 16:28

Then Samson called to the LORD and said, "O Lord GOD, please remember me and please strengthen me only this once, O God, that I may be avenged on the Philistines for my two eyes."

But the Bible also includes examples of folks who walked away from relationship, from God, and never came back. Cain did not yield to redeemed relationship; God spared and protected him, despite his murder of his own brother, but Cain removed himself from the presence of the Lord.[24]

Let's be honest here: Some people are not going to come back, and abandonment is hugely painful. We need to let God heal the part of our hearts that burns with no closure or resolution. If we don't, then we carry abandonment around like luggage that keeps expanding, and eventually we require a bigger suitcase. When we bring it with us everywhere, we start seeing abandonment where it doesn't belong. We can't control people shutting us out, but we absolutely can keep hearts open to not do that to our own relationships. It's up to the Lord to soften the hearts of people, as He did when Saul was about to be crowned the first king of Israel.

> 1 Samuel 10:9, author unknown, but he is recording the words of God
>
> When he turned his back to leave Samuel, God gave him another heart. And all these signs came to pass that day.
>
> 1 Samuel 10:26, author unknown, but he is recording the words of God
>
> Saul also went to his home at Gibeah, and with him went men of valor whose hearts God had touched.

We can leave an open door. Many doors may seem like they are shut forever, and certainly if abusive behavior is involved in any way toward us, the door must be shut out of love and boundary, but it's surprising to me over the years how many truly broken relationships found His Grace Place. Sometimes the fact we are still there, door open (not slammed shut), facing them, approachable, and unconditionally loving brings the angriest of hearts back to us—not because of who we are but because of Who informs our hearts. Grace does that. Pray, and wait. Give space. And ask

Him what He wants you to do when you see someone's back disappearing from you.

In the meantime, the only folks I want to "shake the dust off my feet" to in the biblical sense are those who don't want to hear about my God. I can stay in relationship with them, but the Bible says in Matthew 10:1-15 (as mentioned earlier) that I am not to waste my blessing on them (because they do not want or seek it). So, if you think, "You should be *done already*" with a tough relationship that seems to be going in circles, don't tell that person to "shake the dust off your feet." Jesus didn't abandon people. He moved on when He wasn't accepted, but He didn't abandon. When people leave us standing there staring with a big, painful question mark in our hearts and minds, we need to remember that is not Him; they are not representing Him.

I learned a hard lesson about abandonment many years ago. It sticks with me, even though it requires discipline to remember and live like I believe it, and I do believe it, but, like anyone else, I have a short memory. I sometimes have to relearn it. For whatever reason, coping with people leaving us never seems to get easier, but this is the truth, plain and simple: *No matter who* leaves us stranded, denies us, walks out of relationship, leaves us completely alone, doesn't see the hope that we hold out for a better tomorrow—even if we sit on an island for a while, a solo act, a dry throat waiting on an oasis—*God is enough*. He always is. Having people along for the ride is most awesome and a sure blessing. But at the end of the day, God and me, me and God = enough. He is the Oasis and the Quencher of our souls. When the enemy of my soul tries to whisper: "You are not worthy. You are alone. You aren't good enough for people to stick around and love you through the tough times," God says: "I sent my Holy, Perfect Son to die for you. You are everything to me. Rest here a while. I am yours forever. I will always keep the conversation going. You are never alone when you walk with Me. The defeated cross is My promise, as are My Words recorded in My Book."

When Our Expectations Leave No Room for Him to Bless

I had a friend recently tell me how alone she felt dealing with a major life-shaking event. I understood how she felt because the enemy of our soul wants to always make us feel alone in whatever we're facing. He lies through his teeth to discourage us and keep us from focusing on God's love and promises. Truthfully, though, our inner circle of the safest people to weather the storms of life with is usually very small. It's not uncommon for our greatest-level safety net to include only a few people. If you're feeling like there should be 10 more, there shouldn't be, unless you are not a private person and are superextroverted. There are dear people in my life I consider very good friends, but because they haven't weathered some of the same storms, they express their love more from a distance when I'm hurting in those ways. I've learned to let them do this because life hasn't knocked us around in the same way, and that's not bad. I also am not very good at reaching out to those who've experienced horrible losses that I have not. I definitely express my love, but I'm pretty sure I'm not in their inner circle when they walk through that pain.

Some dear people in our lives will always take a step back when they don't know how to help, but it doesn't mean they aren't hurting for us and don't love us deeply. They perhaps can't express it in a way that may satisfy us. I'm learning to be okay with that. My circle for fighting depression was a different circle than the one weathering parenting woes. Once I let go of expecting more than a handful of folks to care deeply on every issue, I was incredibly free to heal. We may feel like more people should rally around us, but sometimes folks just can't. It's not always that they *won't*, but they *can't* because either they are in the middle of an intense situation in their own lives, or they are simply not the ones God has gifted with helping us through a particular struggle.

> Proverbs 18:24, King Solomon speaking
>
> A man of many companions may come to ruin, but there is a friend who sticks closer than a brother.

Many of us can probably say we've known the "friend who sticks closer than a brother" in our lives; maybe over the course of our lives, we'll have one or two friends that remain true to this verse through everything. But I can also apply it to a friend or two during different seasons of life. The "many companions" are not necessarily those who don't rush to the front to hold us up in a crisis, but certainly not all of them can and do. This verse suggests to me the value of quality over quantity. In any season of our lives, we may have plenty of Christmas cards to send, but only a small handful of those folks will stick close enough in deep relationship. That's how life is. I remind myself constantly that my expectations need to line up with His. Some people will love through gifts, and some will show up emotionally. Gary D. Chapman explains this concept so well in his book *The 5 Love Languages: The Secret to Love That Lasts.*[25] When I'm so busy pointing at who isn't serving up the love exactly the way I want it, I can easily miss the many blessings around me.

There is a flip side to this coin, however: other people's expectations of us. Ah. Big sigh. Lately, I've thought so much about the fact that where we invest is where we reap. We can't complain when people fade out of our lives if we haven't done anything to show we care about them. Who are we not paying enough attention to? That's a question to ask our God because we can't possibly *stick closer than a brother* to everyone at once. We should ask Him to direct our paths.

I used to think that no matter what happened on the other end, in certain situations, I had to keep all the balls up in the air, doing my rightful duty to keep them in motion. Not everybody has to show love the same way, but when folks who regularly demand attention don't offer a gesture of relationship back, it's an interesting indication of the state of the relationship, or at least time to evaluate: Is this a friendship going through a one-way season, or is this a ministry, where I should not expect to receive back? I have found that meaningful relationship is not scattered among 20 people; it's who sticks closest in heart.

The other part about expectations is that, even when it comes to God, what we expect and what we receive may be two different things, but if we're stuck on the expect part, we miss when He has bestowed something on us. Take a look at this example of Peter healing a lame beggar in the name of Jesus in Acts 3. This takes place after Jesus has risen from the dead and has ascended into heaven, and the Holy Spirit has come at Pentecost. The disciples are now bringing the Kingdom of God to others through the word of their testimony and miracles of healing.

Acts 3:1-10, Luke the Physician narrating

Now Peter and John were going up to the temple at the hour of prayer, the ninth hour. And a man lame from birth was being carried, whom they laid daily at the gate of the temple that is called the Beautiful Gate to ask alms of those entering the temple. Seeing Peter and John about to go into the temple, he asked to receive alms. And Peter directed his gaze at him, as did John, and said, "Look at us." And he fixed his attention on them, expecting to receive something from them. But Peter said, "I have no silver and gold, but what I do have I give to you. In the name of Jesus Christ of Nazareth, rise up and walk!" And he took him by the right hand and raised him up, and immediately his feet and ankles were made strong. And leaping up he stood and began to walk, and entered the temple with them, walking and leaping and praising God. And all the people saw him walking and praising God, and recognized him as the one who sat at the Beautiful Gate of the temple, asking for alms. And they were filled with wonder and amazement at what had happened to him.

It's clear in this passage that the lame beggar did not receive what he was asking for. He was being carried to collect sympathy and therefore money. When Peter addressed him in Acts 3:5, "he fixed his attention on them, expecting to receive something from them." Peter is honest that he doesn't have silver or gold to offer, only the healing power of Jesus. From the rest of that account, it seems pretty clear that the once-lame man celebrated his healing. He was no longer stuck on expectations of silver or gold. Peter, by the power of Jesus Christ, had given him something so much greater. Where are we stuck, expecting from people when the gift is sitting unwrapped directly in front of us? Where should our hope and expectation be?

Psalm 62:5, King David speaking

For God alone, O my soul, wait in silence, for my hope is from him.

The Lord Loves Having You There

One of my dearest friends passed on this wisdom to me when I was going through a difficult time and I needed so much just to shut down, retreat, grab for my Father in heaven. Dysfunction Junction had put itself on a wide-load truck, grabbed a police escort, and followed me down the highway. My friend said this at the end of her email: "You can remain hidden in the shadow of His wings. The Lord loves having you there." Oh my goodness! He does? He does! He says so in His Word! Not many people in my life have sent the message: "No matter what happens, how you screw up, or your personal flaws, I will not be irritated by you. I will love you unconditionally. Please always, no matter your mood, come sit under my shelter." I don't know about you, but I find the goodness and shelter of the Lord almost too much to believe at times, except that He offers it, so, ultimately, who am I to pass that up?

Psalm 36:7, King David speaking

How precious is your steadfast love, O God! The children of mankind take refuge in the shadow of your wings.

Psalm 91, author unknown, possibly Moses

He who dwells in the shelter of the Most High
    will abide in the shadow of the Almighty.
I will say to the LORD, "My refuge and my fortress,
    my God, in whom I trust."

For he will deliver you from the snare of the fowler
    and from the deadly pestilence.
He will cover you with his pinions,
    and under his wings you will find refuge;
    his faithfulness is a shield and buckler.
You will not fear the terror of the night,
    nor the arrow that flies by day,

nor the pestilence that stalks in darkness,
    nor the destruction that wastes at noonday.

A thousand may fall at your side,
    ten thousand at your right hand,
    but it will not come near you.
You will only look with your eyes
    and see the recompense of the wicked.

Because you have made the LORD your dwelling place—
    the Most High, who is my refuge—
no evil shall be allowed to befall you,
    no plague come near your tent.

For he will command his angels concerning you
    to guard you in all your ways.
On their hands they will bear you up,
    lest you strike your foot against a stone.
You will tread on the lion and the adder;
    the young lion and the serpent you will trample underfoot.

"Because he holds fast to me in love, I will deliver him;
    I will protect him, because he knows my name.
When he calls to me, I will answer him;
    I will be with him in trouble;
    I will rescue him and honor him.
With long life I will satisfy him
    and show him my salvation."

So, at these crossroads of refreshment, when life has beaten us up a bit, or we simply need to find some refuge to refuel, it's a crazy choice we have to make. It goes against everything the world tells us. Are we going to believe "The Lord loves having you there"? It's completely a faith and obedience issue, isn't it? Not believing that fully doesn't affect our salvation, per se, but it does affect how we live it out. At the moment of receiving that advice, I was befuddled and frustrated because I could not get a confused person in my life to love life more than his chains. I thought I needed a break from that. At the very same time, I was seeking refuge but not fully believing the shelter of His wings was not only an "open house," but it was also chain-free. We have to leave our chains at the door to go in.

They just can't exist there in the same place as His promised protection. To even climb under His beautiful wings, we have to believe they offer shelter, that they are a dart-free zone.

So, I found myself wanting to counsel a person in my life about something I had to be able to do myself. I wanted so much for this dear person to be free and to enjoy what I thought I had learned to enjoy many years ago, His great rest, as outlined well in Matthew 11:28-30, but I needed to fully trust the One Who offers rest. How can I sell something I myself hadn't fully bought? Isn't that how faith is? We have something we want to offer someone in Christ, but we have to first examine our own hearts. Oh, my. Most days that is not fun, but it *is* freeing!

Matthew 11:28-30, Jesus speaking

"Come to me, all who labor and are heavy laden, and I will give you rest. Take my yoke upon you, and learn from me, for I am gentle and lowly in heart, and you will find rest for your souls. For my yoke is easy, and my burden is light."

My sweet friend's advice was not only that it was *okay* for me to take shelter but that *the Lord loves having me there*. It gave me permission to get away from the issue for a few minutes and refuel, but it also held me accountable to much more. What she said went much, much deeper, whether she realized it or not. There is room under those same wings for the person I was longing to help, even though I was temporarily trying to escape him. He loves having him there too. Sometimes I get wicked (Boston adverb) jealous about being under His wings. I want the escape so badly that I want to close the door on the way in. But that's not how God is. We don't have to share Him in the sense that He "runs out." His love is always, unending, spilling out all over the place. So, with this little loving smack of fresh wisdom still on my face, I could go back to the person I was trying to help and say: "Ya know what? There's some room over here under this feather, and whether we share a feather or you take that feather way over there, we are equally loved in His kingdom, and the Lord sure loves having you here."

Free in Him: Clearing Our Attic of Anxieties and Realizing Our "Chains" Are Just Phantoms and Lies

This subject was originally an outline of a talk I gave to a group of moms years ago. I was fresh from my days on the island when so much healing needed to happen, when I lived anxiety and depression as an almost everyday reality. The image of chains started to flash through my head, and I realized that once Christ had conquered death and the powers of hell and had risen again, "It is finished" (from John 19:30[26]) took on a deeply profound meaning. It meant that the chains we all think we are shackled to are really broken off and left at our feet if we put our trust in Christ and what He did for us. Nobody had ever explained this to me before, and I don't recall exactly how I came to this point. This may seem elementary to some, but it was a beautiful image that I was able to carry with me into times of intercessory prayer and ministry; in dealing with situations in my own life, I was frequently called out on whether I lived as if I believed this. I couldn't run from it. It wrecked me for good forever for the Kingdom life He wants us all to live—to live in full faith of "Your kingdom come, Your will be done, on earth as it is in heaven."[27]

For a few moments, let's switch gears and consider the analogy of an attic; we will get back to discussing our chains in a bit. Let's take a look at a first question for those of us with faith in Christ Jesus: If my "attic" is full of anxieties, am I a good witness or help to others? Do I represent my faith well? Do I wear the reality of Christ's victory in my life? Now that is not at all meant to condemn anyone or get people thinking legalistically. We all have tough seasons of life. Because I'm a writer and very right-brained, I more or less bleed words when I'm in pain, anger, frustration, anguish, etc. Very few people in my life don't have the curse of reading my long-winded emails, Facebook posts, or blogs as I process something upsetting. I don't think that makes me a poor witness to Christ; it just makes me openly vulnerable. If you aren't one of those people, you either enjoy the freedom with which those of us who are *those people* express ourselves, or you stopped reading this book after the first 10 pages.

What we do with the anxieties in our attic is what it's all about. It's not that we won't have any. It's that we hold tightly to them, give them to God, or keep trying to cling to them while simultaneously working on submitting them more to God. It's a process. If anxiety is a regular struggle, then this is going to be more of a long-term challenge, and by no means am I clinically addressing the subject. What I am asking is: What does it mean to live in His perfect peace?

Isaiah 26:3, Isaiah the Prophet speaking

You keep him in perfect peace whose mind is stayed on you, because he trusts in you.

This goes back to the chapter on Room 9. For me, it looks like surrendering each worry to His Throne, often over and over again until I let go. It means taking each thought captive and naming each concern, gnawing worry, and devastating "what if"—and telling them all that they must bow to the name of Jesus.

2 Corinthians 10:5, Apostle Paul speaking

We destroy arguments and every lofty opinion raised against the knowledge of God, and take every thought captive to obey Christ.

Psalm 55:22, King David speaking

Cast your burden on the LORD, and he will sustain you; he will never permit the righteous to be moved.

What does this verse say in Psalm 55? I don't know about you, but I feel "moved" around quite often by life. It doesn't even have to be a car accident or a devastating diagnosis. I feel knocked down by injustices, big and small, every day. At bullying. At people misrepresenting the love of Christ. The ESV as well as the KJV both express it as Him not letting "the righteous be moved." He will not allow us to be moved by our circumstances. Um, can I get an Amen? The fallen part is not a promise that we will not fall on our own when we are being sinful. It means that the forces of this world can shove against us, but the righteous will not be moved when we cast our cares upon and trust Him. Being honest about what's in our attic is okay. We all have stuff shoved in there. But part of our honesty is how we go about clearing it out. Are we being good stewards to hand those anxieties over to our victorious Christ, or are we hiding them under cobwebs and Aunt Sally's old sideboard to escape into vices?

Jeremiah 17:7-8, the Lord speaking through Jeremiah the Prophet

"Blessed is the man who trusts in the LORD, whose trust is the LORD. He is like a tree planted by water, that sends out its roots by the stream, and does not fear when heat comes, for its leaves remain green, and is not anxious in the year of drought, for it does not cease to bear fruit."

Okay, let's take a brief look at the home front, because I believe for many of us our first ministry is there in these years of childrearing: If my attic is full of anxieties, how much of myself do I have left to give as a mother and wife? If our attic door is bursting at the seams so everything falls out when we open it, we aren't fooling ourselves, and we certainly aren't fooling our families. Even babies know when we are stressed. This is what always convicts me: an honest view of the attic. We can hide it from many people in our lives but not the people we live with. They see the piles, the dust, the mousetraps of days gone by, and the things we can't let go of even though they aren't doing anyone any good. Just like anxieties. I don't know about you, but I don't want a legacy of anxiety and fear terrorizing my every move, my every decision. If you have a chronic struggle with anxiety, absolutely pursue medical advice. But if we can identify our own red flags and know when they are flying high, we do have some promises we can pray. It takes self-discipline. It takes handing each fear to the Lord. Perhaps the hardest ones are those that concern us about our family. Let's look at some of those promises:

Matthew 11:28-30, Jesus speaking

"Come to me, all who labor and are heavy laden, and I will give you rest. Take my yoke upon you, and learn from me, for I am gentle and lowly in heart, and you will find rest for your souls. For my yoke is easy, and my burden is light."

What? There's a different kind of yoke that is easy and light? I think I may want to trade in what's in my attic for that.

Psalm 34:4, David (not yet king) speaking

I sought the LORD, and he answered me and delivered me from all my fears.

He delivered me from all my *what*? After I first did *what*? There's that word: *sought*.

The verses that keep me afloat when negative thinking and deep-rooted insecurities bare their teeth are the following:

91

Philippians 4:4-9, the Apostle Paul speaking

Rejoice in the Lord always; again I will say, rejoice. Let your reasonableness be known to everyone. The Lord is at hand; do not be anxious about anything, but in everything by prayer and supplication with thanksgiving let your requests be made known to God. And the peace of God, which surpasses all understanding, will guard your hearts and your minds in Christ Jesus.

Finally, brothers, whatever is true, whatever is honorable, whatever is just, whatever is pure, whatever is lovely, whatever is commendable, if there is any excellence, if there is anything worthy of praise, think about these things. What you have learned and received and heard and seen in me—practice these things, and the God of peace will be with you.

I never used to understand *do not be anxious about anything*. It's pretty much impossible on our own. It sounds like a trite, pithy saying. But then I realized it's really a spiritual discipline. Thank Jesus we don't have to carry our burdens alone and have others on the journey with us. It doesn't just end with *do not be anxious* but gives us commands on how to achieve that. We must be *thankful* as we *let our requests be made known to God*— to God, not others. Oh, my. That's where I often slip up. I have to pray the peace of God over myself or a family member who lacks peace, even the kids when they're bickering. That's what guards our minds and hearts. Verse 8 (*think about these things*) is required before the *God of peace will be with you*. When I don't focus on that "whatever" verse, I plummet quickly into the depths. He gives us the tools to stay out of these depths. It's up to us to use them. I wanted other fixes instead: an escape through this or that. Nothing would take it away. Only Jesus.

Please know that I'm not anti-medication or anti-therapy. I think they're both important at different times for different reasons in proper context. Sometimes there is a chemical reason behind depression. But more importantly, I found deeper issues at play in my anxiety: cycles of dysfunctional choices that led me down the Path of No Peace. God was always there; I just had my back to Him. It surely is a daily battle of getting our armor on and *choosing* to keep our eyes on the Savior and not the storm. We can walk over all kinds of water that way, but only with eyes on Him.

> Philippians 4:19, the Apostle Paul speaking
>
> And my God will supply every need of yours according to his riches in glory in Christ Jesus.

Obviously I am not coming at this from a clinical perspective, but here are a few places where our attics start getting full. Our attics are cluttered with these chains:

- Past voices of lies
- Comparisons with others
- Fears about our or our children's future, finances, relationships, health, evil, derailment of our personal plans and goals
- Current lies from others

We must focus on His promises and dwell on what is true, as in the aforementioned Philippians 4:8:

> Finally, brothers, whatever is true, whatever is honorable, whatever is just, whatever is pure, whatever is lovely, whatever is commendable, if there is any excellence, if there is anything worthy of praise, think about these things.

We must *trust*:

> Isaiah 26:3, Isaiah the Prophet speaking
>
> You keep him in perfect peace whose mind is stayed on you, because he trusts in you.

We must remember fresh worry always assaults us the next day. Our inbox —the things vying to get into (and stay in) the attic—is always full of new concerns.

Matthew 6:34, Jesus speaking

"Therefore do not be anxious about tomorrow, for tomorrow will be anxious for itself. Sufficient for the day is its own trouble."

In the moment of His greatest torment, when chaos was about to ensue, when He knew what the rest of His hours on earth would bring, when He could have lingered in the attic, considering all of the "what ifs," Jesus instead offered this prayer to His Father in heaven:

Matthew 26:39-42, Apostle Matthew narrating

And going a little farther he fell on his face and prayed, saying, "My Father, if it be possible, let this cup pass from me; nevertheless, not as I will, but as you will." And he came to the disciples and found them sleeping. And he said to Peter, "So, could you not watch with me one hour? Watch and pray that you may not enter into temptation. The spirit indeed is willing, but the flesh is weak." Again, for the second time, he went away and prayed, "My Father, if this cannot pass unless I drink it, your will be done."

Not as I will, but as you will. The Bible offers this verse for the control freak in us; it's a verse that ultimately commands us to sweep out that attic we keep cluttered with worry.

Proverbs 3:5-6, King Solomon speaking

Trust in the LORD with all your heart, and do not lean on your own understanding. In all your ways acknowledge him, and he will make straight your paths.

As for those phantom chains that seem to still hold us back and choke us in our attics, we can say the following out loud and watch them scatter:

- "Chain of past toxic voices lying to me about who I was and am, Christ left you hanging there and broken off when He ascended. You have no part here."

- "Chain of comparison, you have already been defeated on the cross."

- "Chain of fear of the future, you lie about still being around my neck. You really aren't there. My Father loves me and wants to take care of me. He will take care of me so much more than the sparrow,[28] for that is what He promises."

- "Chain of current lies and deceptions, you cannot squeeze the life out of me. The precious blood of the Lamb was shed for this child. You were 2,000 years ago defeated. You no longer have a voice."

We can look up at a conquered cross and then down at the chains broken and snapped off at our feet because of Christ on the cross, and we take a little peek at that attic, and it's swept completely clean. Let's try to keep it maintained. The Housekeeper has already done the work. We need to stop living like He didn't.

*****

As I wrote this, I received an email from someone who was feeling anxious. Since it applies to any of us feeling that way, especially about relationship issues, I thought I'd share the advice I offered her: "Ask if you need to, but don't assume. Sometimes our bad feelings are only assumptions and speculations doing dark dances in our heads."

Dark thoughts lie to us that our chains are still on and that the attic remains chaotic. They sway slyly to their own music and try to get us to move along to a beat in our minds that pulses and coaxes: "It is *not* finished," when it actually *is*. I think we each need to get honest about what we allow to do dark dances in our heads and ask the Holy Spirit to dance there instead. He's the ultimate "bouncer" and very good at kicking out the bad dancers and clientele. He simply needs us to get real, get humble, and ask Him. It's only then that we will fully understand what it means to be unshackled, uncluttered, and truly free in Him.

Cage

I stretch my longest stretch with fingertips begging to make contact with
his tender heart.
In my mind, through my words,
I cannot reach him.
He hangs his head.
I just don't "get it."

I put my heart next to his, briefly, awkwardly, for as long as he'll tolerate
the embrace before school.
I try to have my heart beat on his,
To see if we can synchronize.
He moves away.
We're still off-beat.

I cradle nervous hands with long fingers that would gift the world with a
gentle touch.
But they do not clutch back.
They rub against each other, pushing away imaginary germ demons.
It's time to wash hands again,
The tenth time in 20 minutes.

I hold him in front of me on my lap as we read.
Bedtime stories bring some ease.
Shoulders lighten, and I am behind,
Holding my breath,
Thanking Jesus for this moment of still,
For his mind to get lost in a story,
Trying to not let my tears break onto his neck and slide down his back.

I drop my bowl as I turn to his breakfast face,
Pained,
Already finding a worry.
From his eyes, I can see it pinging around in his head.
I hate it. More than any human bully I've ever met.

I speak sweet blessings to push back across the front lines.
Reclaim territory. Force a retreat.
I speak the peace of Jesus.
And his face releases.
The cereal box becomes more interesting for a minute.
I might be able to eat a bite now and maybe even swallow past the lump in my throat.
Sharing the table means seeing it all.
Oh, God, please let me be strong.

Getting dressed means second-guessing.
"Did I wash my hands yet? I think I might have touched something messy."
There are sounds of a heated discussion in the bathroom.
A lot of thinking and rethinking aloud.
Where did the happy sounds of yesterday go?
I don't want to open the door
Because if I don't, I hold onto hope I will find the happier child in there again.
Opening it might crush me.

The hat and gloves are on.
"Did you pack the note to my friend, Mom?
Oh no! The bus might come."
The rush and swirl of morning school rhythms are comforting
But raise the panic flag again.
He is rigid as I bless his head and heart for the day at school.
But then a skip.
Just one, but I saw it.
I'll take it and replay it all day in my head while he is gone.

*****

There is a cage I did not build;
I did not give permission for it to be constructed.
And inside, further and further away, sits a panicked heart.
I'm trying to come in, Little Man.

97

I'm still looking for the right key.
Can you show me which one fits this lock?
I'm trying them all, but there are so many.
I really could use your help.

*****

He gets off the bus unwilling to commit to what kind of day he had.
Fifteen questions and statements pour out of his mouth.
I squint to look for the clues, for crumbs, for which key.
I find none.
"I don't want to talk about it" moves quickly into "What's for snack?" and
"I might have touched a tissue at school by accident at lunchtime. Do you
think I can get sick?"
And hope flattens slowly, like a pinhole in a balloon.
I resignedly have him start homework.
And hear him twitch about erasing.
I want to erase the past two months.
Where was I when he entered this cage?
Why did I not grab him back on his way in?

He writes his math work,
And I stop and smell the Mango-rific, something-or-other scent on his hair.
I let my nose glide past those soft locks.
A peace, a prayer, a faith, a trust, a promise.

I will get in there soon, Son.
I will beat back the torment.
I will get both arms in there to pull you out.
And I will slam that hellish door shut,
With the thief of your peace smacked around with God's Truth about you.

And you will skip and jump and laugh and cry freely again.
And I will skip and jump and laugh and cry freely with you as we dance
around the cage
And
Kick it far into the past.

Bonnie Lyn Smith

ADHD: An Unwanted Intruder That Offered Another Opportunity for My Savior to Guide Me

As this book was being polished before heading to my editors, I found myself stopped at a placeholder for the anxiety section. A few weeks went by before I could get back to it. There was a very good reason for that. After a few months of shades of obsessive-compulsive disorder (OCD) and anxiety creeping into my son's life, with no clear explanation of why it had returned, as well as some concerning comments he was making along the way, we came slamming into my daughter's birthday. It's a day I will never forget because my son had a breakdown that day. I won't go into the details, but it was the culmination of weeks of scheduling team meetings at school, re-reading and considering necessary updates to his IEP, making doctor appointments, and requesting that a teacher complete a diagnostic form for our pediatrician. Did I know a diagnosis of Attention Deficit Hyperactivity Disorder (ADHD)[29] was in our cards? Yes, by this time I did. But what I didn't know was why my son was slipping into a very tormented world of OCD and anxiety.

Years ago, I prayed over a friend with extreme OCD. Jesus pulled it right out of her shoulders, almost visibly. As far as I know, as I check in now and again, it was greatly reduced, to the extent she was weaning off medicine. Awesome, right? Yes, every time Jesus heals it is awesome. But my own child was not being relieved, no matter how much I prayed. I would bless him with the peace of Christ, and his anxiety would be alleviated, but he didn't suddenly break out into amazing freedom. Was God going to completely heal him? I prayed so. But just as I carried an epi pen until Jesus healed him of his significant food allergies and I carry albuterol for rare moments when asthma flares, I prayed for wisdom for how to proceed. Maybe there were important lessons I was going to learn through this. Maybe it was a journey God allowed because He was going to use it. Scratch that "maybe." He uses *everything*. So here we were. Here we are, actually. I debated adding our ADHD/anxiety/OCD journey to the book. I am praying for God to show me how to do this and keep integrity for my child. It's a footnote to the anxiety section, but to show how we walk through these trials and find the other side—or often learn to wait in the valley for another side to come into view—real-life examples from my life are needed. Being bare-naked-vulnerable for myself is one thing; my child is completely another. But people need to know how we walk our children through these challenges. I have heroes who went ahead of me in this. I know how badly we all need to walk this journey together.

If you have a child on the autism spectrum, a child with mental health struggles like anxiety, or an ADHD child, this is for you. I pray that you will find something in it that ministers to your heart, encourages you to go on, but more than anything, points to my heavenly Father, the only One Who can sit with us in that place and bring sweet peace in the midst of seemingly endless storms.

I originally wrote this very sensitive blog to a limited number of trusted friends and family. I feel this is really important to understand. I'm only beginning to unlock it myself. This is what a child with ADD/ADHD hears every day of his or her life, from all of us: teachers, coaches, parents, etc. We're mostly well-meaning, but we're all completely guilty of it.

"Sit down, Joey. Stop talking, Joey. Joey, stay on task. Joey, are you cutting correctly? Joey, pack that backpack faster. Did you hear me, Joey? Joey, are you listening? Joey, stop tapping your pencil. This is time to be still, Joey. Joey, are you with us? Joey...Joey...Joey....Joey...."

I get it. I understand how and why it happens. I am guilty of it myself, but this is what my son feels, trapped inside a jail of anxiety about something he struggles to control and is developmentally too young to solve or even know what the adults are so frustrated with. Because my son is such an external processor, I have the benefit of hearing what is often in his head. I'm beginning to realize that it sounds like this:

"I need to worry if I did everything they just said. What did they just say again? I might not have done that. Oh, wait, maybe I did. Oh, I don't know. I might be bad. They think I can't listen. I didn't mean to not do the first three instructions. Maybe I'm dumb. I don't think I have a good memory. I don't know how to sit still. Oh, she might be mad again. Should I put a bandaid on this cut? Wait, did she tell me to get my shirt on? But I need a bandaid on this cut. I'm so overwhelmed, I can't stop crying, but that slows me down, and they think I'm being a baby when I cry."

This morning, I chose to say this (next paragraph). I don't know where it came from except God. He showed me a glimpse of what my son was feeling, and it felt incredibly heavy to carry around. He's so worried about the simple tasks he can't complete that he has retreated into a world where things can be better controlled. He is locked into this: "Did I wash my hands? I can control that. Maybe I washed my hands. Let me do it another time because I'm not sure. That way at least my hands are clean. I know I can do that. Maybe I touched a germ, so let me wash again" and other such small tortures. It's a prison of the mind, and I am committed to daily blessing and praying him into seeing that he doesn't have to live this way.

Me as we waited for the bus: "Little Man, you are amazing just the way God created you. I know you are told all day long to 'stay still, listen, stop talking, don't fidget, did you finish that worksheet, are your boots on, and do it faster,' and that must be really, really hard. And that must make you feel like you don't meet expectations a lot of the time. But you know what? You are a wonderful little boy with a big heart, and I would never think that you did wrong on purpose. People are trying to help you focus, but it sounds like a long day of demands, and I'm so very sorry. You go off today with the peace of God on you. You stop and quietly ask Him for help when you can't please an adult. He knows how pure that heart is inside of you because He put it there, and He knows you are trying your best every day and that some days are very hard and you hurt big inside. I love you deeply, and you don't need to worry all day long if you did everything right. As long as you try, I know you are doing your best work. I'm really proud of you. Don't worry if you did everything right or in the right order. You don't have to be perfect. I'm not perfect. I need God's help too. Every day of my life. I am very proud of the wonderful son and child you are. Go in God's peace, Son. I love you so much."

And it could be that I wanted to see it. It certainly could be. But I felt his shoulders lighten a little. I felt something heavy blow off between us. I felt his painful guard relax. A tiny bit. For the first time in weeks, he let me quickly embrace him. He might have skipped once as he walked to the bus. And I came inside and wept because God showed me what he carries around inside, and it's way too much for a child. Way too much. I hope my reflections somehow help those of you with children who struggle similarly. Thank you for reading.

[Nothing about this post is anti-medicine or anti-behavioral therapy in addition to prayer. We are taking steps ourselves to pursue the best course for our child. It was more or less to share our journey and to open up our adult minds as to what goes on inside the mind of a young child trying to deal with this. It's also not a post soliciting help or sympathy. We are prayerfully taking our own steps. It's a dialogue for parents on this road alongside us. You are not alone.]

I bleed in words. It's what I do. It's my therapy. It's not that I think what I write is great, but I know what my heart meant when I wrote it, so I might rock over and over again reading what my heart said and I typed. I share this section so that I can lay bare the process I went through emotionally sorting out this decline into Scary-Terrible-Unknowns, where the enemy of my soul wanted to hold me captive with no hope. As you can see by reading it, I went back and forth like a yo-yo. This post came a day or two after the one in which my anticipation of the ADHD diagnosis (which later came) was so evident:

I climbed in the top bunk last night and laid down next to a resting redhead, one who was relaxed and calm. I placed my hands around his long fingers and my hand on his head and whispered blessings and peace. I cuddled him with his blanket. I traced where the hairline went around the ear and let my tears fall. Then my oldest came in to claim the bottom bunk and saw his crazy mother up-bunk from him. But he didn't ask. He just knew. So, I got to thinking: Doesn't Jesus climb in the top bunk with us? Doesn't He nestle around us and shelter us with His wings? I absolutely love verse 5: *You will not fear*. Amen and amen!

Psalm 91:1-5, author unknown, possibly Moses

He who dwells in the shelter of the Most High
    will abide in the shadow of the Almighty.
I will say to the LORD, "My refuge and my fortress,
    my God, in whom I trust."

For he will deliver you from the snare of the fowler
and from the deadly pestilence.
He will cover you with his pinions,
and under his wings you will find refuge;
his faithfulness is a shield and buckler.
You will not fear the terror of the night,
nor the arrow that flies by day.

And then a day later:

Like so many mornings lately, I didn't want to get out of my bed and face the heaviness in our house. I didn't want to look at dragons lashing about in the spiritual world, the devil trying to dance on my back and the backs of others. But then the author of Nehemiah spoke from the depths somewhere in my mind and heart: "Do not be grieved, for the joy of the LORD is your strength" (Nehemiah 8:10), and King Solomon declared: "The name of the LORD is a strong tower; the righteous man runs into it and is safe" (Proverbs 18:10). *I want to live in that tower right now, Lord. Thank You for fortifying it for me. Crawling in...leaving laptops and lattes behind. Just. Need. You. Amen.*

Two days later:

Today was a good day. Today he sat on my lap to read a book. He created art. He made a joke. He still exhibited OCD behaviors. But his pained worry face was not as present. Today he was diagnosed with ADHD Combined Type. With today came a big relief of a diagnosis and a big next step. But I feel the hand of Jesus in mine and his and ours. Like his brother and sister both say: "We want the old Little Man back. We really miss him." Today I saw glimpses of him. Down the road I feel he is waiting for me, restored and happy, skipping along and laughing heartily about puppy farts. Until that day when I can find his jovial self again, I'm gonna let God lead me, one step at a time, and I'm going to celebrate each moment when God's glory shines and boomerangs off and through this trial.

It was at this time my husband and I were about to launch my author web site. Oh, exciting! Those were my plans, for sure, but as we all know, our plans are not always the ones God has in mind. At times, we juggle an enormous number of balls in the air and keep them all going for a while. Once in a while they *all* crash down while we keep *only one* in the air. I'm learning to be okay with one in the air. I'm learning to stop thinking it's a failure when I can only keep one up. Sometimes one is far more important than 10. The web site took a back seat. And then came the diagnosis—and my response:

I put my child on narcotics today. Yes, yes, I did. The good news is I have not been "that parent" to judge others for doing this, at least not in my recent memory. I think each person has to make the best choice for their child, or at least try to help in whatever ways that they can. But for me, handing my kid speed to choke down after his breakfast seemed like something I was simultaneously prepared for by God for years (by hearing other success stories) and completely overwhelmed by if I spent too much time thinking about it.

I won't always feel that *what did I just do* feeling that I have today. I won't always take a deep breath and bless his medicine. But today we took a big step together, and we shall see where it takes us.

What I do know is this: He needs to function so we can see the leftovers of what is really going on beyond ADHD. We need to be able to see into the pool of anxiety/OCD and see if there is a drain at the bottom. Does he have a toe stuck there? Can we drain the pool? I also know that God has been preparing us for today for a long time.

When Little Man heard it could help him but only because a doctor thought so (and not that we pop pills for any occasion), he happily took it. He saw hope in front of him. He saw possibility.

I'm not the first parent to face today, nor am I the last. Those of you who have gone ahead of me in this: Thank you from the bottom of my heart.

And for teachers: I love and appreciate you, but I did not do this for you. You will benefit, but you alone were not enough of a reason.

And judgy parent volunteers in the classroom who linger a little too long over my child's classwork, snapping at him to hurry it along and focus: I sure as doggy doo-doo did not do it for you. I'm proud of my sweet boy off meds. You should be half as lucky to have a little man like mine with a wild imagination and big heart. I'll take his off-task focus issues any day to have his character and personality be what they are.

And doctors: I didn't do it for you either. You are awesome, but you alone didn't persuade me.

And Bonnie: I didn't do it for me. I love Little Man exactly as he is, and I don't medicate to make life in the house less frazzled, emotional, or frantic. I would have been perfectly fine still swinging from that tree with him hanging off the bannister and jumping from room to room like Tigger.

I didn't do it for siblings or for his father.

But Little Man: This is for *you*. If it doesn't serve you well, we discard it. If it helps you bring the real functioning you to the surface, we keep taking it. You are the only one who knows if you like hearing all of your amazing radio stations at one time or if it's better to have some help and tune into one channel at a time. Go with God today, Son. I can't wait to hear about your day. Mine will be spent thinking all day about you trying on your new focus and seeing how it feels.

One of the things I am trying to do with the trials of life is look for the blessings and lessons in them. This certainly isn't a new concept, but it is a hard choice to make every day because worries carve out a slippery path for us. We entertain a concern, then a panicked thought, and before we know it, we are not only on our bottoms, but we are sliding down the hill, about to hit a tree. That's me when I walk through this stuff. I'm not good at getting my correct boots on with the right traction so that I don't slip. But the redeeming part is that when I do slide down the hill, I hit a tree, a glorious tree, the one upon which my Savior Jesus Christ died before rising again. That's the tree I want to hit when I fall. How about you?

I came back to my book at one point, after ADHD medication was started. I felt like that was Step One in taking out the anxiety battle and seeing what was behind it. It was then I found that place marker: "Free in Him: Clearing Our Attic of Anxieties and Realizing Our 'Chains' Are Just Phantoms and Lies." Seriously, God? *That* is where I left off? *That* is where you want me to pick this back up again? *Really?* But God doesn't seem to answer sarcasm, not in my experience, anyway. So, I got my laptop back out, and here I am, genuinely living it as I write it. Why? Because I come from it more from His viewpoint now. I have deeper compassion, a new angle, a fresh perspective.

And I leave this section with this thought: As I ask Him daily to sweep out the attic of that which I can't control but threatens to derail me and my child, do I really see my chains as off? You know what helps me? Looking where God is working through others. When I got out of my own way, I saw how my other children were supernaturally strengthened to pick up some pieces lately, to do His work. They may not seem like big things, but they are far more important than even the school team meetings I am arranging. I am being Martha, and they are being Mary.[30]

I end with this story about my daughter, closest in age to Little Man, who saw beyond her own needs for a few hours. It was *not* anything I asked her to do, nor do I think she did it within her own strength. She was listening in her own way to an assignment the Father gave her and empowered her to carry out:

> My kids aren't perfect. We have major areas we are working on in each of them every day like anyone else. Character is so important to us. But today, when I needed it the most, Chickie took several hours of her time and helped Little Man with a made-up project making a "monkey box" (involved old issues of *National Geographic Kids*, an amazon.com box, some glue, scissors, and heaven only knows what else). She indulged his latest obsession, was patient about the very specific "vision" in his head about this box, and saw it through to the end: making sure there was clean-up and everything else, while others of us were out shoveling the driveway. She did something for him I've not been able to do lately. She jumped into his vision and helped him make the latest dream happen. Chickie, I'm grateful for you today. You made me proud. You were leader and loving-kindness at the same time. You were the wings a little boy needed to crawl under. You loved him with Jesus Love, and can't we all use a lot more of that? Sign me up next, Chickie. Will you help me finish this book?

Why We Can't Lead From Our Own "Woundedness"

I recently had a friend in an unfortunate situation that led to consequences having to be lived out. We all have those: friends like that and consequences that we have to each live out. I've been on both sides of that, and both are painful for different reasons. What I could not do during that time was allow my personal triggers to play into that person's unhealthiness (or my own, for that matter). Speaking the truth in love does not mean unlimited encouragement because we think that person needs to "feel good." We can't dismiss people from consequences. And that's one good reason why we can't lead from our own "woundedness": Because we are each wounded in one way or another by our own sin, and we want to think we are consequence-free, so we mislead friends facing similar sins or temptations into thinking they are off the hook.

In other examples, as I write this, I'm in a stuck place relationally with two different people in my life. I wish I could say I'm waiting on their next move. That would really make it simple and take all of my responsibility out of it, but I know by now that's not always how God would have me roll. So, I freshly turn over both situations—both of which have become unhealthy in their dynamics despite my deep love for these dear people—to God every time I want to force my way back in or play the martyr. I am literally in a holding pattern. Why hold back? Because He hasn't given me an answer yet, and it's an area of my own woundedness that I don't trust. But I fully trust Him. Even though I'm not battling an enemy, I can pray His words back to Him, and His promises are fresh and real. So, I want Him to *go before me* and *level the exalted places* because those are some mountains I can't scale on my own. Wouldn't it be better to let Him go first and make a clear path, as it suggests here in Isaiah?

Isaiah 45:2-3, the Lord speaking through the author

"I will go before you
    and level the exalted places,
I will break in pieces the doors of bronze
    and cut through the bars of iron,

"I will give you the treasures of darkness
    and the hoards in secret places,
that you may know that it is I, the LORD,
    the God of Israel, who call you by your name."

Why do I know this promise is for me, too, and not just Israel? Because of the reason He gives for answering: *that you may know that it is I, the Lord, the God of Israel, who call you by your name.* See, if He is going to get glory from it and be known further, it is as real for me now as it was for Israel then. What's more, in Isaiah, God speaks and says His Word does not return empty. I want in on that. I want to pray His words to Him. They are so much better than my own, very broken, very limited-in-perspective ones.

Isaiah 55:8-11, Isaiah the Prophet narrating

"For my thoughts are not your thoughts,
    neither are your ways my ways, declares the LORD.
For as the heavens are higher than the earth,
    so are my ways higher than your ways
    and my thoughts than your thoughts.

"For as the rain and the snow come down from heaven
    and do not return there but water the earth,
making it bring forth and sprout,
    giving seed to the sower and bread to the eater,
so shall my word be that goes out from my mouth;
    it shall not return to me empty,
but it shall accomplish that which I purpose,
    and shall succeed in the thing for which I sent it [emphasis mine]."

Really, my heart's cry should always be for more of His understanding, not to get more of my own way. Doesn't He love both ends of a challenged relationship? So, when I am in the waiting place trying to exercise self-control and let Him lead (ouch!), I need a little extra help seeing the end goal. I need to be reminded that it is *in the path of your commandments* that *I delight*. I need Him to undergird me, to *incline my heart*. I include some pretty impactful excerpts from Psalm 119 because in them I find the courage, the strength, and the heart's cry to do better. *The unfolding of Your Word(s) gives light.* Oh, yes! I need it to unfold, Lord Jesus. *Keep steady my steps. Let no iniquity get dominion over me.* This is why I can't lead from my own brokenness. This is why I must wait for His signal and His direction. Because I want *no iniquity* to *get dominion over me.*

Psalm 119:33-36, unnamed author

Teach me, O LORD, the way of your statutes;
    and I will keep it to the end.
Give me understanding, that I may keep your law
    and observe it with my whole heart.
Lead me in the path of your commandments,
    for I delight in it.
Incline my heart to your testimonies,
    and not to selfish gain!

57-60
The LORD is my portion;
    I promise to keep your words.
I entreat your favor with all my heart;
    be gracious to me according to your promise.
When I think on my ways,
    I turn my feet to your testimonies;
I hasten and do not delay
    to keep your commandments.

105-106
Your word is a lamp to my feet
    and a light to my path.

I have sworn an oath and confirmed it,
　　to keep your righteous rules.

129-135
Your testimonies are wonderful;
　　therefore my soul keeps them.
The unfolding of your words gives light;
　　it imparts understanding to the simple.
I open my mouth and pant,
　　because I long for your commandments.
Turn to me and be gracious to me,
　　as is your way with those who love your name.
Keep steady my steps according to your promise,
　　and let no iniquity get dominion over me.
Redeem me from man's oppression,
　　that I may keep your precepts.
Make your face shine upon your servant,
　　and teach me your statutes.

When I think of the people on the other end of these two separate

relationships, I know they are in pain too. They are silently waiting or

don't know how to proceed. They perhaps also lack wisdom. But I know

He loves us all. As Zephaniah says, He *will rejoice over us with gladness*

and *will exult over us with loud singing*. That is the Lover Who brings

reconciliation to the world, to these relationships I trust Him with, to us

with Himself. That's the Mighty Warrior I want leading me: the One Who

knows certain victory.

Zephaniah 3:17, Zephaniah the Prophet speaking for God regarding the
restoration of Israel

"The LORD your God is in your midst,
　　a mighty one who will save;
he will rejoice over you with gladness;
　　he will quiet you by his love;
he will exult over you with loud singing."

At times, I am still sorting out scars and healing from

woundedness. Ever feel that way?

Jesus, I'm really sorry. I thought I had given that one to You, and yet I keep twitching, so clearly I have taken it back. I want You to have this one to work Your amazing healing in. I want my grimy hands off it. I keep putting new fingerprints on it, but Yours are the only ones I want. May I not let this scar, this condemning voice of the past any longer inform me or speak lies. Take this area and place Your soothing balm over it. You are the balm in Gilead. You are the Great Physician. I praise Your name. Amen.

Jeremiah 8:22, Jeremiah the Prophet speaking

"Is there no balm in Gilead?
    Is there no physician there?
Why then has the health of the daughter of my people
    not been restored?"

Raging Hyena

Sometimes I feel manic. I just do. I am often having the most peaceful day, and then, "Bam!" the rage is right there on the surface. This happened to me a few years ago. I had a relatively quiet, albeit painfully short, kindergartener-free morning. You know those two and a half hours between bus pick-up and drop-off when you can maybe get groceries or exercise, but a shower doesn't usually happen, and only small, minute, seemingly unimportant items get checked off your list? Did a little writing, but not enough to submit anywhere. Chipped away at one or two bills. Started a recipe for yummy after-school cookies for those in my family without food allergies, only to discover we were down to just one egg. Got dressed. (Yes, getting dressed is on my list. If it's not on yours, it should be!)

So, anyway, at 11:40 AM, I begrudgingly went out in the freezing rain to meet my son at the end of the driveway as I heard that bumble-bee-striped chariot barreling down the street. As it pulled to a stop, two cars raced by at speeds I know far surpass the posted speed limit, clearly trying to miss having to wait for a school bus stop. They were going the other direction. As the third one looked like it was about to do the same, I started to scream—not just any scream, but one that called forth a wild hyena ready to pounce on anything and everything standing in the gap between my small cub and me. I have no idea what the bus driver thought, whether she was on my side or simply figured I ran out of coffee, but I put myself in front of the now-stopped third car and glared at the driver with the most horrified look of disgust I could muster. Aren't we women something else?

112

We can get the "ugly" ramped up several notches very quickly when we want to. But the thing is, I wasn't really thinking at that point, only reacting.

I'm happy to report that my cub safely exited the bus and crossed the street, and as we climbed the hill of our driveway, he was asking if I was scared at the same time the woman in the third car gently spoke these words: "I get it. I'm a mom too. I've been there. But I wanted to let you know the bus driver's lights weren't on, and her doors weren't open." I then proceeded to explain how my anger wasn't so much at her but the two cars ahead of her that raced down the street, and as I settled into her very disarming words, I found this kernel of an apology deep within myself: "I'm sorry. Thank you for letting me know. I appreciate that. I didn't know. I was very scared."

And isn't that it, right there, in a nutshell? Doesn't it all come down to us being wildly scared? Aren't we raging hyenas when our world is threatened, or we perceive it to be? I wasn't wrong to rage about my son's safety, but I was wrong to think I'm so right, that my perspective is the only one. Whether or not my incredible anger surfaced purely from the safety angle, or there were a few hormones and a bit of self-righteousness mixed in there as well, my passion needed truth to calm it down. Did that lady quote Bible verses at me? No. But she spoke in a way that is so lacking in our culture today: with compassion and patience. She empathized and gave me the benefit of the doubt. Ironically, this had been my post on Facebook just a few hours before I carried on as I did:

Isaiah 26:3, Isaiah the Prophet speaking

You keep him in perfect peace whose mind is stayed on you, because he trusts in you.

Um, Bible relevant much? Amen! Bring it!

Grace That Changes: One Forgiving Moment at a Time

I performed an interesting social experiment in the past year at a favorite establishment in my town. Folks working there weren't very friendly, to the point I dreaded going in. So, I tried being very kind every time I went, going out of my way to clean up any mess we left, saying something encouraging at the counter, and in general bringing in a consistent smile, no matter what attitude came back at me. I went in more regularly with my kids, having them do homework and lingering, looking for opportunities to bless. It took a few months, but then suddenly, the staff not only knew me by name, but they started going out of their way to also be kind: They brought my kids free food, helped me more with questions I had, and apologized for mistakes even when I didn't complain. Although I'm sure I'm not the reason the entire establishment is friendlier, I was able to show my kids that kindness begets more kindness. Even they have noticed a difference.

So, I keep thinking how deliberate the choice is to love and bless. It doesn't always flow naturally; it is a minute-by-minute choice, but if we employed this same idea everywhere—the car that cuts in front of us for a parking space, the tired clerk at the market counter, the pharmacy technician who doesn't need one more prescription coming in when she's already so behind—how many people could we each reach with love and grace? Too much in this world tears us down. What if that pharmacy clerk was going to go home and drink herself into a stupor again tonight because of problems weighing on her unbeknownst to me? What if the impatient car parker is also impatient at home with his kids, snapping at the least little annoyance? Do we need to cause him more angst, or could grace perhaps make a small dent, leading to bigger dents, in the way he daily functions? Could our choice to extend grace turn around a despairing, tense, hopeless attitude? All I know is grace changed who I am, and the people who offered me grace in my own bad attitudes deserve so much credit; they overlooked the ugly in me and encouraged the beautiful. Grace changes things, one forgiving moment at a time. My mouth can't hold poison and antidote all at the same time. James, brother of Jesus, said it best:

James 3:9-12

With it [tongue] we bless our Lord and Father, and with it we curse people who are made in the likeness of God.

From the same mouth come blessing and cursing. My brothers, these things ought not to be so.

Does a spring pour forth from the same opening both fresh and salt water?

Can a fig tree, my brothers, bear olives, or a grapevine produce figs? Neither can a salt pond yield fresh water.

And here is a fun one for you. I thought it was amazingly descriptive to *clothe himself with cursing as his coat* and have it *soak into his body like water* and *like oil into his bones*. Hello, songwriter! Modifiers and analogies make my heart jump!

Psalm 109:17-18, David (not yet king) speaking

He loved to curse; let curses come upon him!
  He did not delight in blessing; may it be far from him!
He clothed himself with cursing as his coat;
  may it soak into his body like water,
  like oil into his bones!

Summertime presents some nice opportunities for learning how to relate better to one another. I bet if you're a parent of kids still at home, it does in your house too. One of the rules of my house is: "If you come to any of us with accusations, anger, or emotional response of any kind, you may not walk away when you are in the middle of receiving a response. If you are not prepared to hear out a response to a problem/accusation you put forth, you should not present it in the first place." I told my children that I know adults who do this to me all of the time. They drop their emotion down but run off and sulk without sticking around to hear another perspective. Any issue or relationship worth working out deserves to have both people heard. We better ourselves with stronger, committed relationships if we learn to develop this one important concept. I see this as part of the blessing/curse idea. Working through misunderstandings or upsets needs to be approached from a stance of blessing. Blessing invites openness and vulnerability. Cursing shuts relationships down. I don't want cursing to enter my *body like water* or *my bones like oil* as the Psalmist depicts for us, which suggests to me a "soaking in." Toxic interactions have a way of soaking in and permeating so many areas of our lives. Grace and love do just the opposite; they cover us:

1 Peter 4:8, Apostle Peter speaking

Above all, keep loving one another earnestly, since love covers a multitude of sins.

Along the same lines, I had a difficult "issue of character" discussion with one child at bedtime one night. It wasn't a huge deal, really, and it was only one area of correction, but this child struggles to receive constructive criticism no matter how delicately it is presented. I waited to make sure it sank in and shared that we all have to be able to take feedback and ask God if it's something He wants us to correct. Then, because this child bruises easily from feedback, I spent the falling-asleep moments listing all of the things this child does well, areas where I am very pleased, and at Item Number 20, the slight smile gave way to slumber, and peace climbed beside us and laid its head on the pillow as well, a welcome companion. That is not how I conduct myself every day, but when I consult God and come from a standpoint of blessing, informed by His living Word, it is a much more peaceful way to do life.

Just as mourning comes in waves, so does His grace. It rides in on constant tides like a covering of love that soaks into every pore until it fills the heart. There is never grief without grace, if we'd only learn to keep our feet in the Living Water, facing the oncoming surf, not fearing the raging storms, but instead standing steadfast to receive as He gives. If only we stood there in great faith and expectancy, we'd quickly find He *never ever* stops giving. We're the ones who lose hope or courage and walk away from the source. His waves of grace chase us and lap at our feet, desiring to heal, to nurture, and to be received, but if our backs are to those waves as we walk away, we never even know what was there for us, what we failed to discover as we walk back inland to where discouragement and fear are ready to take hold and plant roots—only because we gave those dark thoughts permission again. I don't want to give them permission anymore. I want to sit in tide pools of never-ending grace at the feet of Jesus. If you trust Him, you can sit there too!

Whose Court Is the Ball in Anyway?

About a year ago, I received a message from a dear friend struggling with a similar relational problem as I was at the time—one that had gone on for years without a clear end, not something trivial. In her message was that fabulous question: "How do I know when to contact them? How do I figure out whose court the ball is in?" That's a loaded question, and I certainly can't pretend to answer that catered to each situation and relationship, but it got me thinking about the higher calling we are held to when we believe Christ is our Savior, a higher calling to love and not easily dismiss or discard. The following was my reply at the time:

Ah, Dear Friend:

You have tapped into some issues I'm still working through. Those are all brilliant questions, ones I am still asking myself, and how I wish God would drop the "this is how you deal with this relationship's particular dysfunction and what your response is to be, and when" manual into my lap. I've been essentially begging Him for years.

That said, I can share my recent struggle. On a special occasion recently, I didn't want to call this person. In fact, it made me sick to my stomach to call until I did, and sadly, even then I felt empty and sick. My conversations with them are one-sided; they're self-absorbed and in defensive posture always; they won't fully disclose, and if I disclose anything, I get criticized or mocked. My wise husband asked afterward why I felt I needed to call. We sent a card to lovingly acknowledge them. Isn't that good enough?

As for how to know *how* to contact, I don't remember how you all exactly function. For me, sometimes the safest bet is a quick email: "Thinking of you. Hope you had a nice _____. We are x,y,z right now (one safe line about something you feel you can share but doesn't make you feel too personal if you don't want to be). Love, _____"

I know we can't always rely on email as the only communication, but since it's there, if you don't feel personally ready to call, at least you ease their hearts that you care and are thinking of them. Calling or time in-person, whenever possible, is always best for hearts to be fully heard, though. There is no substitute for it.

Sadly, because we are the ones who have exposed the problem, the ball is often in *our* court. It's in our court because we are healing, because we are learning better ways to handle problems, and because they may never pick up the ball. But just because it's in our court doesn't mean we always have to pick it up right there and then. If we need to hear clearly from our Father in heaven first, if we need a bit more healing time, if we need an inspired reason to call and say something, waiting itself isn't sinful, unless you are waiting out of spite.

That's a long way of saying:

1) They may never know to pick up the ball, or even if they do, they may never pick it up because they feel stuck. This is an opportunity for our (well, actually *His*) grace to come in, but...

2) We need to have our "grace suit" fully on before calling. Calling itself accomplishes nothing if we don't call with the agenda Jesus would: To simply love and speak truth. If we have a ramped-up agenda: Wait. If our heart is smarting from the last encounter and we know we might explode if confronted on anything, even something mundane: Wait.

What matters most, going forward in trying to model safe, healthy relationship, is that the following is communicated:

> Grace
> Unconditional love
> Listening ears, if needed
> Forgiveness
> Patience
> Gentled-heartedness
> Meekness
> Humility

and all fruit of the Spirit.

> Galatians 5:22-26, Apostle Paul speaking

> But the fruit of the Spirit is love, joy, peace, patience, kindness, goodness, faithfulness, gentleness, self-control; against such things there is no law. And those who belong to Christ Jesus have crucified the flesh with its passions and desires.

> If we live by the Spirit, let us also keep in step with the Spirit. Let us not become conceited, provoking one another, envying one another.

Even if you don't call on that special occasion but call a few weeks later, what matters isn't the legalism of calling on a specific day. Those are the old rules. Those are the rules that call down perfection, shame, fear, condemnation. We operate with new ones now. What matters is you call clothed like Christ in the above-mentioned ways. That will make all of the difference in the world in the future, regardless of their response or even an ounce of change. Why? Because they are indicators of who *you* are now, not them, and your victory is getting off that phone knowing you put those clothes on before you called. Even if you mess up or get angry or have a moment when you slip into old stuff, the new you is trying to wear the garments of Christ and carry them everywhere. And slip-ups, when confessed and turned over to Christ by believers, are covered by grace and that cross.

Those are my thoughts.

Loveyou!
Bonnie

God's timing is amazing because I had just spiritually battled one of my relationships over and over again in my own heart and mind. I was still a bit in the clutches of processing my recent incident of grabbing the ball sitting in my court—the results weren't pretty or nice. The other person involved still doesn't give one indicator of liking me. But I did what God called me to do, so there's a peace that flows, regardless of how back and forth that ball gets volleyed, or even if it stays right where it seemingly taunts us. We move it when the Holy Spirit tells us to move it. When we go ahead of Him, we often do so much damage. So, yes, the ball is in our court. Grace is an action. So is love. I'm going to remind myself to live where perfect peace is because perfect peace doesn't depend on the ball. It depends on the saving grace of our amazing Savior and trusting in the goodness of His Father, *Our Father*. That's Whose courts we sit in waiting for the next move, sometimes simply resting there. And there is Isaiah 26:3 again. Geez, Isaiah, do you have to keep being so relevant?

Isaiah 26:3, Isaiah the Prophet speaking

You keep him in perfect peace whose mind is stayed on you, because he trusts in you.

Feeding the Heart of the King

This topic is hands-down one of my all-time favorite Bible references. It comes up all of the time. It is constant counsel not only for me, but also for others. On several occasions I have had friends tell me that they had a significant issue to work out with a spouse, an authority figure in their lives, or a difficult person in general (or several of those categories at once). Immediately what comes to my mind is the "Esther principle."

Esther was the Jewish queen in the Bible who needed to get the ear of her very intimidating king (of Persia). He didn't exactly ooze grace and understanding, and he could banish or kill her for any reason at any time. He wasn't coming in from any part of her perspective: vulnerable woman, disrespected Jew, desperate servant of his (as his wife). Before she could present any of her wishes to him about the fate of her people, she decided to feed him and his staff a few meals. Um, yes, feeding a man as a way to his heart is nothing new; it's in the Bible! Sister Girl prepared two banquets, not just one. She needed him to see her heart clearly, and in order to do that, she made sure his needs were met first. Brilliant! Relevant excerpts from Esther's account are at the end of this chapter for reference.

So, as I offered this counsel to several friends, not all of them sharing my faith, my point wasn't whether or not they actually fed "their king (or queen)" a delicious meal. My intent was for them to find a place of loving their spouses with a humility that would open ears for listening, stir vulnerability, soften hearts. Or, if it wasn't a spouse but some person in authority over them, I encouraged them to maintain a similar posture, presenting a reasonable request when the time was right. Timing is everything, as we see from Esther's example. Now, please hear me in this: We are *not* talking manipulation or even favors. This is entirely about figuratively "washing feet"[31] in a way that shows someone you are trying to open communication, that you care about what he or she cares about. Mostly I have applied this to marital relationships, but even when having to confront a father figure or an authority of some kind, this can be useful if done with integrity. It's about grace and caring; but it's also very much about not bulldozing in with our requests and instead being honoring and respectful. Esther knew her place in that kingdom and that queens before her had been kicked out. She had much at stake. She needed to be prayerful, seek counsel (from Mordecai, her cousin), and wait on the Lord with her timing. That "wait on the Lord" part means "patience," by the way, which most of the time feels very inconvenient, I know, but it keeps us from going before the Lord in our decisions and actions. I'm not very good at that fruit of the Spirit (patience, Galatians 5:22-26), but I know it's necessary, and it's a command after all:

> Romans 12:12, Apostle Paul speaking
>
> Rejoice in hope, be patient in tribulation, be constant in prayer.

I have seen wives take this step toward their husbands (and vice versa), and they have been able to communicate better what was important to them, to see more eye to eye. So much of the stuff of life gets in the way and makes us defensive. A gift of love can be so disarming. An attitude of humility and yielding can go a long way to opening doors. Again, I'm not talking about receiving abuse of any kind. *Please hear me on that.* I have seen spouses move closer to each other exercising this principle, deep issues of the heart be heard, and the other party feel respected and honored. The effects can be long-lasting, but we can't bail halfway. We have to be willing to go the distance—to make the extra meal, figuratively speaking. We have to be willing to go further in our personal sacrifice, to bow lower. It's not about getting our way but rather about reaching a place where we can feel heard and successfully negotiate significant issues. We simply cannot effect change or work through conflict from a place of hurt, no matter how tempting. We must only lead with love, respect, honor, gentleness, and good will toward men. Otherwise, our voices lose the ability to carry far enough to reach listening ears.

Let's take a look at how Esther managed her way through some life-threatening tension. Relevant excerpts are included. It's a long read, but I think it's worth examining her example in its full context.

Esther 4:9-17, most likely written by a Persian Jew

And Hathach went and told Esther what Mordecai had said. Then Esther spoke to Hathach and commanded him to go to Mordecai and say, "All the king's servants and the people of the king's provinces know that if any man or woman goes to the king inside the inner court without being called, there is but one law-- to be put to death, except the one to whom the king holds out the golden scepter so that he may live. But as for me, I have not been called to come in to the king these thirty days."

And they told Mordecai what Esther had said. Then Mordecai told them to reply to Esther, "Do not think to yourself that in the king's palace you will escape any more than all the other Jews. For if you keep silent at this time, relief and deliverance will rise for the Jews from another place, but you and your father's house will perish. And who knows whether you have not come to the kingdom for such a time as this?" Then Esther told them to reply to Mordecai, "Go, gather all the Jews to be found in Susa, and hold a fast on my behalf, and do not eat or drink for three days, night or day. I and my young women will also fast as you do. Then I will go to the king, though it is against the law, and if I perish, I perish." Mordecai then went away and did everything as Esther had ordered him.

Esther 5:1-8

On the third day Esther put on her royal robes and stood in the inner court of the king's palace, in front of the king's quarters, while the king was sitting on his royal throne inside the throne room opposite the entrance to the palace. And when the king saw Queen Esther standing in the court, she won favor in his sight, and he held out to Esther the golden scepter that was in his hand. Then Esther approached and touched the tip of the scepter. And the king said to her, "What is it, Queen Esther? What is your request? It shall be given you, even to the half of my kingdom." And Esther said, "If it please the king, let the king and Haman come today to a feast that I have prepared for the king." Then the king said, "Bring Haman quickly, so that we may do as Esther has asked." So the king and Haman came to the feast that Esther had prepared. And as they were drinking wine after the feast, the king said to Esther, "What is your wish? It shall be granted you. And what is your request? Even to the half of my kingdom, it shall be fulfilled." Then Esther answered, "My wish and my request is: If I have found favor in the sight of the king, and if it please the king to grant my wish and fulfill my request, let the king and Haman come to the feast that I will prepare for them, and tomorrow I will do as the king has said."

Esther 7:1-7

So the king and Haman went in to feast with Queen Esther. And on the second day, as they were drinking wine after the feast, the king again said to Esther, "What is your wish, Queen Esther? It shall be granted you. And what is your request? Even to the half of my kingdom, it shall be fulfilled." Then Queen Esther answered, "If I have found favor in your sight, O king, and if it please the king, let my life be granted me for my wish, and my people for my request. For we have been sold, I and my people, to be destroyed, to be killed, and to be annihilated. If we had been sold merely as slaves, men and women, I would have been silent, for our affliction is not to be compared with the loss to the king." Then King Ahasuerus said to Queen Esther, "Who is he, and where is he, who has dared to do this?" And Esther said, "A foe and enemy! This wicked Haman!" Then Haman was terrified before the king and the queen.

And the king arose in his wrath from the wine-drinking and went into the palace garden, but Haman stayed to beg for his life from Queen Esther, for he saw that harm was determined against him by the king.

Esther 8:1-8

On that day King Ahasuerus gave to Queen Esther the house of Haman, the enemy of the Jews. And Mordecai came before the king, for Esther had told what he was to her. And the king took off his signet ring, which he had taken from Haman, and gave it to Mordecai. And Esther set Mordecai over the house of Haman.

Then Esther spoke again to the king. She fell at his feet and wept and pleaded with him to avert the evil plan of Haman the Agagite and the plot that he had devised against the Jews. When the king held out the golden scepter to Esther, Esther rose and stood before the king. And she said, "If it please the king, and if I have found favor in his sight, and if the thing seems right before the king, and I am pleasing in his eyes, let an order be written to revoke the letters devised by Haman the Agagite, the son of Hammedatha, which he wrote to destroy the Jews who are in all the provinces of the king. For how can I bear to see the calamity that is coming to my people? Or how can I bear to see the destruction of my kindred?" Then King Ahasuerus said to Queen Esther and to Mordecai the Jew, "Behold, I have given Esther the house of Haman, and they have hanged him on the gallows, because he intended to lay hands on the Jews. But you may write as you please with regard to the Jews, in the name of the king, and seal it with the king's ring, for an edict written in the name of the king and sealed with the king's ring cannot be revoked."

The way I see it, we can apply any of these accounts in the Bible to our own lives. If it worked for Esther, why not for us? But the thing about the Bible is this: We have to follow the heart and obedience to God behind it if we are going to try out a scenario. We have to be prayerful and make sure it had an edifying result. For example, I don't suggest putting our younger brother (Joseph) in a cistern when we get jealous.[32] But seriously —where are you finding communication hard, your perspective not heard, a need to break down a wall of pride between you and another? Where do you need to feed the heart of a king or queen before moving into a confrontational subject? It has moved mountains in my life. What can it do in yours?

Uh, Oh. Chick Fight: When Our Hearts Are Not Understood

I have found, over time, after evaluating relationships and their many complexities and intricacies, that who we really are shows up between extending the olive branch and waiting to see if it is received. Who we are is at its most raw in the waiting place, not knowing if rejection and condemnation are coming—or grace. My prayer:

Oh, God, let me be a grace-pourer and not a "twitcher," who stews in the valley. Let me think the best, hope for the best, and extend the best of myself while I wait for the storm raging around me to quiet. Let my own soul not be battling but resting in You. Thank You that when I ask You, You fight for me. You bring Your truth into situations, and You invite me to rest in Your gentle, humble heart. Laying in Your lap, Daddy. Snuggling up tight until the storm passes. I'm grabbing onto the hem of Your garment like a favorite blankie and rocking myself in the comfort of Your love. Amen.

Matthew 11:28-30, Jesus speaking

"Come to me, all who labor and are heavy laden, and I will give you rest. Take my yoke upon you, and learn from me, for I am gentle and lowly in heart, and you will find rest for your souls. For my yoke is easy, and my burden is light."

Exodus 14:14, Moses speaking

"The LORD will fight for you, and you have only to be silent."

Exodus 14:14 requires something of us that is very interesting: to fully let Him have the battle. We can't keep a piece of it and let Him have the rest. We can't have our own weapon in hand and then ask for His rescue, while we stand at the ready to battle where we think He isn't doing a good job. We have to honestly mean: "It's Yours and Yours alone." Being silent is an act of obedience, faith, and trust. If we can't manage the still (silent) part, why do we expect the rescue? Backing up, the verse before Exodus 14:14 is this:

Exodus 14:13, Moses narrating

And Moses said to the people, "Fear not, stand firm, and see the salvation of the LORD, which he will work for you today. For the Egyptians whom you see today, you shall never see again."

Ah, Moses declared it! This was right as the Egyptians were pursuing the fleeing Israelite slaves and before Moses parted the Red Sea and took them across to safety. Talk about stress and discord! This was no chick fight. These were nations at war with each other, long-term slaves breaking free. And what does Moses do as he leads his people? He declares it! That's truly the essence of faith, isn't it? It's saying: "We believe you, God. You say You will show up, and we trust that." If Moses can do that on the verge of a massive exodus out of Egypt after years of his people being enslaved, how much more so can we turn over our relationship disputes to God?

I'm not saying He will lead the other party of our dispute into an empty sea only to have the waters crash over that person, as He did the Egyptians, or that we will *never see [that person] again*, as discussed in the context of this verse. What I am saying is that we need to work on the *be silent* part and declare our trust in Him *before* deliverance happens. Sometimes in the middle of relational misunderstandings, big and small, I whimper out a quiet: "Um, I trust You, Jesus. That is all." Because I simply have no solution, no answer, no eyes to see the completely exposed heart of the other person. But He does.

I have a difficult phone conversation coming today. Yes, phone. (It must be serious if I'm getting on the phone because I'm not in any way a phone person.)

Dear Lord, I have no clue what to say, so I'm just going to lick my shut-up-sicle, and as a dear Kwaj buddy phrased it, my "grace-sicle" as well, and listen until You give me words. Maybe listening is all that is needed. Maybe that is part of what being still means. And when/if the barbs come flying at me, please don't let me feel pride and get defensive. Let me be a listener and help me quiet this storm. If You're in the boat with me, that should be no problem. You have a history of calming storms like this one, so I know You can do this. Amen.

Psalm 46:10, author unknown, but he is recording the words of God

"Be still, and know that I am God.
  I will be exalted among the nations,
  I will be exalted in the earth!"

Psalm 107:29, author unknown, but he is recording the words of God

He made the storm be still, and the waves of the sea were hushed.

Luke 8:22-25, Luke the Physician narrating

One day he got into a boat with his disciples, and he said to them, "Let us go across to the other side of the lake." So they set out, and as they sailed he fell asleep. And a windstorm came down on the lake, and they were filling with water and were in danger. And they went and woke him, saying, "Master, Master, we are perishing!" And he awoke and rebuked the wind and the raging waves, and they ceased, and there was a calm. He said to them, "Where is your faith?" And they were afraid, and they marveled, saying to one another, "Who then is this, that he commands even winds and water, and they obey him?"

As I write this, I already have an answer. Thank You, God: The olive branch is finally received. Weapons have been put down. Real communication has been ushered in. Wow. I started the phone conversation with: "Guess what? I'm just calling to listen to you, so go ahead. Tell me everything on your heart, and I'm not going to respond until you're ready." And that made all arrows fall out of her quiver, and she simply said: "I miss you." It's amazing to me that when we take the peaceful, disarming approach, much more can be accomplished and fewer hurtful words can be said.

Thank You, God! People matter to You: both sides of the argument. I just love that, because as You might already know, ahem, I screw up at times. Thank You for loving both of us enough to get us out of the ring and into Your rainbow of promises. Amen.

I don't do well shoving problems under a carpet. If they never get taken out, shaken out, and aired out, the carpet stinks more and more. I don't believe in forcing people up against a wall with issues to be dealt with, but I also feel completely disempowered when the other party in any given conflict shuts down, goes silently hostile, and walks away. That is a form of passive-aggressive control by the other person, unless there's a nice "Hey, I need to regroup and think on this, but I'll get back to you soon." Words matter. We need to make sure we don't use words that shut people down, but now that I'm a big girl, I expect to have big-girl conflicts that get resolved in big-girl ways. Often, the healthiest boundaries are the ones that say: "Can you get back to me if you would like me to gently grace you through this, or maybe you don't want my grace but you plan to come back ready to interact after a while?" But no matter which words we use, we need to decide if we can have enough self-control, patience, and self-sacrificing love to wait on His deliverance, to let Him go ahead of us. I don't want to be standing in that Red Sea when He calls it from split waters to crash back down on the divide. I want to be standing victorious on the other side, knowing He led me across because I waited for each instruction, because I trusted Him fully in my relationship with the other person.

Oh, God, help me not to ever think I can part the sea on my own, by my own power or strength. Amen.

One of the many things I love about the Lord is that He loves the people on both ends of these exchanges so deeply that He lets us almost exhaust ourselves with a careful letter or phone call and much prayer before a conflict resolution because He protects all of His sheep so much. One afternoon about two years ago, when my husband and I were completely wrung out composing a letter in a painful situation, I went for a nap and started praying. I felt the Holy Spirit show me some of the pain of the other parties, and I started to sob and to intercede in prayer for them. Of course, it wasn't the first time we have prayed for these dear ones, but it was a beautiful picture of being truly knit together with a love that only God can give us for other people. It certainly wasn't something I planned ahead of time. Nor was it convenient after several iterations of struggling with this issue. But afterward, I said to the Lord in my head:

There's a different version to write, isn't there?
And He said, "Yes."
But I'm tired, and this is so hard.
And He said, "I know. But I love them so much too."

Of course I knew that, but I loved the journey He took me on to show me that. And isn't that really the point?

What Do We Do With Garbage Dumped at the Wrong Curb?

James 4:1, James, brother of Jesus, speaking

What causes quarrels and what causes fights among you? Is it not this, that your passions are at war within you?

Scenario 1, Healthy Interaction:

Person 1: "This is bothering me. Can we talk about this?"

Person 2: "I don't see it that way, but I'll try to understand better."

Scenario 2, Unhealthy Interaction:

Person 1: "This is bothering me. Can we talk about this?"

Person 2: "Well, I can't understand why you are attacking me because my life is so horrible, and I have XYZ problems, so how could your issue even come close to being valid? How dare you add to my pile?"

Yup. Had this Scenario 2 conversation today, and I was Person 1. I need to remember this when I respond to folks as well: to aim for Scenario 1. Our own pile of stuff is not relevant when someone comes to us with a *separate* issue. Oh, boy, am I guilty of this at times, which is why it's also one of my biggest triggers: when people can't hear me because they are so busy reciting their own woes from a separate situation. Each relationship has its own stuff to talk through. What happened in XYZ relationship has little to do with ABC relationship. One of my 2013 mottos was: "Please don't bring the wrong garbage to my curb. If it's mutual trash, let's work through it and sort it out. If it's garbage you share with someone else, please deal with it on that curb. I can only clean up my own garbage." Now, that doesn't mean I won't listen or let someone bounce possible resolutions off me. What it does mean is that I need to be careful not to dump my own garbage at the wrong curb.

Ephesians 4:15-16, Apostle Paul speaking

Rather, speaking the truth in love, we are to grow up in every way into him who is the head, into Christ, from whom the whole body, joined and held together by every joint with which it is equipped, when each part is working properly, makes the body grow so that it builds itself up in love.

What do we do when the other person thinks his or her garbage belongs at our curb? Does it? What does *speaking the truth in love* mean? Is that permission to draw a boundary? Recently someone (not a consistent person in my life) felt the need to tell me about a grudge she's been carrying against me for almost three years. Um, wow. That's not at all to be taken lightly. As much as Dysfunctional, Ugly-Sinner Me would like to dismiss that and not think about it, Healthy, Healed, Sanctified, Whole Me needs to consider that information, if only to examine my own heart out of love and respect for the other person. Usually at these times, I ask myself a few questions:

- What is wrong/so unhealthy about our relationship that the person couldn't express honesty sooner?

- Am I unapproachable, or does this person avoid conflict until she's built up her arsenal?

- Is this a person whose point of view is healthy/valid for me to consider?

- Does God want me to consider this, or is this coming from brokenness in the other person that has nothing to do with me?

I am finding that this is partly what truly walking in His amazing peace is: It's listening for discernment on what to pay attention to and what to ignore. Despite the painful dagger aimed rightly or wrongly at me, I know Whose I am and to Whom I belong, and I know how He sees me.

Whenever He wants me to know something, it's a gentle rebuke through trusted sources. So just like I did a few days ago when a person who barely knows me aimed her own pain and brokenness at me, I am going to give this one to God.

God, if this is truly my garbage, will You expose Your Light on it and show me my wrongdoing? I am going to rest in You and wait. I'm waiting at the curb to know if You would like me to pick this up, look at stench in my own heart, and let You replace it with Your beautiful aroma. Otherwise, I don't want to pick up the stink from another source because then it won't go away. It needs to be cleansed on the right curb. No matter which curb it sits on, it needs You. Let me know if it needs me as well. Amen.

If I have expressed compassion, grace, and any humility I felt appropriate to folks in these kinds of interactions, then the rest belongs to God. He is the healer of hearts, not me. I can walk in great peace because I know that, at the core, frequently these painful exchanges or misunderstandings may come from such misplaced hurt in the other person. And if not, He is so incredibly faithful to show us where we have responsibility.

Matthew 18:15-17, Jesus speaking

"If your brother sins against you, go and tell him his fault, between you and him alone. If he listens to you, you have gained your brother. But if he does not listen, take one or two others along with you, that every charge may be established by the evidence of two or three witnesses. If he refuses to listen to them, tell it to the church. And if he refuses to listen even to the church, let him be to you as a Gentile and a tax collector."

Now, this verse is Jesus's instruction on how to handle sin in the church, but I think we are wise to take a look and see where our responsibility begins and ends, whether we are the one bringing the garbage to someone's curb or we are the recipient. Why is the church asked to get involved? Because at times we need a third party to help us realize whose garbage it is. Sometimes our own perspective is clouded. Surely this is why the Israelites appointed judges in Old Testament history before the time when Israel had a king to rule over them. The people couldn't handle that without a judge hearing directly from God. Hmmm. But I also see a final boundary at the end of that statement. If *he refuses to listen* despite consensus among the witnesses and church, what are we to do? I read that as: not accept the garbage. This cuts both ways. We need to be willing to hear wise counsel when we have sinned against someone as well as willing to make a clean break when we are wrongly accused and the other person can't let it go. We need Him to tell us how to proceed.

This brings me back around to my original point, which had little to do with sin but more to do with people bringing their unrelated "stuff" to the table when we are trying to directly interact over shared stuff. How do we get to the place where people stop redirecting to their own stuff? I haven't been able to fully answer that yet, but I think it is about getting closer to the true meaning of *speaking the truth in love* of Ephesians 4. That's not a license to slam people around and put a smile or Bible verse on top of it. Although this verse is specifically referring to interactions with people who share belief in Christ, what relationship wisdom deposits can we find in that bank? Here's what I see:

Again, Ephesians 4:15-16, Apostle Paul speaking

Rather, *speaking the truth in love, we are to grow up in every way into him who is the head, into Christ,* from whom *the whole body,* joined and held together by every joint with which it is equipped, when each part is working properly, makes the body *grow* so that it *builds itself up in love* [emphasis mine].

What will happen when we put grace and love on our interactions? *We will grow.* Does it matter if the other person shares our faith, how we then apply this verse? No, because the idea is, as a part, each ligament *grows and builds itself up in love*. What is that? Our own sanctification as believers (for those of us who are).

So, when there is a tough conversation and we want to be heard and to model to another person what that would look like, we may or may not change their garbage-dumping habits. But we will be working out more of our own sanctification, letting Him purify us and make us more reflective of Himself. I used to think I was put on the planet to police the self-absorbed. What I learned was that for each ounce of garbage wrongly cast at me, I had already cast pails of it at Him. Face to the floor. Humbled. I revisit the wrong curb every day of my life. But for my precious Jesus, I'd still be riding the truck around town thinking I could set everyone else's garbage right. What I found out is that I need to get off the truck and go through my own trash. Maybe if I do this enough, others around me will realize that we all have piles to sort through, but when we are on this journey together, we can put the bags down and come listen to one another, building one another up. We can stop assuming we are the only ones sorting trash. We can stop demanding our own spotlight, and as the verses in Ephesians 4:15-16 suggest to the believer, we can *grow up in every way into him who is the head, into Christ.*

Do Those Praise Freaks Know How Hard Life Can Really Get?

I go to a nondenominational church with a mixture of folks in terms of praise expression. Some jump up and down with hands raised, as if trying to reach God in heaven right on the Throne in that very moment, and some are more reserved in their demonstration of worship, which is a euphemism for: They stand still, emit some expression on their faces, fold their hands, and tolerate the rest of us. Neither way is right or wrong. I find myself both amused and completely blessed by our awesome variety; it takes all kinds, and I delight in diversity.

So, as I was sitting in church this past Sunday, I started noodling over how passionate praise might come across to someone in pain. Why? Because as I look around, I know some of the stories of the people sitting there: the seemingly yet-unanswered prayers and heart cries, emotional pain, disappointment, anger, and tough situations. In some cases, I don't know the personal stories, but I feel the emotion when I look into their eyes or see their posture. I imagine there's a big "I'm waiting, God, so where are You?" floating around in their hearts and minds. And I think I might understand a little what might be going on inside their thoughts—maybe not each situation, but some of them. I've been there. I've wondered about those crazy praise freaks and how they could possibly muster that much enthusiasm in church, let alone in life in general.

I dedicate this discussion to all people, past/present/future, who have felt/are feeling/will feel completely numb during worship and might not understand what is happening in those moments and might even feel discouraged by it. Depressed/frustrated/angry peeps in church often look at those in more praiseful/worshipful stances (or seasons of life) and think it's all "pie in the sky" and that we've not hit any hard bumps like they have. It's good for them to know that a lot of those people have walked through tremendous trials and distress to get to that worshipful place. They've had to wait on the Savior to rescue them. They've had to be face-to-the-floor humbled. I myself am one of those people. I may go through rotten seasons again, like anyone else. I surely hope I still keep praising Him, but I know myself: I have a bad memory. I might find myself once again resenting the praising folks who seem to have a passion for Christ that hits the roof and back again.

I've found that usually the ones so desperately praising Him know how high the stakes once were or currently are. *So very high*. When I was depressed, I honestly thought that they were all fakers with no real hard knocks in life, but I was wrong. It turned out that the opposite was actually true: They had already hit rock bottom and knew how much they needed the Savior. They had looked with empty, desperate stares into the face of the Father as their last resort, and He answered them. A posture of praise is an act of trust, a leap of faith, a thankful heart for things past and things *not yet accomplished*. It is obedience. It is not mere happiness. It is bringing honor to the Father of lights, from which all good gifts come. It is acknowledgment. It is confirmation of covenant relationship.

James 1:16-17, James, brother of Jesus, speaking

Do not be deceived, my beloved brothers. Every good gift and every perfect gift is from above, coming down from the Father of lights with whom there is no variation or shadow due to change.

I refer to one of my absolute favorite accounts in the Old Testament, not only to inform us of what praise really is, but also to remind us of the consequences of a despising heart. We don't always feel like praising, but that's a lot different from resenting others for making that choice, regardless of their current situations—even in spite of them. I include the entire chapter here for context, as it is important to realize what King David is celebrating: the ark of the covenant[33] (or ark of the Lord) brought to Jerusalem as a resting place for it.

2 Samuel 6, author unknown, but he is recording the words of God

David again gathered all the chosen men of Israel, thirty thousand. And David arose and went with all the people who were with him from Baale-judah to bring up from there the ark of God, which is called by the name of the LORD of hosts who sits enthroned on the cherubim. And they carried the ark of God on a new cart and brought it out of the house of Abinadab, which was on the hill. And Uzzah and Ahio, the sons of Abinadab, were driving the new cart, with the ark of God, and Ahio went before the ark.

And David and all the house of Israel were celebrating before the LORD, with songs and lyres and harps and tambourines and castanets and cymbals. And when they came to the threshing floor of Nacon, Uzzah put out his hand to the ark of God and took hold of it, for the oxen stumbled. And the anger of the LORD was kindled against Uzzah, and God struck him down there because of his error, and he died there beside the ark of God. And David was angry because the LORD had broken out against Uzzah. And that place is called Perez-uzzah to this day. And David was afraid of the LORD that day, and he said, "How can the ark of the LORD come to me?" So David was not willing to take the ark of the LORD into the city of David. But David took it aside to the house of Obed-edom the Gittite. And the ark of the LORD remained in the house of Obed-edom the Gittite three months, and the LORD blessed Obed-edom and all his household.

And it was told King David, "The LORD has blessed the household of Obed-edom and all that belongs to him, because of the ark of God." *So David went and brought up the ark of God from the house of Obed-edom to the city of David with rejoicing.* And when those who bore the ark of the LORD had gone six steps, he sacrificed an ox and a fattened animal. *And David danced before the LORD with all his might. And David was wearing a linen ephod. So David and all the house of Israel brought up the ark of the LORD with shouting and with the sound of the horn.*

As the ark of the LORD came into the city of David, Michal the daughter of Saul looked out of the window and saw King David leaping and dancing before the LORD, and she despised him in her heart. And they brought in the ark of the

139

LORD and set it in its place, inside the tent that David had pitched for it. And David offered burnt offerings and peace offerings before the LORD. And when David had finished offering the burnt offerings and the peace offerings, he blessed the people in the name of the LORD of hosts and distributed among all the people, the whole multitude of Israel, both men and women, a cake of bread, a portion of meat, and a cake of raisins to each one. Then all the people departed, each to his house.

And David returned to bless his household. But Michal the daughter of Saul came out to meet David and said, *"How the king of Israel honored himself today, uncovering himself today before the eyes of his servants' female servants, as one of the vulgar fellows shamelessly uncovers himself!"* And David said to Michal, *"It was before the LORD, who chose me above your father and above all his house, to appoint me as prince over Israel, the people of the LORD—and I will celebrate before the LORD. I will make myself yet more contemptible than this, and I will be abased in your eyes. But by the female servants of whom you have spoken, by them I shall be held in honor."* And Michal the daughter of Saul had no child to the day of her death [emphasis mine].

At this point in time, David had already been chased down by the previous king, King Saul, who wanted to kill him. He had been engaged in warfare between two houses of loyalty: those who wanted Saul's family to continue the kingdom and those who wanted David to carry through with the anointing to be king that he received from the Prophet Samuel. He lost his best friend Jonathan (Saul's son) in battle, faced a long war between his own house and the house of Saul (now dead), and was anointed King over Judah first and then Israel. All of this is recounted in 1 Samuel 18 through 2 Samuel 5. At the end of 2 Samuel 5, at the age of 30, after being crowned king of Israel, David conquered Jerusalem and, with the Lord's help, defeated the Philistines. That was his point of view as the ark of the covenant entered Jerusalem. He was victorious, yes, but he had just weathered several battles in his life as well as losses. This wasn't a rejoicing because life was light and fluffy.

The lessons I see in it are that David was worshipping unabashedly, *"uncovering himself today before the eyes of his servants' female servants, as one of the vulgar fellows shamelessly uncovers himself"* and all. He knew the stakes had been high. He probably also knew life wasn't going to remain easy. He was now king over Judah and Israel! But he saw the Lord's faithfulness as the ark of the covenant came into the city he had taken as his own.

Note his first wife Michal's reaction to his uninhibited praise. She *despised* him, enough to speak boldly against him to his face. Um, wow. But let's also look at who she was: Saul's daughter. Bitterness much? Perhaps she, too, couldn't get past her own sense of loss, confusion, circumstances. But what were her consequences?[34] Verse 23: "And Michal the daughter of Saul had no child to the day of her death." Wow. I'm guessing we are left to deduce that the Lord was pleased with David's worshipful heart and not so pleased with Michal's hardened one. Her heart was divided between two kingdoms—her father's line and her husband's—and also between what was right before man and what was right before God.

So what does that mean for us? Well, we can conclude that God expects us to worship in spite of circumstances and that He blesses a praising heart. I'm not sure Michal's sin was not praising so much as it was despising and speaking against the purity of praise that her husband displayed. We don't always experience passionate worship. I'm not suggesting that makes us sinners. Rather, I think the sin is in our critical spirit toward others who are currently standing on that holy ground. We need to remember it is holy ground where people are praising the Lord.

Psalm 22:3, King David speaking, KJV
But thou art holy, O thou that inhabitest the praises of Israel.[35]

We also need to keep in perspective the notion that David was a "praise freak" for God because he also knew firsthand how hard life could get. If we're in a season of pain and disappointment, we should consider that the people around us who are praising God—either with arms tightly to their sides or with wild abandon—likely know exactly what He has brought them through and therefore trust Him for their future. We might not be ready to parade half-naked through the streets like King David, but we should take a lesson from those who praise God with great passion. They have something figured out: The presence of God is the only place to be, no matter what you are feeling. I want to live in that place too. I want to lay prostrate on that holy ground in complete surrender when madness swirls around me. Our only other choice is a hardened heart like Michal, and blessings did not flow forth from her choices. I want to be where the blessings flow because it's there that I know I'm in the presence of my beautiful Savior.

1 Thessalonians 5:16-22, Apostle Paul speaking

Rejoice always, pray without ceasing, give thanks in all circumstances; for this is the will of God in Christ Jesus for you. Do not quench the Spirit. Do not despise prophecies, but test everything; hold fast what is good. Abstain from every form of evil.

Sweep the Floor

Recently I ended up in the middle of a difficult situation in which the parties involved in an event I was helping to plan were in a lot of personal pain. One of them had greatly misunderstood some counsel and encouragement I had offered another party. It quickly spread to others planning the event. Unfortunately, the event coincided with a time of loss and genuine grief, and, like all obstacles that the enemy of our soul sets up to take what was meant for good and twist it, it got pretty ugly before it got better. But it thankfully did get better.

While it hurt to have my heart so incredibly misunderstood, I knew that if I was prayerful about it, the amazing thing is that I would hurt for all sides. That's because the Holy Spirit informs believers in Christ in perfect unity. I could be angry, disappointed, disillusioned, and disheartened, but if I truly sought the Lord, I would feel what everyone felt to some extent. *And I did.* I was in pain for all of us; to be honest, that was really hard because nobody was validating that, and I'm a Validation Chaser some days. I'm not sure they ever knew that I carried around several portions of pain on their behalf. There are no badges of "well done" handed out when these scenarios happen. We often walk them humanly alone.

As luck would have it (or not), this unfortunate situation coincided with the event we were all going to be participating in together. I'd be lying if I said I wasn't a ball of nerves as the day of the event approached. But I knew two things for sure: I knew God loved all of us and that I therefore had the capacity to show His love despite my own insecurities. I knew He'd be with me. (I guess that's three things that I knew.) Anyway, the day of, I brought my humbled heart (in some ways it was more of *fully bashed pride*) in the door of their home and asked God what to do. I could feel the heaviness in the air. I had set this event into motion before the misunderstanding. The tension was palpable. There were choices: Walk away. Rage. Be passive-aggressive. Be a martyr. Be spiteful. We all know the enemy of our souls knows how to whisper those recordings into our ear. But God? God is a different story altogether. This is what He said: "*Sweep the floor.*" Um, what? But I didn't have to ask twice because that sounds just like Jesus. You know the more you get to know Him, the better you catch on when wisdom is coming from Him. I couldn't deny the calling. It was a call to defuse a potentially emotion-fired few hours by "going lower." What else could I do but ask for a broom?

Matthew 5:38-42, Jesus speaking

"You have heard that it was said, 'An eye for an eye and a tooth for a tooth.' But I say to you, Do not resist the one who is evil. But if anyone slaps you on the right cheek, turn to him the other also. And if anyone would sue you and take your tunic, let him have your cloak as well. And if anyone forces you to go one mile, go with him two miles. Give to the one who begs from you, and do not refuse the one who would borrow from you."

To be fair, the people involved in my situation weren't evil or bad in any way. But regardless of circumstances or even misunderstandings, the message is to love deeper, bow lower, serve greater.

John 15:12-17, Jesus speaking

"This is my commandment, that you love one another as I have loved you. Greater love has no one than this, that someone lay down his life for his friends. You are my friends if you do what I command you. No longer do I call you servants, for the servant does not know what his master is doing; but *I have called you friends*, for *all that I have heard from my Father I have made known to you.* You did not choose me, but I chose you and appointed you that you should go and *bear fruit* and that your fruit should abide, so that *whatever you ask the Father in my name*, he may give it to you. These things I command you, so that you will *love one another* [emphasis mine]."

I don't know about you, but I want to be Jesus's friend. The only way I see this as a possibility is to do what He commands. He has made all things known to us. He is not withholding. If there was something else we were supposed to be doing other than loving as He has loved us and humbling ourselves, I'm pretty sure He'd be telling us. As much as I may not find it convenient or pleasant in the moment when I am making the choice, *bearing fruit* correlates with *loving each other*. How on earth do I do that? By *asking in His name*. I don't see another option.

The thing about brooms is: They sweep away only the surface dirt. We had some real prep work to do to make the floors shine for this event. Likewise, with my own intentions, I couldn't fix this big mess that had happened. I could only do my part on the surface. The Lord had to get in and scrub us all clean. So the next action He asked me to take was reaching for a mop. Great! That sounds a lot like, *"Lower still." Okay, Lord, I hear Ya. I need to come in as You would: to serve.* When two brothers were vying to sit at the right and left of Jesus in His Kingdom, His response was this:

Matthew 20:25-28, Apostle Matthew narrating

But Jesus called them to him and said, "You know that the rulers of the Gentiles lord it over them, and their great ones exercise authority over them. It shall not be so among you. But whoever would be great among you must be your servant, and whoever would be first among you must be your slave, even as the Son of Man came not to be served but to serve, and to give his life as a ransom for many."

And at the Last Supper, the night before His crucifixion, He washed the feet of His disciples (John 13) and challenged them to do the same for each other. With that in mind, despite the fact my human inclination was to run out the door and escape the entire afternoon—and my sin nature called me, taunted me, told me to abandon—the call was clear, and mop away I did.

What happens when we do this? Does it always end up looking like glorious, instant reconciliation wrapped in a sweet little bow? No, I can't say that it does, not always at the time. Often God still takes time to heal hearts. But in those few moments of me lowering myself, it didn't ultimately matter what the results were. What mattered was the voice of God whispering His plan to me, taking the lead (because I thankfully submitted this time), letting His child learn the valuable lesson of *"Go lower."* I could see Him clearly only in that place where I was in the Throne Room asking my God for the royal scepter, to lend me His ear like Esther[36] asked her king. To do this, I have to follow His example, and in so doing, I glimpsed a tiny snippet of the heart of God. If nothing else at the time, I could at least find joy in that because that was between God and me; regardless of tension still floating in the atmosphere around me, I obeyed my Savior, and whenever I do that, there is peace of heart.

I knew He'd mend the relationship eventually or clear a path for better future interactions, and He later did, but through tears of relief, I drove home knowing I had cleaned the Throne Room for a little while. When I did, it worked out best when I focused only on the dirt in front of me, which belonged to *me*, but if I lifted my head to search more of the surface area of the floor, I quickly forgot for Whom I was actually cleaning. I needed to look down and manage one small stroke of wet fibers at a time. *Always*. Because it's not *my* throne room. And, really, it's not my floor either.

James 4:7-10, James, brother of Jesus, speaking

Submit yourselves therefore to God. Resist the devil, and he will flee from you. Draw near to God, and he will draw near to you. Cleanse your hands, you sinners, and purify your hearts, you double-minded. Be wretched and mourn and weep. Let your laughter be turned to mourning and your joy to gloom. Humble yourselves before the Lord, and he will exalt you.

NOT JUST ON SUNDAYS

When There's a Station for Dysfunction Junction—Wait for It—Right in the Church!

Ouch. That really hurts. That's a hard topic. I can see sparks flying already. Get your seatbelt on. This might hurt a little because it's true of all of us. If we attend church and think we haven't made a stop at this station, we are deceiving ourselves. Because this is such a delicate and difficult subject, ask God before reading this to prepare your heart. In writing it, I had to examine my own.

Sadly, I have found church to be a breeding ground for both judgment and grace. When people live only by Law, they offer condemnation. When they understand they are sinners saved by grace, they live out that grace. But, as broken as it is at times, church is exactly what God would want: a place where even the "prodigal's older brother"[37] can work out his sanctification in safety. I love that about Jesus, and it helps me not get my britches in a rumple at church when I understand that we are all equal in His sight.

Want to know something scandalous? (Chances are you know it already; you just might not say it out loud.) *Pastors stop at Dysfunction Junction too.* I am not going to write much here because I am not targeting any particular pastor along my life's journey. I had one I adored who ended up needing a lot of grace at one point, and yet, for me personally, that did not take anything away from the years he was an amazing pastor. In my early twenties, I worked closely with a pastor and saw his every side. Yup, he needed huge portions of grace, *just like me*. And I've worked with campus fellowship staff leaders who needed that same grace, *just like me*.

148

We want to put them on a pedestal, but the truth is, they often struggle to fully project grace because, like so many of us, they are often only beginning to understand it. They are still being sanctified, just like *all* believers in Christ. Does it mean they aren't qualified shepherds of their flock? Not at all. But they need to have mentors, too, and they need to be open about it. Pride is the scariest block to growth in any of us.

What has disappointed me over the years, in a nutshell, hasn't been finding out that pastors sometimes lack grace. It's been when they won't open this wound to Jesus, seek help, be honest about it. When they can't share that with their sheep, their sheep often end up feeling like little children who couldn't please their perfectionist parent. It leads to sheep with a failure complex. When grace isn't functioning from the top—or at least leadership isn't striving toward it or having honest discussion about it—the lack of it trickles down and cripples. I think one of the biggest struggles pastors face is thinking they have to be strong for everyone and not allowing grace to touch them too. I wish I could gather them up (ones I have known and loved and even others I meet along the way) and wash their feet. And bless them. And hold them like a mother curling up behind her child and waiting for the healing to flow. Once we know this about pastors, *boom!* we can have grace for them.

I told you reading this would hold us all accountable. I can't even publish this book until I'm sure I genuinely understand this and am living it. That's what grace does: It bulldozes our preconceived notions and leaves us accountable. Grace is dangerous! I love gulping it down, but it completely freaks me out at the very same time.

If you're in church and wondering why you encounter some dysfunction there, it means, in some ways, that the church is functioning as it should be: a place where sinners start taking on more attributes of the God they are made in the image of once they turn their lives over to Him for Him to complete a good work in them.

Philippians 1:3-6, Apostle Paul speaking

I thank my God in all my remembrance of you, always in every prayer of mine for you all making my prayer with joy, because of your partnership in the gospel from the first day until now. And I am sure of this, that he who began a good work in you will bring it to completion at the day of Jesus Christ.

If you see people raising the bar to grow in great grace and Christ-like behavior: awesome! If you find others working out their issues just like you are, it's not a red flag necessarily, unless the church corporately remains stuck. But most people entering the fellowship of other believers in a church setting are hopefully committed to grow in their relationship with Christ and to obey Him more, taking on more of His character (the fruit of the Spirit in Galatians 5:22-26).[38] There is no perfection this side of heaven, but, rather, within a healthy church, you should see a committed desire to grow to be more like Christ and to help others to do the same.

On the other hand, if you see a church that is content to remain stagnant right where it is, that only has grace but no personal growth,[39] or conversely, one where grace cannot be found: Be cautious and prayerful. In a church seeking God's guidance, a corporate commitment to grow in the knowledge and wisdom of Christ will be evident. Grace is a wonderful thing, but it is in no way an excuse or free pass to stay where we are and not grow or to overlook obedience to God's Word. Grace without personal growth is loosey-goosey and undefined. On the contrary, a lack of grace in a church fellowship leads to a church of various levels of amateur judges holding court. Thankfully, God intended grace and growth (through the Law, His Word) to go together. As everything He has made, it is the perfect balance, the best guardrails for us to walk inside, the healthiest boundaries, and a beautiful way to live out and "love out" this life together.

2 Peter 3:17-18, Apostle Peter speaking

You therefore, beloved, knowing this beforehand, take care that you are not carried away with the error of lawless people and lose your own stability. But grow in the grace and knowledge of our Lord and Savior Jesus Christ. To him be the glory both now and to the day of eternity. Amen.

Samson and Delilah, the Shih Tzu Variety

As I write this, I am considering driving 12 hours to Ohio to buy two Shih Tzu puppies. Have I ever raised puppies before? No. Did I grow up with dogs? No. My vast experience involves rescuing a 13-year-old Yorkie 18 years ago. So why on earth would I get two pups at once? Because I'm an expert after watching endless small dog care and training videos on the Internet for a few weeks. I could probably run my own talk show on the subject at this point. But the real reason we are crazy enough to consider two? It's really rational, so hold onto your seats.

We finally agreed on names, but there are two: Samson and Delilah. Two names = two dogs. My daughter said I could name them that if we got two. And that was that. (And no, she does not call the shots in our family despite how this story sounds.) Somehow, some way, Salad Boy and I bought that logic, hook line and sinker. Salad Boy has come a long way, considering he didn't even want dogs. Four years with two females in your house dropping little snippets about dogs into every conversation tend to wear one down. That, and if we get a dog, we want the majority of its lifetime to fall during our kids' childhoods. Well, Kids Number Two and Three. Kid Number One is mourning the passing of time from an animal-free house to one with two fluff balls in it. He's not only not enthused; he has stated his "anti-dog" case multiple times. Too bad. He has had 13 years of an animal-free home. For the next five years of his residency, he will need to adapt.

We wanted our tiny dogs to have names bigger than themselves. We also thought it very appropriate that Samson would have hair that kept growing, considering his biblical namesake (read on). Should we groom

him? Biblical Samson lost his strength when his hair was cut. Hmmm.

> Judges 16:15-17, author unknown, possibly Samuel
>
> And she [Delilah] said to him, "How can you say, 'I love you,' when your heart is not with me? You have mocked me these three times, and you have not told me where your great strength lies." And when she pressed him hard with her words day after day, and urged him, his soul was vexed to death. And he told her all his heart, and said to her, "A razor has never come upon my head, for I have been a Nazirite to God from my mother's womb. If my head is shaved, then my strength will leave me, and I shall become weak and be like any other man."

Kid Number One is morally opposed to the name Delilah. He doesn't think

we send a good message naming a cute puppy we love after a vixen in the

Bible. Point taken. I get it. For the record, Moses, Gideon, Abraham, and

Shakespeare were on the name list when there was talk of one dog. I

suppose those are more noble in his mind. But the truth is, we are all

Samson and Delilah in one way or another, right? Honestly, but for the

grace offered to us by Christ's victory on the cross over death and His

ascension, we all have pieces of us that can relate.

In the famous Bible account, Delilah uses her wiles and female

charm to seduce truth out of Samson about the source of his strength,

divulging this secret to the enemy, who then captures Samson and gouges

out his eyes. It makes sense that the enemy would want to subdue Samson;

he presented a very real threat with his amazing strength, plus he had God

on His side (before the haircut). For the lure of money, Delilah,

approached by the Philistines (Samson's enemy), determined to get his

secret out of him.

How many of us are Delilah? We want a shortcut to something:

money, fame, attention, a relationship we want to force, etc. How many of us take the enemy's bait to not wait on the Lord? Granted, Delilah didn't seem to be answering to Samson's God, but her character isn't that far from our man-flesh character, is it? How many of us hear that enticing whisper and buy it the first time? How many of us fake relational interest in someone to use them in some way? How many of us try once, twice, three times to "work another person over" to get what we need from them? How many of us do the passive-aggressive "But if you love me, you will XYZ" line in a marriage, with our kids, in a friendship, or even with someone we want to strong-arm into committing to us? I hate to say it, but I see this dynamic all of the time in upper elementary school girls. It's in our DNA to "work it." It's in our flesh nature. We aren't powerless if we have Christ. We can choose to not act that way. But Delilah's sneaky character is only one or two quick choices away for any of us.

And how about Samson? Are we easily fooled and misled by not *being wise as serpents and innocent as doves* as Jesus calls us to in Matthew 10:16-17? Granted, He was speaking to the disciples at the time who would be arrested, tortured, etc., for their profession of faith in Him as the Christ, but we, too, are called to be discerning.

Matthew 10:16-17, Jesus speaking

"Behold, I am sending you out as sheep in the midst of wolves, so be wise as serpents and innocent as doves. Beware of men, for they will deliver you over to courts and flog you in their synagogues."

Clearly Samson wasn't considering the wisdom of Proverbs 13, since the writing of Proverbs 13 came more than 100 years after Samson's account.

Proverbs 13:19-21, King Solomon speaking

A desire fulfilled is sweet to the soul,
    but to turn away from evil is an abomination to fools.

Whoever walks with the wise becomes wise,
  but the companion of fools will suffer harm.
Disaster pursues sinners,
  but the righteous are rewarded with good.

With his weakness in sexual desire, Samson lost his discernment and forgot to *walk with the wise*. He became a *companion of fools*, and *disaster pursued* him in a big, bad way. He certainly knew what Delilah was about, as she tried to get the information from him four different times. But his own personal desires caused him to not walk away. He let her wear him down, and in that one moment, he forsook his Father God.

No judgment here. How often does my Samson heart flirt with a need, want, or desire and let me listen to enemy voices about who I am? How often do I let others rob me of joy by listening to their toxins: gossip, persistent slander, persuasion about something wrong? How often do I say: "God, if you don't mind, I'm going to ignore this command or warning and hang out over here for a while, but I won't be polluted by it, no worries." Uh-huh. Sit in the pigpen with people of ill intent, and see how quickly you, too, start to stink. Perhaps the scariest line in this entire account is this:

Judges 16:20, author unknown, possibly Samuel

And she said, "The Philistines are upon you, Samson!" And he awoke from his sleep and said, "I will go out as at other times and shake myself free." But he did not know that *the LORD had left him* [emphasis mine].

Why *should* God stick around when Samson had essentially blown off His instructions and slept in a soiled bed? God was clear about the source of Samson's strength. God never backed out of the deal; Samson did. And, like those of us who have put our faith in Him, God has such an amazing history with Samson (read Judges 13-17), yet Samson betrayed what he knew for what was unknown. He was dipping from a different well, and he was going to come up thirsty because God didn't tell him to draw from that well. How often do we act outside of God's instruction? Um, speaking for myself: often.

So, I find two upside-down-mop dogs that dust my floor at their short stature (and will always be underfoot) to be excellent reminders of who we are without Christ or when we step outside the blessings of God. I don't see their names as necessarily symbolizing their sin. I see them as God sees us when we repent: forgiven and clothed in righteousness. God gave Samson one more chance,[40] honoring one more prayer, even though it meant Samson's end. He let him honor the name of the Lord one more time. I understand why my 13 year old is morally opposed to the names, but I hope the two fluff balls at our feet daily reflect the grace evident in their namesakes. Samson and Delilah made it into the Bible. God felt they were important enough for us to know about. They were not heroes in their sin, but they were examples God used to teach us. They played a part not only in history but in showing Who God is and who we can be.

The Bible doesn't follow up Delilah's story. We don't know if she ever made better choices or continued to seduce for gain. I suppose that's where my oldest son's sense of justice and morality struggles with the lack of purity in that name. But we have a chance to see the Samsons and Delilahs of life redeemed by sharing the truth of Christ. People walking in that impurity can be told the great story of redemption offered to all on that cross. With biblical names that "beg the question," perhaps our family pets can be part of telling that story to others. Or maybe Delilah will taunt

Samson true to her name, and I'll have to come down firm with her in training. Sometimes God does this with us, but I am always better for it.

That's the very beautiful and very sad thing about choices. When people ask me why this and that decision wasn't yielding results or being blessed, I tend to be honest—not in a judgmental way, but in a way that says: "Well, within these parameters, God promises to bless. Outside of them, He doesn't. We don't have to choose to live within the parameters, but outside of them we're essentially on our own." Samson made some choices outside of God's protective law. It wasn't until his repentance that he could come back under God's grace, but not without consequence. His gouged-out eyes were not reversed to seeing ones. His shame had already taken place. His enemies had already had a good laugh. But under God's grace and protection was a new day, one where Samson could have one last hurrah—but only to bring God more glory because that is what His blessings are for.

That's why the screw-ups in the Bible can still be great names. Ultimately, it's why our story isn't over yet either. That's why I celebrate this story in the Bible: It's another amazing place where we find hope. Where we find God's protective boundaries. Where we see the potential of our sin. Where we also see we can pick ourselves up again in humility and ask Him to help us the rest of the way. Where we can see on our darkest day that He can still use us. That's why I find these names worthy of attaching to something I will dearly love. Because the Father loves us that way.

As I finish this, in the course of only 24 hours, I have discovered a local acquaintance's Shih Tzu is expecting and that we can have some of her puppies. Wow. I don't even have to drive to Ohio! My kids are ecstatic, and I'm out buying crates. Stay tuned. I'm sure we are not done with lessons from Samson and Delilah. If my kids have their way, the dogs may someday get their very own book deal!

Dear Advent: Where Are You?

We observe Advent in our family. We started a few years ago to slow us down and build anticipation for celebrating Christ's birth. Scratch that. Make that: We *attempt* to observe Advent in our family. It has built on itself over the years. In the beginning, it was as complicated as a LEGO® Advent calendar of new small constructions to make every day. This had nothing to do with Christ, but it was incredible fun. Then we started reading through pieces of Luke for the Sundays leading up to Christmas, gathering around the table, lighting candles, and singing songs about wise men, angels, shepherds, and the Christ Child each appropriate week. One of my favorite times was when my youngest son was born between the first and second week of Advent. One week I was swollen with child, relating well to Mary, the Mother of Christ, at this time of year, and the next week, I was nursing a screaming (but very cute) redhead as we attempted to sing carols and welcome our new family member into our Christmas traditions.

Later on, Advent included reading some great books put out by Kregel Publications: *Jotham's Journey: A Storybook for Advent* and *Bartholomew's Passage: A Family Story for Advent.*[41] Our Children's Ministry directors introduced us to these, and they have been a fun addition. I must admit, the readings can get long, but I've always been a fan of reading while the kids finish their meals. It keeps the fighting and arm farts at bay. Some years we add in a chocolate countdown calendar, and each day we read a tiny part of 25 days of the events leading up to the Savior's birth written on ornaments my sister gave us years ago. But this all makes us sound like Advent experts, people who "have it down pat," who live in this world where the weeks leading up to Christmas are peace and joy, serenity and patience. Nope. In reality, we play "catch up" to doing four LEGO® sets, three days' of marathon readings from an Advent book, and Tuesdays of doing our Sunday song and candle time. Advent competes every year with the Robotics State Championship (when we make it that far), a Christmas-themed dance recital, homework projects, and frantic shopping/mailing/wrapping/Christmas card writing. Yeah, Advent gets the back burner. I almost laughed my way up to the pulpit the year our family was asked to do the Advent reading one Sunday. I wanted to read the verses and then grab the microphone and say: "This isn't really what it looks like on a daily basis, People!" Thankfully, I knew to feed the cynic in me a shut-up-sicle. But I felt that. I felt like Scrooge that year.

So, this year, I've gone in search of Advent, and you know what? I've had a little help from two unlikely partners: our Shih Tzu puppies, Samson and Delilah. I'm pleased to say Samson and Delilah arrived on the planet on my birthday, and we brought them home the first of December. In anticipation of their arrival, I went into Christmas prep. All gifts were bought, wrapped, and sent off (mostly) to family and friends by the day after Thanksgiving. Our tree was up November 30th. The kids' gifts were wrapped and in their hiding place as well. They had even wrapped each other's. Although Christmas cards weren't sent yet, I was able to avoid Black Friday shopping and walk into an empty post office to mail my packages. Could I have done this while training nine-week-old puppies? Perhaps. But they were the perfect excuse to slow down, enjoy our pets, and be done with the consumer frenzy early. If it wasn't bought by now, we didn't need it.

The dogs were our big gift this year. Scratch that. Our biggest gift was giving ourselves Advent fully, recognizing the Gift we have been given in the Christ Child and taking the time to breathe that in, instead of rushing through LEGO® projects, the readings, the songs. Do Robotics, dance, and holiday parties and commitments threaten to derail Advent again? Of course. But this year, *they* come second. They will know their proper place as gifts from God in terms of talent and opportunity. They are *because of* Advent, not in spite of it.

James 1:17, James, brother of Jesus, speaking

Every good gift and every perfect gift is from above, coming down from the Father of lights with whom there is no variation or shadow due to change.

Luke 2:1-12, Luke the Physician narrating

In those days a decree went out from Caesar Augustus that all the world should be registered. This was the first registration when Quirinius was governor of Syria. And all went to be registered, each to his own town. And Joseph also went up from Galilee, from the town of Nazareth, to Judea, to the city of David, which is called Bethlehem, because he was of the house and lineage of David, to be registered with Mary, his betrothed, who was with child. And while they were there, the time came for her to give birth. And she gave birth to her firstborn son and wrapped him in swaddling cloths and laid him in a manger, because there was no place for them in the inn.

And in the same region there were shepherds out in the field, keeping watch over their flock by night. And an angel of the Lord appeared to them, and the glory of the Lord shone around them, and they were filled with great fear. And the angel said to them, "Fear not, for behold, I bring you good news of great joy that will be for all the people. For unto you is born this day in the city of David a Savior, who is Christ the Lord. And this will be a sign for you: you will find a baby wrapped in swaddling cloths and lying in a manger."

I also made another choice during Thanksgiving weekend. As much as I wanted to drive down to Pennsylvania to go shopping with my sister and see my extended family, I had to stop and consider the ridiculous speed with which we had been going for the past few weeks. As much as my kids wanted to pile into the car and head to cousins, aunt, uncle, grandparents, I simply couldn't do it. I knew we needed to rest, watch *Star Wars* all weekend, stay in our pajamas, make pies, put up a Christmas tree, and sit quietly. We don't stop and rest enough as a culture.[42] I'm very guilty of this. But when I find myself on edge, snapping, stressing, and panting, I know I need to go back to Matthew 11:28-30, the verses sprawled out in beautiful script on the front wall of my childhood church.

> Matthew 11:28-30, Jesus speaking
>
> "Come to me, all who labor and are heavy laden, and I will give you rest. Take my yoke upon you, and learn from me, for I am gentle and lowly in heart, and you will find rest for your souls. For my yoke is easy, and my burden is light."

I hope you can drink these verses in deeply, knowing His deep rest in your weary soul whether it's seasonally Advent or not, because at the end of the day, Advent is how we choose to live our lives—or not. Expectant, joyful, observing Sabbath in Him, resting in His grace of finished work on the cross and a promised "completed work" in those of us who believe.

> Philippians 1:3-6, the Apostle Paul speaking
>
> I thank my God in all my remembrance of you, always in every prayer of mine for you all making my prayer with joy, because of your partnership in the gospel from the first day until now. And I am sure of this, that he who began a good work in you will bring it to completion at the day of Jesus Christ.

Part 3
When Love Stops at My Door, and His Name Is Jesus

I don't know why I am amazed afresh each time this happens, but God truly fills us in places where we have a deep need. He fills the voids left behind by broken things when we yield and ask Him. It's a great reminder to stop looking at what we think "fails us" and start acknowledging more where love shows up. Love showed up today via two friends 3,000 miles apart in messages I needed God to speak to my heart. Neither person knew the current storm in my mind, where old lies of self-doubt were playing on rewind and repeat: one of those smaller battles that you don't necessarily involve others in until it becomes large enough that you suddenly need help. Well, before it escalated or I even cried out, God sent reinforcements in the form of two emails that delivered timely messages from people who don't know each other. It was God reminding me He loves me and provides, *always*. Love often takes on a very unique form, if we are willing to look for it.

This section is dedicated to all of those smaller moments in life when we need a hand reaching down from heaven, and suddenly—sometimes without a prayer formed on our lips yet—there it is. Obviously, there are longer stories too, but those that are included here are meant to get us tuned into the everyday—not only where we see Him working, but also where He offers us opportunities to stop at someone's door in the name of His great love. These stories hopefully speak for themselves; they belong to all of us. I am not unique in my experiences, but I hope they serve as encouragement that a very real Savior moves among hearts—and moves hearts—every single day in so many magnificent ways.

I include here my favorite fellowship song. My husband and I used to sing it at Christian Student Fellowship (CSF) of PA when we were college students. Our campus minister at the time, a beautiful man and martyr for the Word, who lost his life to gang violence in his early thirties, taught it to us. The message sticks with me. May this be our forever song while we walk this earth.

The Servant Song

Will you let me be your servant,
Let me be as Christ to you?
Pray that I might have the grace
To let you be my servant too.

We are pilgrims on the journey;
We are brothers on the road.
We are here to help each other
Walk the mile and bear the load.

I will hold the Christ light for you
In the night time of your fear.
I will hold my hand out to you,
Speak the peace you long to hear.

I will weep when you are weeping;
When you laugh, I'll laugh with you.
I will share your joy and sorrow
Till we've seen this journey through.

When we sing to God in heaven,
We shall find such harmony,
Born to all we've known together
Of Christ's love and agony.

Richard Gillard of New Zealand, 1977

Bus Driver Angel

So, I went to drop Chickie off today at Sheriff Camp, and the bus driver was standing outside and struck up a conversation with me, very deliberately. It went on for a topic or two until we got to the subject of the original sheriff who started the camp (he committed suicide during an investigation of his use of campaign funds). Then the bus driver said to me: "The devil is alive and well." So, I responded: "Yes, he is, and he whispers in people's ears, and if they don't know the solution, they often believe him," thinking how sad it was the sheriff believed the only answer to his problem was to take his own life. Suddenly the bus driver responded with words about the reality of spiritual warfare (battle of good versus evil) and boom! We were off talking about the Lord! It felt like God had him seek me out. He was a man in his late fifties who used to be a cop before retiring and was told to drive this bus to Sheriff Camp. He said he simply wants to be doing what God has planned for him every day. Wow, me too!

Then, in the middle of the conversation, he spoke something directly into my life about a very specific situation that we have kept private to protect those involved. He just spoke it and said: "So, it doesn't matter what you're going through (I hadn't said anything about any of that) because God is bigger, and even if you are in the middle of XYZ (XYZ being the *exact* situation and not a common one someone could guess), you know He's got it. It's not really your fight. He is the One Who scoops the waters into the ocean and measures the mountains" (he quoted

Isaiah 40). He said to be encouraged, because if you follow the Lord, He's got it, and it's not ever been in our control anyway.

Isaiah 40:10-14, Isaiah the Prophet speaking

Behold, the Lord GOD comes with might,
and his arm rules for him;
behold, his reward is with him,
and his recompense before him.
He will tend his flock like a shepherd;
he will gather the lambs in his arms;
he will carry them in his bosom,
and gently lead those that are with young.

Who has measured the waters in the hollow of his hand
and marked off the heavens with a span,
enclosed the dust of the earth in a measure
and weighed the mountains in scales
and the hills in a balance?
Who has measured the Spirit of the LORD,
or what man shows him his counsel?
Whom did he consult,
and who made him understand?
Who taught him the path of justice,
and taught him knowledge,
and showed him the way of understanding [emphasis mine]*?*

Okay, so I already knew and believed all of that, but this man did not know me or the situation. But He knew God, and God had him seek me out and say this to me to encourage me. So, be encouraged, because when you pray, provision comes in very supernatural, specific, personal ways. This man wanted to bless someone, but God pointed him to me; he was obedient and carried through. When people ask me how I know God is real, one reason is because this kind of thing happens to me all of the time when He uses another person (often strangers) to deliver a very personal, direct message to me. I believe He does it for all of us, but we don't always have our eyes open enough to see it. I was able to share it with those involved in this very specific situation as well.

Where can you be looking for God to be speaking to you through another? Could it be the kind nurse drawing your blood? The stranger stopping to help you pick up your dropped coupon in the grocery store? The parent, formerly unknown by you, who just happens to be sitting next to you at basketball practice as you talk about your struggles over your son's IEP; maybe she has gone before you and has wisdom, or maybe she works in special education. It could be the gentle hand on your shoulder as you frantically get through the pharmacy with three kids in tow, with someone saying: "It's okay. I remember those days. Take a deep breath. You're doing great." He gave us each other, and He uses people to bless us whether they believe in Him or not. Maybe you're somebody's assignment today, or maybe you're on a mission yourself. Here's what the Apostle Paul encourages believers in Christ to do and to be for other people. The last line summarizes it well. His point is that we build up other believers, and in so doing, we are equipped to bring the Good News of Christ to the world.

1 Thessalonians 5:4-11, Apostle Paul speaking

But you are not in darkness, brothers, for that day to surprise you like a thief. For you are all children of light, children of the day. We are not of the night or of the darkness. So then let us not sleep, as others do, but let us keep awake and be sober. For those who sleep, sleep at night, and those who get drunk, are drunk at night. But since we belong to the day, let us be sober, having put on the breastplate of faith and love, and for a helmet the hope of salvation. For God has not destined us for wrath, but to obtain salvation through our Lord Jesus Christ, who died for us so that whether we are awake or asleep we might live with him. Therefore encourage one another and build one another up, just as you are doing.

When the Gardener Comes: What I Want to "Perch in My Branches"—And What I Don't

James 5:13-18, James, brother of Jesus, speaking

Is anyone among you suffering? Let him pray. Is anyone cheerful? Let him sing praise. Is anyone among you sick? Let him call for the elders of the church, and let them pray over him, anointing him with oil in the name of the Lord. And the prayer of faith will save the one who is sick, and the Lord will raise him up. And if he has committed sins, he will be forgiven. Therefore, confess your sins to one another and pray for one another, that you may be healed. The prayer of a righteous person has great power as it is working. Elijah was a man with a nature like ours, and he prayed fervently that it might not rain, and for three years and six months it did not rain on the earth. Then he prayed again, and heaven gave rain, and the earth bore its fruit.

Today, a dear friend gave me this verse, so I share it. I share it because I want to be like Elijah, not for a sense of my own power (I have none), but to have my faith be so Elijah-like strong and my mind so much like Christ, that when I pray for someone, what is spoken happens. I don't think the inclusion of this story in the New Testament is an accident. Read 1 Kings 18 for the full context.[43] The Lord allowed Elijah to speak weather to happen. What? That's right. He told the evil King Ahab to expect wet weather that was highly unlikely, considering the drought. Is our faith like that? Do we trust God for answers that cannot be seen anywhere on the current horizon? Do we pray with expectant hearts?

I thank God right now for the amazing answers coming in: some slow, some swift, but all with His signature. He listens to each detail, and even with the tiny faith of a mustard seed, we can approach His Throne of grace. I want the marriages/relationships being prayed for reconciled, the addictions ended, the heart's desires for children or marriage or ministry or provision granted, the sick well, the broken-hearted comforted, the lonely friended, the losses restored. I want the birds in His garden to *come and*

170

make nests in its branches today because they know the love of the Father for them. I want to offer them His peace and His provision. I want to *sow in His field* and watch seedlings turn into sprouts, and then a tree, a home with many branches to rest on.

Matthew 13:31-32, Apostle Matthew talking about Jesus

He put another parable before them, saying, "The kingdom of heaven is like a grain of mustard seed that a man took and sowed in his field. It is the smallest of all seeds, but when it has grown it is larger than all the garden plants and becomes a tree, so that the birds of the air come and make nests in its branches."

I would be remiss not to mention this famous passage, spoken by Jesus, when discussing how we even have healthy branches to perch on:

John 15:1-8, Jesus speaking

"I am the true vine, and my Father is the vinedresser. Every branch in me that does not bear fruit he takes away, and every branch that does bear fruit he prunes, that it may bear more fruit. Already you are clean because of the word that I have spoken to you. Abide in me, and I in you. As the branch cannot bear fruit by itself, unless it abides in the vine, neither can you, unless you abide in me. I am the vine; you are the branches. Whoever abides in me and I in him, he it is that bears much fruit, for apart from me you can do nothing. If anyone does not abide in me he is thrown away like a branch and withers; and the branches are gathered, thrown into the fire, and burned. If you abide in me, and my words abide in you, ask whatever you wish, and it will be done for you. By this my Father is glorified, that you bear much fruit and so prove to be my disciples."

The key here is remaining in Christ. We may have all the right intentions or even accreditations in the world in wanting to help people, fix a situation, or "do good," but bearing real biblical fruit comes only in trusting in Christ, remaining in the Vine. And with that comes an entirely different side: a willingness to be pruned. As the verse suggests, we are pruned to *bear more fruit*. But it doesn't say that part is pleasant or fun. I've read it several times looking for that, and it isn't there.

At times, the signs are all there for quite a while, but when we finally allow ourselves to see a disappointing situation in its fullness, one that we had tried so hard to make better, it is almost crushing. But the best part of it is that on the flip side, there was so much hope, so much love (within us), that kept us going in the first place, that we can look back and say: "I honestly gave that my all. I gave it the best of me, always hoping and praying for the best." We don't have to stop hoping and praying for the best, but we absolutely need to check now and again if our hope is in Christ or ourselves. That's the difference between being connected to the Vine and being a branch dying on the ground, completely cut off from its life source.

More frequently than I care to share, I feel the dead fruit being pulled off the branches for me. And it hurts—*a lot*. Sometimes it costs me a relationship or something I enjoy. But whenever that happens, I know a lighter, more productive time is ahead. It's a guarantee. After all, mourning dead fruit in my life is a pointless exercise, even though I fall into the trap of wanting to cuddle it for a while before letting it drop off. Dead fruit is not life-giving when it's hanging dead on your own tree. If you think about it, it's only dead because it didn't remain in the Vine. It didn't get nourished by the Gardener. It's not as if He were passive about it. He actually cut it off. I don't always like that, but I can trust it. When the dead fruit falls off, suddenly the branches bear more fruit and grow to welcome other birds to perch there. Dead fruit, or more room for new birds? The Gardener knows exactly what He is doing, and it's a beautiful, loving example of healthy boundaries and incredible growth.

I truly want only what He wants to perch there. How about you?

What His Provision Looks Like on a Daily Basis

As I dropped off a timid daughter at the bus for Sheriff Camp a while back, I felt like a nine-year-old girl again. It made me sad because she usually embraces these moments with such a stoic and sure attitude, but then I forgot, until just a few minutes before, how much she dreaded dealing with the "mean girls" in her grade, and how, after this past year, she was enjoying the summer break. So, at home before we left, I prayed (out loud) peace of heart over her and that no matter who showed up from that group, that God would provide her with at least one solid friend she could count on who wasn't already buddied up or paired up with someone.

And there was Madisyn (sister of a dance friend), my saving grace. She had a seat ready to share with Chickie, and in that older-sister, confident way, took Chickie under her wing. Before she got on, I told her: "See: Madisyn is your answered prayer today. Perhaps you are hers as well." And I saw the tightness of stress leave my daughter's face through the bus window. My heart went back to that peaceful place it needs to be when you send your child off for day camp, knowing she's going to be okay. *Thank You, God!* This is His provision walked out on a daily basis. These are the short prayers surrendered to Him for results and then Him revealing Himself through answers that cut directly through the problem or concern and bring peace. This is how I want to do problems, by asking Jesus to help me. I do not want to miss out on seeing Him in action simply because I do not ask.

James 4:2b-3, James, brother of Jesus, speaking

You do not have, because you do not ask. You ask and do not receive, because you ask wrongly, to spend it on your passions.

"Just Keep Swimming, Just Keep Swimming"

Last night, I dreamt I was a well-muscled Olympic swimmer who, whenever someone confronted me, made them watch me swim the length of the pool several times. I woke up, and my clothes fit better. Coincidence? Yes, I admittedly have issues. But I think what's really behind that is warring in prayer. I think the message in my dream was that with Christ, I have the upper hand. Prayer is power. I've been trying to do a *lot* more of that lately on behalf of so many dear ones, and as a result, my prayer muscles really are getting stronger!

> Romans 15:13, the Apostle Paul speaking
>
> May the God of hope fill you with all joy and peace in believing, so that by the power of the Holy Spirit you may abound in hope.

I love "so that" in a sentence. When the God of hope fills us with all joy and peace, *in believing* (which is our part of the deal), we may *abound in hope by the power of the Holy Spirit*. I'm so on-board with that. Hook me up to that power source, please. I have none on my own when I'm unplugged from it.

> Luke 10:19-20, Jesus speaking to 72 disciples he sent out, and to us
>
> "Behold, I have given you authority to tread on serpents and scorpions, and over all the power of the enemy, and nothing shall hurt you. Nevertheless, do not rejoice in this, that the spirits are subject to you, but rejoice that your names are written in heaven."

The enemy of our souls comes whispering in our ears, telling us everything around us is negative and crashing down, that we can't hold this one person up well enough because this next trial is about to plow into another one, etc. I love the last line in the Luke passage about not rejoicing over the power, but rather that we are acknowledged by the Father with our names written in heaven. It keeps us from a holy power trip. But I also love the promise that we have the *authority*, in Christ, to overcome *all* power of the enemy.

And you know what I say?

Hey, puny enemy of my soul: Watch Him help me swim the length of this trial! And watch Him help me swim it with others during theirs. Have you seen my God-shaped muscles lately? They aren't mine. They are all His, and He helps me get through those waters. Watch, and be amazed! God is swimming with me. I'm not alone like you want me to believe. I've got the best Olympic swimmer in the universe doing laps at my side!

God Is Dancing in the Dance Studio, and He Dances Better Than I Do

Yesterday God revealed Himself at a time when I wasn't expecting it. Boom. He was right there. He invades time and space to let Himself be known. I *love* it. He used another person to minister to me in the middle of an ordinary scenario in my schedule. He is extra-ordinary, but He meets us in the ordinary, the everyday, and says: "You are mine, beloved, and I delight in you." He didn't show Himself in some huge display of power that turned all heads in the room. He quietly whispered in the "crowd."

I was dancing in an adult summer class. Not sure "dancing" is the appropriate word. It might not get the nod of approval from my competitive dancer daughter. But I was being brave and fulfilling a promise to be in a recital with my daughter. At that time, the other adult dancers, who were really good and/or teachers at the studio, showed me a song they were performing to in the summer dance show. The song was a prayer, a worship song. They only half-realized this, but it completely meant something to me. It was God saying He was right there, being worshiped in a place that wasn't a church, a sanctuary, or a Christian concert. And that was mighty cool.

Truth is, He is always there, but He wants to know if we're paying attention, if we recognize Him when He pops into interaction with us, when He uses someone to bless us. Where can we see the Savior today? Let's learn to not be shocked that He engages with us. It's His heart to have relationship with us. We should come to expect it and delight in it. He is worshipped in a dance studio. Does He come to karate too? Methinks He does.

Speaking for myself, we Christians can be so uptight at times, limiting God to some holy sphere that touches nothing earthly. Have we forgotten the Holy Son of God touched down on earth and walked among us? This is what I think of whenever folks tell me to stay in Christian-only activities. What are those anyway? If God is everywhere among us, I'm not sure how we define what those are. I can see Him easily in the churchy moments. I want to look for Him outside that context. I want to see Him loving the people who haven't stepped inside His holy temple yet. I want to dance with Him in the dance studio.

One of my favorite verses is found in Leviticus: "I will walk among you and will be your God."

Oh, Lord, this is what I want. I want to wake up and hear Your voice whispering "Good morning" to me. I want to walk alongside You in the grocery store, the dentist office (oh, especially the dentist office!), in my neighborhood, and running the kids to their activities. Amen.

Leviticus 26:11-13, God speaking through Moses

"I will make my dwelling among you, and my soul shall not abhor you. And I will walk among you and will be your God, and you shall be my people. I am the LORD your God, who brought you out of the land of Egypt, that you should not be their slaves. And I have broken the bars of your yoke and made you walk erect."

Let's not limit our minds to church, Folks. It's a wonderful place to be to worship together in unity. That is very important. But God doesn't just hang there while we get on with the rest of our week. He's up to a lot of other really cool stuff. Let's follow Him around and be part of it. I'm in! Are you?

Why I Go to Church

The entire story before this one talks about where to recognize God's presence outside of church. This begged a question as to why I even go to church. If you didn't grow up in church, or did, or either way, you simply don't get the whole "church" thing, this one is for you.

While Sundays are not my "day to be a Christian," since I would hope and pray that I reflect Christ every day of my life (some days not as well as others, perhaps), I get so excited to go worship Him together with other believers, to pray, to hear His Word with more clarity, and to be refreshed in the midst of others who share my faith. Who He is is alive and living in me and in His Word every day, but on Sundays (or sometimes Saturday night), I get to celebrate that with others.

For me, church isn't "checking off that social or even religious box for the week," which means I look forward to it. To me, it isn't a building or even an institution. To me, it is where some of His peeps gather at a set time to give Him honor and praise, to hear from Him together, to sit at His Throne together. I can sit at the Throne in my own home. The building makes no difference. But when we gather together (even when it's in someone's home or prayer meeting), it is incredibly meaningful to me. I like sitting at His feet and keeping my eyes gazed up at Him for a dedicated hour and a half: such a refuge from the worries of life.

I don't do it because it wins me favor with Him or scores any suck-up points with God. I don't do it so I can say what a great Christian I am to others or have my kids all dressed up once a week (we wear jeans half of the time). I do it because I want to love Him back, give Him that time with others, and rest in Him for a set-aside time. It's a time of fortification for whatever stuff hits the fan the rest of the week, and it surely always does for any of us one way or another, right? For me, it's a taste of the forever I look forward to someday singing with angels in His glorious presence, one day fully revealed to me.

> Matthew 18:20, Jesus speaking
>
> "For where two or three are gathered in my name, there am I among them."

Luke describes so well what church should look like when we are all consulting the Lord in our actions and interactions and as we become more like Him:

> Acts 2:42-47, Luke the Physician narrating, referring to the early Christian church
>
> And they devoted themselves to the apostles' teaching and the fellowship, to the breaking of bread and the prayers. And awe came upon every soul, and many wonders and signs were being done through the apostles. And all who believed were together and had all things in common. And they were selling their possessions and belongings and distributing the proceeds to all, as any had need. And day by day, attending the temple together and breaking bread in their homes, they received their food with glad and generous hearts, praising God and having favor with all the people. And the Lord added to their number day by day those who were being saved.

Bring it! We need to all pray in unity that we look much more like *that*.

Wal-Mart Marcy

Not too long ago, I ran into a sixty-something woman in Wal-Mart trying to buy BPA-free microwavable containers. She needed them for packing and reheating kale soup for her daughter, who was struggling her way through chemotherapy. She asked me for help reading labels, which is how I know God was at work, because I'm so anal about label-reading as it is, having a food-allergy child in my house for many years.

"That's so wrong," I thought to myself, "that this poor woman has to watch her offspring suffer through this," but we all know how wrong it is because we've seen this scenario somewhere with folks we know and love. It's heartbreaking. So after helping her find the BPA-free containers, I asked if I could have the first name of her daughter so I could pray. She was very grateful. If you are a praying person, please ask Jesus to restore what has been eaten from Marcy's life and grow healthy cells, flushing out the toxic ones. When I can, I like to align my prayers with God's promises in the Scripture because they are God-breathed and life-giving.

Joel 2:25-27, God speaking through Joel the Prophet

"I will restore to you the years
    that the swarming locust has eaten,
the hopper, the destroyer, and the cutter,
    my great army, which I sent among you.

"You shall eat in plenty and be satisfied,
    and praise the name of the LORD your God,
    who has dealt wondrously with you.
And my people shall never again be put to shame.
You shall know that I am in the midst of Israel,
    and that I am the LORD your God and there is none else.
And my people shall never again be put to shame."

After we parted ways, I went into another aisle and was so overcome with Christ's love for this woman and her daughter Marcy, I started to weep. [Yeah, this is why I can't go out anywhere in public; this happens to me more often than I share.] I hate cancer like everyone else, but I was grateful God answered a prayer on my heart today: "What do you want me to do today? Whom can I bless?" I didn't do anything but meet a prayer need—and only because He put me in her path. I am asking Him to bring me back somehow into that woman's life to hear a good report someday: that those soups are no longer necessary. Who in your life needs this restorative prayer from Joel?

His Kenyan Rose

My sister and I were at a Christian conference in Pennsylvania, about a year ago, and were walking back from a long conversation in a coffee shop during one of the break times in the conference. On our way, we noticed an African woman walking very closely to us, seeming to need help. After some inquiries, we discovered her name was Rose, she was from Kenya, and she was trying to find a building where she would be taking an aptitude test for her profession. If I recall correctly, she was a nurse's aide, which was another cool God connection because my sister is a perioperative nurse. She needed some help with a confusing address. As we walked with her more, we discovered she hadn't been long in this country, having left sons and other family behind in Kenya, and that as of yet, because of some holdup in an embassy somewhere, they had been unable to join her.

We spoke of many things together in the thirty minutes we spent with her, and we were able to offer prayer, right there on the streets of a quaint Pennsylvania town. It wasn't much. We don't deserve medals for this. But she was a believer in Christ, and it seemed like He had matched us up together on the street at the same time to mutually bless each other. We were reminded of needs beyond our sister time, and she was able to find help from likeminded, safe folks like us. To this day, we continue to interact on email. Again, it wasn't much. We didn't launch a campaign to get her son over to the States or even procure a better job for her. It was clear that was a struggle. But as nice as it would have been to accomplish that, our interactions were much simpler than that. We often think unless we solve a major issue like world hunger, our smaller moments mean little.

We connected with Rose for a little while and shared the fellowship of believers. We prayed for her, and she for us. Maybe two years from now, she will still remember that. Maybe not. But I believe God is very pleased when people reach out to one another, believers or not. She is His Kenyan Rose first and foremost. When we see people this way, it humbles us, it teaches us about God, and it shows us how we are not alone in this world because He brings us all together—on city streets and through the cyber-universe. Rose taught me to stop and look around. She reminded me of the struggles of an ex-patriate, which I once was. She demonstrated that among cultural barriers, God was bigger and could help us communicate and love each other in His Spirit.

We may never have Rose's particular challenges. It's tempting to think our personal trials pale compared with some of hers. But we are not to compare each other in this way. In God's eyes, we are the same. We are each walking opportunities to connect with others: *all* others—not just those who share our faith. When we do share our connection in Him, the Bible says to edify each other and encourage good works.

Hebrews 10:23-25, author unknown, but he is recording the words of God

Let us hold fast the confession of our hope without wavering, for he who promised is faithful. And let us consider how to stir up one another to love and good works, not neglecting to meet together, as is the habit of some, but encouraging one another, and all the more as you see the Day drawing near.

Rose seemed to already be doing those on her own. Her profession was to take care of people, often through thankless jobs. She also seemed to stop and acknowledge a lot of fellow Africans on the street, some her countrymen, some not. In our few exchanges, she made me a better person. She renewed and refreshed my thinking. She helped me be more aware. And isn't that *always* a *good* thing?

Sticky Notes From God

For every area of crushing brokenness, insecurity, deep pain, or rejection, there is someone He sends to counter it, as if to say:

> No, My Child. That other thing is *not* you. Do not listen to that. That doesn't even match My Word. Instead, listen to this person whom I sent. They say things that match what I say in My Word. Learn to know the difference. They are reflecting who I think you are, and I think you are beautiful and full of purpose because I love you and I made you.

And when that happens, I know that He really sees us. He truly hears us. He knows how another person did not properly steward his or her relationship with us, and He speaks new life into us. The deal is that we have to learn to recognize the countering voices of love that He sends. We have to tell the negative to "bug off" and think only on these things:

> Philippians 4:8, Apostle Paul speaking
>
> Finally, brothers, whatever is true, whatever is honorable, whatever is just, whatever is pure, whatever is lovely, whatever is commendable, if there is any excellence, if there is anything worthy of praise, think about these things.

A dear friend of mine from my island days came to visit; sadly, I was away at the time, so she and her husband hung out with Salad Boy and the kids without me. She was unaware of the incidents I encountered the week I was gone, but when I came home, she had left me sticky-note messages all over my house, reminding me of God's love and her friend love. She had no idea the heart returning home needed to see and feel something tangible that was the opposite of rejection and the very definition of love (my own family also reminded me of that). He knows what we need, and He sends messengers to deliver the messages. We are not always tuned in to see it, but He does this. And I love it! *Open my eyes to see it more, Lord! You are awesome!*

So, I got to thinking how God also leaves us sticky notes. They are all over our Bibles, sure, but they are also penned by those who love us, like my sweet island friend. Salad Boy and I don't write each other notes a lot in the everyday rhythm of our lives. I wish I could say, being a writer, that I wrote him long confessions of my love, daily, but alas, I do not. But in a rare moment when he felt inspired, as he left for work, Salad Boy said: "Have a great day at work, Honey." I didn't, at that time, work for regular pay. Not yet. But it doesn't matter if it is a writing day or a "keeping house" day or a "running around on errands" day, he gets it. He gets every bit of it, and I just love him to pieces for it. He was my sticky note from God that day. It was verbal, but it was a blessing.

Sometimes we are the ones writing the sticky notes. One day, this was my sticky note to a friend of mine who did not share my faith. Life had taken her down a road where she had taken a bite out of the bitter apple one too many times. Don't we all get to that place some days? I wanted to speak some of His Truth to her. She didn't magically embrace my faith. We often need a whole stack of sticky notes speaking truth to undo the untrue, hateful ones we have received:

> I have many thoughts, and I probably can't get them all down, but I do hear you on feeling betrayed, abandoned, disappointed. I think when so many people have poorly reflected back to you your worth, it is easy to think they are reflecting God as well with their awful choices to be devastatingly hurtful. I can understand why that feels like it is God acting (or not acting in some cases). This is a great discussion for a time when I can go more in depth, but I encourage you to realize humans failed you over and over again, but God knows that and has a heart that aches for you. This may not make sense right now or feel real. I had to spend a lot of time getting "human" out of my way of seeing God. Humans can really disappoint and screw it up sometimes. They kept getting in the way of me

seeing God. It's hard to distinguish. It's hard not to feel left out in the cold at times, especially after all of your rotten experiences. I hear you on feeling like you "did all of the right things" or "followed all of the right rules." I am sure He sees that. The coolest part for me in my faith (or perhaps the biggest relief) is that, while I want to do all of the right things because I love Him, my relationship with Him isn't dependent on that. I don't have to be perfect or measure up.

I want to be praying for you that the lies and untruths that all of those people (those who abused their responsibility to "tend your heart and soul") spoke to you will scatter and that God's love for who He made you to be will be the only voice you hear. I am still clearing out my own cobwebs and telling old tapes playing in my head to stop, but each time I do, I see myself through God's eyes more clearly. It's the only version of me I fully love—because He does.

What's Your Good News?

When a dear friend who recently suffered a devastating loss sent me an email with the subject line "Good News," I just about broke several keys on the keyboard getting over to click on that message. It had been fewer than two short months since the love of her life died unexpectedly and tragically in a white-water rafting accident. So you see, "Good News" was not what I was expecting as an email title from her. But that's simply who she is. Even in the face of a torrent of pain, this friend has something positive to share.

Another dear friend experienced painful abandonment in the past year. In a recent phone call from her, she told me how she saw God's grace and peace over a situation that would make most of us scream and wail. Good news? Really?

A lovely young mother (and growing friendship of mine) spoke during a church share time that she had sought the Lord for answers and breakthrough for her child for years, and breakthrough had finally come. She mentioned that through the difficulties, "But God." *But God?* Really?

Unlike these bearers of good news, we all know people who choose to sit in Negative Land, with or without real reasons to be there, and they can't seem to do anything but state the impossibilities right before them. And let's face it. So many things *are* proven impossibilities in the human realm. Pancreatic cancer isn't a diagnosis you want to receive. Neither is a chromosomal disorder in your unborn fetus. A loss typically can't be undone. An unfaithful, unrepentant spouse seems like a tall order for redemption. I'm not saying Jesus can't heal people in these conditions and situations. I'm merely acknowledging that some things are sucker punches that we can't imagine being undone.

And what if they're not undone?

My friend did not get her sweet boyfriend back this side of heaven. My other friend's situation still looks bleak as she picks up the pieces of a life wrecked by another person. While the third friend is currently enjoying breakthrough, there were many years she quaked and trembled waiting on His answers.

We discussed this very topic in our junior high Sunday School class the other day. Where is God acting in the middle of the storm? The answer coming in may be "no" or "wait," but that does not mean He isn't revealing Himself somehow. So, what is the good news during dark times? My favorite Old Testament person to consult is King David, who knew his share of personal failings and difficult circumstances:

Psalm 34:17-18, David (not yet king) speaking

When the righteous cry for help, the LORD hears
    and delivers them out of all their troubles.
The LORD is near to the brokenhearted
    and saves the crushed in spirit.

Psalm 145:17-21, King David speaking

The LORD is righteous in all his ways
    and kind in all his works.
The LORD is near to all who call on him,
    to all who call on him in truth.
He fulfills the desire of those who fear him;
    he also hears their cry and saves them.
The LORD preserves all who love him,
    but all the wicked he will destroy.

My mouth will speak the praise of the LORD,
    and let all flesh bless his holy name forever and ever.

The good news is that the Lord is *near to the brokenhearted*, He hears the righteous (those made right by the cross and putting their faith in Jesus) when they cry out. He is always *kind in all his works*. He is *near to all who call on Him in truth. He fulfills the desire of those who fear Him. He preserves all who love Him.*

That is the good news: the Good News! It is unchanging, unlike our lives. It is always true. It is where these three friends, and many more, have found their strength, their joy, their hope, their good news when life smacked them around. Can you get your mind behind that? Can you place your trust in Him Who died for you? If you can, these promises are for you too. God isn't a vending machine, as Salad Boy and I often tell our junior high students (who regularly prove to be significantly smarter than the two of us put together); we say this more to teach ourselves than to teach them. Circumstances don't always change instantly, but the God walking with you through them is faithful, and He never changes.

Hebrews 13:6-8, author unknown, but he is recording the words of God

So we can confidently say, "The Lord is my helper; I will not fear; what can man do to me?" Remember your leaders, those who spoke to you the word of God. Consider the outcome of their way of life, and imitate their faith. Jesus Christ is the same yesterday and today and forever.

When Horror Comes to Town: The Boston Marathon

I have a policy I like to follow. It's fairly simple. "Don't give evil the spotlight." Now, one could argue that we have to make sure evil that is hidden around the world comes to light. I agree with that. But, in general, don't let the evildoers get much airtime. Talk about the heroes. Let evil crawl back under the floorboards and cower in shame. This was pretty much my approach when we heard about the Boston Marathon bombings, which sent a shockwave through the Boston area on April 15, 2013.

Let's start off by saying that nobody close to me was injured. I knew people who were there, but I didn't live the fear the way so many in this area did. When the subject was still at large, I was a safe distance away. So, I was admittedly looking at this through the lens of one removed from the situation. A direct victim would have another vantage point, I realize. But from my vantage point, I was asked by a friend to offer some thoughts. Where is/was God in this? Where is He in any horror, really? Some of my processing spilled out over social media before she even asked, and the posts more or less looked like this, sequentially, as I struggled to formulate a response:

> The Boston Marathon explosions and an armed robbery in our town the same afternoon. Evil takes its 15 minutes, but I take comfort in this:
>
> > 1 John 4:4, Apostle John speaking
> >
> > Little children, you are from God and have overcome them, for he who is in you is greater than he who is in the world.
>
> Evil assaults for a little while longer, but it does *not* have the final say. Best approach to take is to pray and defeat this evil with His

good. Yes, horror still happened. But let's not give it any more power than it took. Community will rally. Prayers will go up. People will unite. The power of love and His bright Light are stronger and better, and the darkness shall soon scatter, coward that it is.

I want to say this to anyone currently dealing with high levels of anxiety, depression, or fear: Stay off Facebook right now. Inform yourself as you need to on the Boston news (briefly), but don't soak up the fear. We have to be wise, yes, but 152 posts later can take an already anxious person and put him or her on the edge. Soaking in the fear will only entangle you in more fear. Please don't spiral. This is horrific, yes, but don't let this one evil man take control of you today. If your depression or anxiety gets out of control, please call someone to help you.

Tonight when it was Little Man's turn to pray, he asked in a quiet little voice if he could add an extra prayer on his heart to what he had already decided to pray for. We all said, "Yes," and he said: "And dear Jesus, please help the bad guy (Boston bomber) in the hospital who lost a lot of blood to get enough blood again." I am incredibly humbled by that statement because I'm not there quite yet, but I should be. So, I acknowledged that was a loving thing to do and held my breath, and Oldest picked up on what should have been my parenting moment and said: "The Bible says to pray for your enemies, Buddy, so you did the right thing." *Thank You, Lord, that the children hear You clearly even when I don't.*

When awful, unexplainable horrors and tragedies strike us, it's fascinating to watch a seven year old process it. He is re-enacting the heroes—not the scenario—by making sure the good-guy Star Wars LEGO® police guys get the bad LEGO® bandits. I love that for two reasons: One, I can see a little boy with an innate sense of fighting for justice, and I don't get uptight about LEGO® weapons because God made him a warrior-protector, and nothing about me wants to squelch that. Two, kids have to make sense of their world and try to put it back in order after these kinds of events remind them of horrible possibilities. If some LEGO® casualties end up on my floor in a defeated heap, it's worth it to have Little Man feeling safe again.

My favorite place to be after a week of tragedy and horror like this? With praying people seeking the face of God. *Oh, how my heart has found solace. Oh, how peace has rested on my head in Your presence, Lord.* I know none of us has slept well this week. I know we all feel unsettled and shaken, hating the awful injustices and darkness of this world that we have to explain to our kids or reconcile in our own hearts. If anyone would like prayer, message me. I'm happy to pray for you. We need to lift each other up at times like this and be directed toward the source of hope and peace. Prayer requests don't have to be about the latest crisis. It can be anything, and you don't have to share major details. And you don't have to share my faith for me to pray for you. Just know you are loved.

I know it didn't feel like it last week, but the good guys often do win. Another story wrapped where the bad guy's 15 minutes are over. The Merrimack Bank Bandit has been caught.

Last week felt very unsafe on several levels. I totally get that, although compared with so much of the world, we are very safe. But once in a while we need to acknowledge how powerless and frail darkness is when all is said and done. As scared as we can be at times, darkness is more scared that light will shine on it and expose it for what it really is. May this bandit get not only justice but help where light can push out all darkness gripping him and have a soul that is free, like the thief on the cross.[44]

Acknowledge the goodness in the world, and the things that lurk in the dark fade in importance. Inform as you need to, but don't give this evil the fame it seeks.

Take heart. This evil has about 30 seconds left before it is snuffed out. Just sayin'. It has an expiration date. Evil always does.

Do We Come to Serve or to Be Served?

I'm listening to two women at a table near me as I write this. One woman cuts the other one off halfway through whatever she says to talk about herself; she's amazingly skilled at weaving everything back to herself. (I have found that is its own art form.) She's not *hearing* her lunch mate. I am, from one table over, but she's not. Lately, I have to say: I know the feeling. People dynamics fascinate me. How many of us don't really listen? How many of us think our stuff is way more urgent and important and don't walk into a time with another person carrying a servant's heart that says: "How can I bless and listen to you today? What's on your heart?" People railroading over other people's voices is a pet peeve of mine because inside all of us, at least from time to time, is a little squeaky voice trying to get louder and be truly heard. I frequently have to tell mine not to passionately scream by the time it finally gets a chance to speak. I often have to say (to my own voice): "I know you've waited a while, but you don't need to holler now that someone's actually listening."

For some reason, this whole battle over who gets to talk more reminded me not only of a few scenarios in my own life, but also of James and John. Many Bibles break this section into a little subheading called: "The Request of James and John." I'd like to suggest that many times it's more of a demand, a sense of entitlement, an assumption of why they're (and we're) really there. I think "request" is a euphemism here because James and John had a wrong heart attitude that went a little beyond "polite request," in my humble opinion.

Mark 10:35-45, Apostle John-Mark narrating

And James and John, the sons of Zebedee, came up to him and said to him, "Teacher, we want you to do for us whatever we ask of you." And he said to them, "What do you want me to do for you?" And they said to him, "Grant us to sit, one at your right hand and one at your left, in your glory." Jesus said to them, "You do not know what you are asking. Are you able to drink the cup that I drink, or to be baptized with the baptism with which I am baptized?" And they said to him, "We are able." And Jesus said to them, "The cup that I drink you will drink, and with the baptism with which I am baptized, you will be baptized, but to sit at my right hand or at my left is not mine to grant, but it is for those for whom it has been prepared." And when the ten heard it, they began to be indignant at James and John. And Jesus called them to him and said to them, "You know that those who are considered rulers of the Gentiles lord it over them, and their great ones exercise authority over them. But it shall not be so among you. But whoever would be great among you must be your servant, and whoever would be first among you must be slave of all. *For even the Son of Man came not to be served but to serve, and to give his life as a ransom for many* [emphasis mine]."

So, getting back to my point, how many times do we enter a situation, even with someone familiar or intimate, and assume we are there to receive? How many times do we (those of us who talk to God and His Son Jesus) say the following: "Father, what would you have me do in this meeting? How can I bless?" So many times we enter gunning for what we can take, what we need to get off our chest, what we can walk away with. That's like this delightful, raw, honest slice of Mark 10 (verse 35):

And James and John, the sons of Zebedee, came up to him and said to him, "Teacher, we want you to do for us whatever we ask of you."

Um, can you imagine saying that to a Holy Savior, the Son of God, or—if you aren't fully "there" yet in realizing Who He is, as they may not have been—the amazing Rabbi you've been walking with a while? The one doing miracles and calling down the power of God when His Father wills it to heal people, drive out demons, raise the dead? In some ways, demanding to be the center of attention at times can be like that. James and John are more or less saying: "Me, me, pick me! Pick me!" preschool-style. That's so much like our one-way conversations. We don't ask what we can bring into it. We demand that our need and heart's desire are met and frequently forget what the other person needs.

I love—no, I *adore*—what the Savior says, which is essentially: "Go lower. Lower still. Serve." Well, I'm paraphrasing. What He actually says is: "Whoever would be great among you must be your servant, and whoever would be first among you must be slave of all." Um, wow. I know we often think that "acts of service" mean going to a charity event, volunteering, maybe even with our kids. But what if we were all to put on that posture before doing *anything*: that meeting with a teacher with whom we don't always see eye to eye, lunch with a friend, phone call to a difficult relative? What if we *"came not to be served, but to serve"*? How fantastic would that be? For one thing, our expectations would be where they need to be toward everyone but God: lower. He came to "give his life as a ransom for many." Not much tops that, and therefore, we should spend more time giving, not whining about not getting. That has been a real struggle of my life: to shake off my self-scripted expectations of other people (and to not twitch about their expectations of me as well).

If we're blessing other people, His blessings toward us keep pouring out, so we never have to worry that we won't receive, as long as our heart isn't in "martyr mode," seeing how much attention we can get for our sacrifices or looking to please and perform. I imagine James and John licked a few shut-up-sicles after that conversation. What rebuttal could one possibly have to the Son of God saying He came to serve? I think personal goals, expectations, and agendas have no choice but to drop into their proper place when we follow His example. When He orders our steps, we lose our status as "takers" and become contributors, lovers of His people, ministers, evangelists, life-lay-downers, and feeders of His sheep, and we accomplish far more than we would in Self-Absorption-Ville. We feel significantly more fulfilled as well.

Getting back to the two ladies at lunch. The more I sit here, the more I hear the quiet spirit inside the listener. The more I see that she chose to be a serve-r today. I see where my own attitude started out critical because what I couldn't see at the beginning of my little time next to her was that she didn't get her back up about her overwhelming friend. She's not overwhelming her because she clearly came to nurture her today. I hear that now. And I am humbled. Because my little tiny perspective can be off-kilter. I don't see as He does. Not until I ask Him. I'm just like James and John and get too big for my britches. We all do. Thank God *"For even the Son of Man came not to be served but to serve, and to give his life as a ransom for many"* (Mark 10:45). I need to spend a little more time reading about Him and talking to Him because without Him, that whole serving business doesn't come naturally.

Suddenly You Find Yourself Marrying Him All Over Again

This book landed itself right in the middle of three key milestones in my life: my 40th birthday, my last child entering full-day school, and my 20th wedding anniversary. Because we don't have family nearby and for a host of other reasons, we figured out pretty quickly we couldn't get away on our own without the kids this year to celebrate the special occasions. So, we stretched out our celebration this year. We don't normally make such a fuss, and although we didn't go on a special getaway or buy diamonds and pearls, we found ways to make it meaningful and significant, to remember the ride, savor the celebration, and make it linger. Twenty years has a lot of "stuff" in it. It's not smooth sailing, this relationship stuff; it's hard work. Twenty years ago, I said "I do" at the ripe old age of 20, having just graduated college and come back from Japan. What could I possibly have known about the journey ahead (and 11 big and small moves in 20 years)? But God did, and I thank Him for each golden moment, each instance of growth, and each amazing blessing.

So, after spending months thinking about it, I prepared for celebrating 20 years of life with Mark in two of my favorite ways: I drank copious amounts of espresso and wrote him a tribute. But I even went one better: I *accidentally* arranged for us to say our vows at the beginning of a Sunday morning service the weekend before the big day. Yeah, *accidentally*. It all started with our pastor putting out the plea to honor marriages of 20 years or more on special anniversaries to encourage long, committed marriages in our community. I figured that meant I'd tell him, and we'd be prayed for or acknowledged with one sentence from the front on a Sunday morning. I didn't picture spotlighting myself, and I mostly wanted to honor Mark. So, I sent an email to the pastor, and despite about three exchanges where he said: "Come up front and we'll renew your vows" and I said: "Yeah, that's okay. I don't even know where my vows are. Mark isn't really a 'come up front and renew your vows' kind of guy," that message apparently did not get through. I came home one afternoon to an email sent out to our entire church, complete with our wedding photo, marriage vows with our names inserted in them, and the announcement that Mark and Bonnie would be renewing their vows at the beginning of the next Sunday service. Um, wow. All kinds of wow.

After getting over my own shock from that email coming in (as well as emails of congratulations following it), I spent time consulting with my older two children on how to break it to their dad; much to my chagrin, they told me I couldn't wait until the morning of. It took two days, lots of dress- and shoe-shopping later, and one lame email telling Mark to check his Google account (and to be sure to have a suit and tie and get to the church on time on Sunday), and then came that nervous laugh, the one I've heard in awkward moments over the course of many years. What's even more pathetic is that we were in the same room on separate computers when I emailed him. Yup, because that's how I roll. I'll leave the shades of how red his face turned and the discussion following to our own little locked-up closet of memories reserved for only us, but many points for Salad Boy because he took it pretty well. Next came the news that I involved a few outside-of-the-church friends; he quickly forgave me my enthusiasm when that proved a smart move since we had no photographer until they showed up and were handed our little Canon.

I will never regret that day. In some ways it was more special than in 1993. Before this day, I somehow associated marriage renewals with folks who had broken their vows and were now publicly sharing the victory of putting a marriage back together again or those marking a milestone like a 25th or 50th anniversary. But after getting up on that stage and seeing three growing versions of ourselves staring back at us (some with awe and some with the teen angst of "Hurry up and do your silly adult thing and then get me off this stage!"), I was sure we had just done something so significant. We essentially said: "We know what this actually means now, and even so, we'd still do it all over again." How crazy is that?

I realize this isn't everyone's story. I know some people have not repaired their relationships, had to leave situations for reasons of abuse, or never knew this kind of companionship; I have deep compassion for those circumstances. But I think that in today's society, each year we all inch along toward lengthier marriages, flying in the face of what our discard-everything culture always tells us, is to be celebrated. And so, I collected my thoughts and wrote this tribute to Mark. But it's a tribute to God more than anyone, because without Him as the center where we recalibrated—often—Salad Boy and Latte Girl may have long ago pitched this whole holy matrimony thing and bought the lie that good things don't last. Marriages—and all good gifts—need tending, faith, patience, perseverance, and humility. No short order, but they can last because they come from God.

James 1:17, James, brother of Jesus, speaking

Every good gift and every perfect gift is from above, coming down from the Father of lights with whom there is no variation or shadow due to change.

Back to Salad Boy: He gave me permission to share this tribute because the sentiments speak to what both of our hearts say as encouragement to hurting marriages. I hope you find something healing in this if your marriage is in a tough season. Or perhaps it will remind you that you have much to celebrate in your own marriage as well. Maybe you just began this journey and you want to look ahead to what people mean by walking out their vows, when action often has to model the words we spoke to each other in the beginning. Or maybe you want the dream of a forever romance, but this is so sobering, you find it wise to walk another season or so before committing yourself long term to the one you love.

Whatever place you find yourself in, marriage or not, I hope you see the truth of what spiritual warfare marriage can be up against. It's not something to go into without all of our armor fully on—not against each other but against everything that tries to tear our union down. Because marriage was designed to model Christ's relationship with His Bride, the Church, the enemy will do all he can to make it seem unachievable, stained, less than radiant. The only way to keep her sparkly and new is to keep turning back to Christ for renewal, whether you *accidentally* end up on a stage reciting your vows again or not. This is included in this section because we need God in our marriages, *desperately.*

Ephesians 5:25-27, Apostle Paul speaking

Husbands, love your wives, as Christ loved the church and gave himself up for her, that he might sanctify her, having cleansed her by the washing of water with the word, so that he might present the church to himself in splendor, without spot or wrinkle or any such thing, that she might be holy and without blemish.

To Mark on the Occasion of Our 20th Wedding Anniversary

I used to think marriage had to mean saying yes all of the time together. I have found the opposite to actually be true. So much of what we do, as long as we stay on the same page and look up to our Father in heaven, is to stand in the gap and say, "No!"

No, we will not let that trespass into our home.
No, we will not let old lies inform us.
No, we are not stuck in unhealthy patterns.
No, we will not tolerate that behavior under our roof.
No, we are not okay with that influence on our children.
No, we will not engage in negative thoughts or behaviors.
No, we will not go down that path.
No, we will not compromise our standards or faith.

But it's not so much always saying no to *each other* but rather taking a stand against that which seeks to infringe upon the health of our *oneness in Christ*. It's about standing at the threshold of the doorway and not letting certain things through—but only because we are standing together and He is with us. The minute we forget that, the snake at our feet slithers in. It's a choice every day—and sometimes every minute.

But it's a lot of yes too. It's a lot of:

Yes, I will choose to assume the best about you.
Yes, I will serve you even when I feel selfish.
Yes, I will look up to Him when I have no clue what to do here, how to reach you.
Yes, I will humble myself.
Yes, I will listen to you deeply even though I'm half asleep and my day has been long.
Yes, I will accept that you are not me, and I will not attempt to make you into my own image.
Yes, we are in charge. The kids are not.
Yes, we are a priority to each other.

Mark, we have looked several difficulties in the face together and roared back at darkness, declaring that His Light is real and that the dark must back way off! I guess I'm actually the one roaring if you walk past our windows on any given day, and you are the one who stands incredibly strong and deep but quiet-spirited. It's an amazing balance God put together. I'd still be roaring if you hadn't come along and put a softer muffle on it. I'd still be raging there on the side of the road, and perhaps, just perhaps, you wouldn't have found how incredibly wise your own voice is if you didn't have to counter, encourage, and challenge me at times. Together we've come closer to the middle, and that middle is Him.

We have faced 11 moves in 20 years. We have faced down the last dimes in the bank with two extra mouths to feed at the time, losing housing, praying through the terror of a critically ill infant, the strain of grad school and marriage, taking turns letting each other achieve some dreams, the painful waiting: When is it going to be *my* turn? When is it going to be *your* turn? We have lived far from our families and moved around the world and back, adjusting three small kids to life on a tiny island and then back to the culture shock awaiting stateside. We saw one of us buckle under into dark waters of depression and get back up again, pushing aside voices of death. We have shuttled from temporary home to temporary home. Like anyone else on this journey, a few loud voices in the dark have *tried* to have a say at us. We roared back. We roared back together. In Jesus, we had victory. The enemy sometimes flicked us and laid little molotov cocktails at our feet to distract or discourage us, but Jesus put out the fires, and we safely walked out. We walked away stronger, and any scars are hopefully used completely for His glory. We are learning how to usher in His peace and trying to model for our children how to flood Him into every area of life.

We have partially raised three very different but beautiful children, and in these 13 years of childrearing so far, we have seen His amazing hand in all of it: every bully, every sickness, every desperate time of personal growth, every moment of needing creative and supernatural parenting wisdom from the Best Parent there is. We have seen food allergies, decades of migraines, and more importantly, *F-E-A-R* leave our home, all in the precious name of Jesus. We walk more and more with chains off, more unafraid, more bold, getting up more quickly when we fall down again.

So, in from your morning run you came the other day, Mark, in the USAF sweatshirt you used to wear when you would walk over half an hour from your campus to mine to date me. When I was at college and saw the man in that sweatshirt walk in, I knew my day was about to get much brighter. Hadn't seen that on you in a while. Wow! I think my breath suspended in mid-air for a few moments. You are still my same cadet, only now you've been entirely mine for 20 years, and when you walk through the door like that, two decades later, I still think: "Is he really here for me?" There are three kids running around that look like you, and most of the mail has your name on it, so I kinda think that you are! And I want you to know that is incredibly awesome! And I'm so grateful to Him for 20 years with you. May the next 20 be even more steeped in Him. Happy Anniversary!

Part 4
Words That Bless Our Children and Knowing Who We/They Really Are

Little Man: "Mom, when I look into Rufus's (stuffed animal) eyes, I see things."
Me: "Um. Like what?"
Little Man: "I see broken things, like pieces of something."
Me: "Little Man, I will go look into his eyes and check, but it's okay. You are an artist in your heart. You see the extra things so many of us don't see."

About a year ago, a few mentors in my life, unbeknownst to each other, offered me some very valuable wisdom around the same time. It was so confirming. I love it when God does this for us. It's beautiful. I have an annoying tendency to walk around and keep saying: "Jesus, is that You?" He therefore knows to give me a few folks to bang it into my head. Anyway, each, in his or her own way, taught me to pray blessing over my children: To thank God for the vision He was slowly giving me for each of their lives and to pray in strength where there was weakness. I have never looked back! It has made such an incredible difference in my life and my children's. It has not only changed my prayer life; it has changed my perspective toward my own children. It has given them a beautiful, tangible vision of a Lord Who walks beside them, who never forsakes them. If I do nothing else right on this parenting journey, I really believe this one will have lasting impact.

In this section are ways I try to find the blessing to speak over my children, ways to affirm who they are and what they were created to be and do. I end this section with a sample from tributes I wrote them on different birthdays. I think the more we do this, the more we help nourish and build up strong little people who can battle their day to day and come home to a refuge. Parenting isn't a journey in which every season is sweet icing and lollipops. I've sat around my Moms' Prayer Group table many, many times over the years when one of us was weeping with the very real struggles of trying to guide, love, and create healthy boundaries and discipline for her children (from toddlers to teens). We will sit around my table biweekly many more times over the years passing the tissues. It isn't easy. But on the days that stink the most, we need to have a ready list of what is good, right, noble in our kids and speak it to them—speak it to them often.[45]

Philippians 4:8, Apostle Paul speaking

Finally, brothers, whatever is true, whatever is honorable, whatever is just, whatever is pure, whatever is lovely, whatever is commendable, if there is any excellence, if there is anything worthy of praise, think about these things.

How Do You Parent an Extrovert If You're an Introvert, and Vice Versa?

My first child is a lot like me in some ways. He is content with a good book for *hours*. The phone is his enemy. If he sees and interacts with another person every couple of days, he's all set. He's content being pensive and learning. All three of my kids have different areas of intensity. He is intense academically and requires huge pieces of my brain to keep up. When he has spent enough social energy (which equates to one hour of church), he retreats to his room to think, read, research, compose music for multiple instruments, or iTouch. (I'm not really sure that's a verb, but it is now.) It's almost easy to forget he's around, except when he's in my presence asking me some obscure science or math question. Parenting him has been "comfortable," because my husband and I are both bookworm introverts. My son and I read dictionaries for fun in our free time. We more or less "get" each other, at least at this point.

From one introvert to another, I offered this wisdom to my son before a youth retreat:

> If you are feeling followed around by anyone, chances are the other kid may find you a comfort. If you need personal space, try not to passive-aggressively give off an irritated vibe. Be honest that you might go lay down or read for a bit in the cabin because you're tired. It's okay to need that time to regroup. Take it before you start stressing out. This is how I always had to handle being away in groups of people. Still do. Oh, and last thought: Good luck being technology-free all weekend. You will do great!

Along came Child Number Two. She is a real mix of "vert." But as a young child, her extrovert side wore me out. With adults speaking to her in almost any context, she was freakishly shy, but when she was with peers, she always wanted to be surrounded by them—not just one or two, but the *whole class*. I could tell stories about her inviting *all* of her Marshallese classmates over during lunch break from school during kindergarten. I used to curl up in a ball and cry when she was in her preschool and kindergarten years, and her social energy with peers in one week exceeded my capacity to be with people in an entire year. It was so hard to strike a balance between not giving up too much of what was comfortable to me and trying to meet her needs at the same time. I have always admired her for that. Her social ability astounds me. I want to be her, but I am not, and I long feared not meeting her needs enough in this area.

Then along came Child Number Three. And there simply are no words, really. None. He talks to himself at night if everyone else is otherwise occupied. He can strike up conversations with any child or adult. Where Child Number Two enjoys children her age, Child Number Three wants to engage with every age. My husband and I used to take turns taking him to the playground because, inevitably, he'd go beyond introducing himself to new friends and bring parents over to meet us. Salad Boy and I aren't unfriendly, but sometimes after a long day of work or home, we enjoy flying a bit under the social radar. We made more friends during his playground years than perhaps we had in our adult lifetimes. Little Man's winsome character is hard not to want to be around. He is quick to find the humor in situations but not at others' expense. He is a good listener. More and more, while I appreciated who God made me and Oldest Child to be, I saw amazing strengths in the other side of the social spectrum. I'll admit it got on my nerves at times, but overall, I have learned to love and admire the differences. We all are starting to see the benefits to the blend of personalities in our home.

As a side note, I offer this one thought for extroverted parents and their introverted kids. (A friend and I have this conversation all of the time over her knitting and my consumption of ridiculous amounts of coffee.) Let the child know even you occasionally feel this way—introverted or overwhelmed socially—(if you do) or know adults who do. It makes her feel less alone and that she can approach you more. She may see you as socially "together" since you have an extroverted side. That can make an introverted or inward kid feel that the extroverted parent has no social issues. Transparency is beautiful and vital! Keep snuggle-up, quiet moments with her, but let her be alone too.

So where am I going with all of this? I have two children who overall are the opposite side of the spectrum from me socially. Their needs are different. My worst fears are that I will look like I favor the one more like me socially, that we will somehow cater to the majority, that we will undermine or make the other "verts" feel "less than" by heavy sighs or demonstrative irritation, or that we will not speak enough affirmation about the different giftings each of our children has. How do we do this when our selfish nature says (if we are introverted): "Stop talking. Leave me alone. I'm in my cave," or (if we are extroverted): "What is *wrong* with you? Don't you ever feel anything? Or express anything? Are we left to guess who you are?"

First, we are told we are each made in His own image.

Genesis 1:26-27, Moses narrating

Then God said, "Let us make man in our image, after our likeness. And let them have dominion over the fish of the sea and over the birds of the heavens and over the livestock and over all the earth and over every creeping thing that creeps on the earth."

So God created man in his own image,
   in the image of God he created him;
   male and female he created them.

["Us," by the way, is the Triune God: Father, Son, and Holy Spirit, Who were since the beginning of time, always.] So, if we are each made in God's likeness, guess what that means? He is both introverted and extroverted! Okay, that might be taking it a bit far to label God that way, but the overall point is: It levels the playing field. We all resemble our Maker.

My next point is that in 1 Peter, Peter (the disciple) exhorts us to use our different gifts to serve others, *as good stewards of God's varied grace*.

1 Peter 4:10-11, Apostle Peter speaking

As each has received a gift, use it to serve one another, as good stewards of God's varied grace: whoever speaks, as one who speaks oracles of God; whoever serves, as one who serves by the strength that God supplies--in order that in everything God may be glorified through Jesus Christ. To him belong glory and dominion forever and ever. Amen.

Now, I know the Bible isn't explicitly referring to the introvert/extrovert terms, but we can surely read it there. First of all, those "speaking" (and don't we know those gifted in that to the nth degree?) and those "serving" almost could be delineated as the extroverts who are socially using their gift, and the introverts, who often, not always, find themselves more behind the scenes meeting needs.[46] They are both valuable. We are called to use what we have. The Bible doesn't say one is better than the other. It simply says to use our gift to serve others as *good stewards of God's grace*. It also explicitly states that grace has various forms. Amen? But they each require stewardship: The speaker should be careful how he represents *oracles of God* if He has gifted him in this way, and the serving person should only do so with *the strength that God supplies*. What does that do? It keeps us humble and also honoring in using our gifts.

So, in parenting the other "vert," I have to draw from this very grounding wisdom in 1 Peter. I have to guard my attitude toward what I don't fully understand, and I need to have God's vision for the other reflection of His image. Hopefully in the next few pages, how we bless our children in their differences will come through.

What's Really Behind the Things That Drive Us Nuts?

Not giving a creative person the time, space, and materials to do his "art" is like slowly starving him from the inside out. I am trying to find that balance, and I am learning from my youngest guy. His hands are not the strongest, and his fine motor skills need to develop and be refined, but he sees himself as an artist as he shapes Amazon.com boxes with endless materials to create amazing treasures. I have to remember that although all of the assorted scraps I call "trash" (like Dum Dum wrappers) get under my skin after a while, when he stocks them up like a squirrel, he sees future masterpieces. What I like to think I see in words, he sees in everyday stuff around him. Okay, Little Man, if you need a card table in the family room with endless junk on it and a used mailing box, and that keeps you from begging for more screen time, then have at it, Child! Can't wait to see what you make. Maybe we should sell a few of those items at our lemonade stand this summer to afford storage.

That was a lovely story, wasn't it? I wish I could say my perspective looks that delightful and calm all of the time. It doesn't. I occasionally rage. But it is an area I am turning over to the Lord so He can help me find a way to bless instead of speak labels onto my children. I'm not a big fan of any label. The label "ADHD" may help a child get the help he needs on an IEP, and within the context of a school system, that may be entirely appropriate and helpful, but I do not want to look at any of my children as limited by their weaknesses. I don't want to say: "You forever will have attention issues." I want to say: "It will be awesome to see how

God uses all that phenomenal energy for creative works to bring Him honor someday and help people!" But this takes daily praying through what may perplex me or drive me nuts and asking God for words that cancel out the "You never wills," "You always," and "You have to stop XYZ-ings" that our kids hear every day. Some of it is necessary. A lot of it is not. Here's what it looks like when I ask my Father in heaven to give me words. I won't taint your minds with what it looks and sounds like when I don't. You're welcome.

I was challenged this past weekend to speak to my kids more about their God-given gifts and abilities, how the Lord is shaping their hearts, and whom I see them growing to be. It builds on some of what I have already been doing, but I love saying: "_____, you have been given a tremendous heart for others, tender toward people and all of God's creatures. You are sensitive to the hurts in others and respond with great compassion." Or "_____, you have been given a warrior spirit to stand up for injustice and speak His Truth when He calls you to it." Or "_____, you have a kind, gentle heart that speaks quiet strength, safety, and protection. You lead softly, with delightful humor and deep thought. You know His Word inside and out, and now may it go from your head to soak deeply into your heart."

And, really, what's actually behind the things that get under our skin is simply that: our own skin. We are just as annoying and frustrating at times. But we're adults and have more authority to misuse or mishandle. *Or to bless.*

James 3:9-12, James, brother of Jesus, speaking

With it [tongue] we bless our Lord and Father, and with it we curse people who are made in the likeness of God.

From the same mouth come blessing and cursing. My brothers, these things ought not to be so.

Does a spring pour forth from the same opening both fresh and salt water?

Can a fig tree, my brothers, bear olives, or a grapevine produce figs? Neither can a salt pond yield fresh water.

"I'm Just Going to Curl Up With You Until You're Ready!"

In a recent message with a friend trying to get her sweet, inward daughter to open up about a hurt, she told me she has her keep a communications journal, in which they privately exchange and write responses to each other. I thought that was brilliant. I have heard of ideas like that before, but knowing someone putting it into practice and having success with it made an impact on me. I need to remember that one for the nonverbal communicator in my house. Anyway, she was worried she was scrambling for the right approach. I thought she did great! God truly gives us the right words and ideas for our children and will give us more as we need them. I wouldn't want to parent without Him.

One of my favorite parts of her message to me—she was asking me for wisdom but ended up giving me some—was her statement to her child: "I'm going to curl up with you until you're ready!" when this young teen couldn't find words yet for her feelings. And she laid on the bed with her, quietly hanging out as tears started coming—and later words. It wasn't a quick fix. It required patience, a deep well of unconditional love, and incredible faithfulness. She wasn't going anywhere until her child felt safe.

What struck me was how much God is like that! He is very much like that. Sometimes I don't have any words, not even a groaning, only a "stuck," low-grade inner moan or long sigh that is rumbling to the surface but hasn't fully taken shape yet.

Psalm 23, King David speaking, KJV

The Lord is my shepherd; I shall not want.

He maketh me to lie down in green pastures: he leadeth me beside the still waters.

He restoreth my soul: he leadeth me in the paths of righteousness for his name's sake.

Yea, though I walk through the valley of the shadow of death, I will fear no evil: for thou art with me; thy rod and thy staff they comfort me.

Thou preparest a table before me in the presence of mine enemies: thou anointest my head with oil; my cup runneth over.

Surely goodness and mercy shall follow me all the days of my life: and I will dwell in the house of the Lord forever.

And He comes beside me, as in Psalm 23. Before *He leadeth me beside the still waters* and *restoreth my soul*, He quietly waits. He doesn't push me. He takes steps with me when I'm ready. He doesn't rush me because He is at peace. I'm the one stirring. He is at peace because He knows it will be okay and because He *is* peace. He can see what happens at the end of our trial. In some ways, we understand that our kids will get through tough times because we've weathered life, but unlike the Father, we don't walk in His peace about a hurting child until we take on the Father's mindset. Until we *take every thought captive* to have His mind, we stress and twitch and agonize as parents. But when we believe and trust that He will bring help as He always does, we can be the peaceful parent too. We might not yet see the outcome, but we know the Father in heaven Who does.

2 Corinthians 10:5, Apostle Paul speaking

We destroy arguments and every lofty opinion raised against the knowledge of God, and take every thought captive to obey Christ.

I realized, in this exchange with my friend, that I more often post on social media parenting stories that are successful in my house than the ones that aren't, although I try to be as transparent as possible so people know it doesn't always smell like roses either. I figure one thing out, often belatedly, and then that child either moves on to another issue, or another child has an issue. Because the children are all so different, not many of my specific parenting strategies remain the same. We have to fine-tune our approach for each one, and it feels like a full-time job emotionally. But God is faithful when we ask Him. He *loves* for us to consult Him and dialogue with Him, even in the most panicked of moments. Let's seek Him together. After all, He's been doing this parenting gig perfectly for the longest time.

He Loves Making Weakness Strong

I offered these thoughts to a friend this morning, based on awesome counsel I had received. I'm leaving it as is, in its original message form. I think it speaks for itself.

> Pray the peace of Christ over her as she leaves for school every morning. I bless each kid with their weakness, because every weakness, He can make strong! He loves making weakness strong. For my little guy with attentional and fine motor weakness, this is my prayer every morning as I place my hand on his head or hug him: "I pray the peace of Christ over ____. I bless him with strong hands, good self-control, great attention, safety, good health, and bless his loving heart, in the name of Jesus. I rebuke all flu germs in the name of Jesus." I'm that specific. I speak strength into weakness and acknowledge his God-given strengths in the name of Jesus. It not only reminds him as he starts his day who and Whose he is, but it sends him off in peace and knowing God goes with him. And when one day his hands are strong and he has amazing talent using them (who knows? piano player? artist? etc.), he will remember Who delivered him and made him strong. I do this tailored to each child every morning. Before you give me credit, about a year ago, a few mentors in my life suggested this. It has made *all* of the difference in the world. As different needs come up, we add/subtract them from the blessing.

So, okay, what does this mean, when all is said and done? Is it mind over matter? No. The reason it isn't is because folks who want to engage in "positive thinking" may change their attitude for a few hours here and there, but they aren't calling on the life-giving power of the Word of God or a relationship with Jesus. Why is speaking a blessing over my children effective? Well, first and foremost, it reminds them to Whom they belong, Who defines them, Who has set forth a plan for their lives. Many different things will try to define us over the years: family, school, education plans, peers, religion (I don't mean our relationship with Christ; I mean "the church of comparison" and other people making up definitions for us that are not in the Bible), romantic life, career, finances. But really, our weaknesses and strengths are not necessarily what those other people will say that they are. They are only what Christ says they are, and unlike other people, He has the power to make us strong in our weakness.

2 Corinthians 12:9-10, Apostle Paul speaking

But he said to me, "My grace is sufficient for you, for my power is made perfect in weakness." Therefore I will boast all the more gladly of my weaknesses, so that the power of Christ may rest upon me. For the sake of Christ, then, I am content with weaknesses, insults, hardships, persecutions, and calamities. For when I am weak, then I am strong.

So, when one of my children is told he has a developmental delay, weak upper body strength and fine motor difficulty, and attention deficit, I don't throw those diagnoses out the window. But I do consider them in light of what God says. If we buy into anything but God or His Word defining us, we get so led astray. We see limits where there is potential. We are a work in progress. How do I know my weak-handed child won't end up a surgeon some day? Why not? Who would get the glory from that witness? Who would get the credit? Educational specialists who declared his weakness in his early life? They may be used in his rising above it, certainly. But can they take that kind of pronouncement and turn those hands into steady, surgeon hands? No, but our God can. And He loves to use other people along the way whom He has gifted for that purpose.

Ready for the shocker? They don't have to be believers! That's right. He uses all of His creation to bless, whether they are participants willing to give Him glory or not. Maybe that isn't a shocking thought to some of you, but I think believers often put themselves on a high horse as being the only ones with gifts and talents that can be used for His glory. Nope. It's just that those who don't believe don't know or aren't willing to give Him credit yet.

I pray similarly over the child with social issues. I speak the possibilities into that child's life, of overcoming or weakness being used as a strength, but only in the mighty name of Jesus. I don't want that child to ever think that happened in the maturing process alone. It happened because we asked God to do it. We asked Him to help us see the possibilities of *a future and a hope* through part of His lens. We consulted with Him and asked Him to partner with us in every moment in life. God has plans way bigger than what we can imagine for our kids in our finite minds. The cool thing is that His plans often involve His glory shining out all over the place, such as when He took something like a speech impediment or weakness (like Moses[47]) and turned that person into a strong leader used for His purposes. He didn't change the disability; He made him powerful in spite of it. He provided because He always does.

Jeremiah 29:11-13, Jeremiah the Prophet narrating

"For I know the plans I have for you," declares the Lord, "plans for wholeness and not for evil, to give you a future and a hope. Then you will call upon me and come and pray to me, and I will hear you. You will seek me and find me, when you seek me with all your heart."

When the Past Comes Calling and Bangs on Our Door

Today one of my children spoke words that were a huge trigger for me. They didn't know it, even though they were indeed being negative, and their attitude behind it still needed to be addressed. But it's interesting, isn't it? The idea that we have to be on guard even as adults that we don't let our own gunk get in the way of responding to these moments with our children or children close to us. I was a bit ashamed of myself. I was not mean, but I heard more behind what was said than what was really there. They couldn't possibly know what was behind those words.

At times, I take the time to explain why I don't want them saying something like that again. This time I simply needed to apologize for the reaction. One of my life's goals (I'm sure it's everyone's) is to keep the next generation from having to take ownership of brokenness from former generations, including my own very broken self. They will have their own. They don't need mine or that of the generation before me, and so on. So, once in a while I have this conversation:

> I'm sorry for the reaction. You couldn't possibly know the pain behind your innocent comment, nor is it your fault, but I would ask that you don't make that comment again. It would be respectful of what you haven't had to walk through if you just wouldn't. Can you perhaps say what you wanted to say this way—xyz —and then I would both understand you and not misunderstand you at the same time.

I adore this whole Proverb (16), but here are the most relevant verses from it. It truly speaks for itself. May we be *discerning, sweet in our speech, persuasive,* full of *good sense, a fountain of life, judicious, gracious,* and *healing* in our responses to past triggers and in all ways when we speak to people, particularly our children.

Proverbs 16:21-24, King Solomon speaking

The wise of heart is called discerning,
    and sweetness of speech increases persuasiveness.
Good sense is a fountain of life to him who has it,
    but the instruction of fools is folly.
The heart of the wise makes his speech judicious
    and adds persuasiveness to his lips.
Gracious words are like a honeycomb,
    sweetness to the soul and health to the body.

I'm His Bon. Oh, Yes, I Am!

Do you have a nickname you are fond of? I have a few extending all the way back to childhood, but the one that seems universal as a derivative of my name is "Bon" or "Bon-Bon." Often, people have the courtesy to ask permission to call me that, but at other times, they slip into it as if we've known each other for years. Some people can get away with that, but with others, it doesn't feel quite right. Isn't that true of anything super-familiar and intimate to us? Sometimes it's that a person has earned the right to be that familiar with me, or calling me that fits our rapport. I don't know what it is, but nicknames have to be spoken to us by the right folks.

As I was typing a prayer out for a friend, a prayer I was e-speaking (another awesome made-up verb for ya) over her and sharing what God put on my heart, I signed it to God this way: "Love, Your Bon, Lord. Amen." I'm His Bon, and I love it! It so works with God. Do you look at yourself this way? You should. I may have been decided as "Bonnie Lyn Fitzgerald" at birth and later added "Smith" on my wedding day, but God knows me as "Bon." He knows the most intimate details of my life, more than anyone else, including my dear spouse. He can call me anything He wants to, but somehow "Bon" just fits—not because we are equals, but because I feel that rapport with Him that is easy and light. He sees us as Isaiah reports in Isaiah 43:1. I love being *called by name* by the Lord. I love being *His*.

> But now thus says the LORD,
> he who created you, O Jacob,
>   he who formed you, O Israel:

"Fear not, for I have redeemed you;
I have called you by name, you are mine."

Recently I opened an envelope with the words "Bonnie Lyn" on it. It took me back to all of the many love notes and cards my sweet grandmom would send me. She used to call me that, and she was a voice of unconditional, unwavering love, hope, and encouragement in my life. This envelope came from a current, dear mentor in my life at a time when I needed that hug from the Father calling me by my full name, like my grandmother did with such love and approval. Right before that envelope came, I had been feeling beaten down, but for whatever reason, scripted so beautifully on that envelope, those nine letters took me back to a place of warmth, where I was always accepted in her presence, to receive her all. No matter how old we get, at times we need that assurance. We can talk about blessing our kids until we are blue in the face, but we can't do a whole lot of blessing until we see ourselves as His kids, and if we believe in Him, that's exactly what we are.

Galatians 3:23-29, Apostle Paul speaking

Now before faith came, we were held captive under the law, imprisoned until the coming faith would be revealed. So then, the law was our guardian until Christ came, in order that we might be justified by faith. But now that faith has come, we are no longer under a guardian, for in Christ Jesus you are all sons of God, through faith. For as many of you as were baptized into Christ have put on Christ. There is neither Jew nor Greek, there is neither slave nor free, there is no male and female, for you are all one in Christ Jesus. And if you are Christ's, then you are Abraham's offspring, heirs according to promise.

Dolly in a Stinky Sack of Potatoes

A while back, I found myself in quite the predicament. I was in a massive cleaning frenzy Labor Day weekend, partly out of the jubilation of kids going back to school and fewer hours of my day straightening up rooms, and partly motivated by the plan of getting a puppy (or two) in the upcoming months. All of a sudden, I was ready to sell half of the contents of our house, although I admit I was a bit focused on Happy Meal Toys, G.I. Joes, and abandoned Rescue Heroes. I was pretty much obsessed. In my cleaning madness, if a particular toy didn't have a category (Trio, LEGO®, Superhero, Lincoln Log), it was getting the boot.

So, it stands to reason that there it was: on my beaten-down-and-managed-to-many-times-get-back-up-again futon couch, a tiny 5-inch doll named Dave. (So many items in our house are named Dave. My youngest has fantastic self-esteem.) Its hair was incredibly matted, the paint on its face was almost wiped away, but it had made it through two across-the-world moves and 10 years of play. It probably deserves some kind of award for that, seriously. Because it's the tiniest of the dolls, it apparently had a special place in my kids' hearts as Dave. They each have a doll representing them, and this one represents my youngest. Well, it's in the kind of shape one wouldn't even donate it, not even as a play toy to a dog. And so, in the middle of my cleaning mania, I *could have* stopped to make an intelligent decision, but I didn't. I saw something ugly and ridiculously shabby and tossed it. Hey, they weren't in the room to fight me on it. It's been ages since they all played with their mini representations of themselves. And that thing was almost scary-ugly. If it could talk, it would surely scream "Boo!"

But there comes a moment when you know you crossed over into a decision you can't turn back. Something starts to creep in and not feel right. You can't quite let it go. It more or less haunts you. While it's not all that untypical of my seven year old to have his "She Threw Out Some of My Stuff" radar go off within minutes of my offense, this time he was spot on and immediate, except it started off so sweetly like this:

"Hey, do you know where Dave is? I just saw him on the couch a minute ago."
I played dumb: "Dave? Who's Dave?"
That didn't go well, at all, because the conversation instantly turned to panic:
"Oh no! You didn't throw him out, did you, because he's me, and..."

What followed was a long list of why this inexpensive, disgusting, plastic-and-cloth toy was precious and important. Gulp. (At this moment, I seriously started to wonder if the real Dave could see through walls. It's almost scary how he always reads me with impeccable accuracy.) Then, sniffing out discord to see if she could help or simply be in the know, in came Middle Child trying to find out what was going on. I had to repeat my performance, and it wasn't at all pretty. So, I did what any other guilty mother would do and practiced some awesome conflict-avoidance: "Oh, Honey, I'm sure he'll turn up. I'll look for him as I clean. You know how things like that always show up somehow, under something. We need to be patient."

I'm pretty sure those last few statements rank right up there as Mother Lies. Yup. Pretty sure. But as soon as the kids left the room, I started retracing which trash cans the doll and its clothes ended up in so that once the school buses rolled away in the morning, I could search in peace and not face Child Wrath and Condemnation. As I reminded myself in bed that night of the task at hand before Trash Day, I realized in complete horror that the doll went out with a stinky, rotting, leaky bag of potatoes, and the doll's clothing ended up in Coffee Ground Hill. So fun. Tomorrow would be so much fun.

As I watched the last bus roll down the street the next morning and found my tongs and extra trash bag, setting out at the task at hand into the busted-open old heap of trash, I looked down, holding my breath, and saw one, lonely, desperate, plastic arm reaching out from under some potato rot nastiness. And it took my breath away. Literally. But it spiritually took my breath away as well. That was me. I was Dolly in a Stinky Sack of Potatoes. At times in my life, I had reached up, rotted by my own sin and the corruptions of this world, waiting for His mighty hand to pull me out. I had been marinating in my own stench of all of the things I did to put Him on that cross.

Whenever I have been pulled out of that mire, like the doll, I was too dumbfounded and numb to be immediately grateful. I had to let the fresh air of His Light and love wash over me. I had to learn what grace looks, smells, tastes like. I had to remember my baptism, washed clean in His glory, and reflect on the Lord's Table. Dave the Dolly went right into the washing machine, hoping to get rid of the stains and smells that attached themselves to him from his time in the garbage of this world, just like the prodigal son had to shake off the smells of the pigpen in Luke 15.[48] Dave the Dolly and his clothes were washed fresh, baptized in a new beginning, loved enough to dig through the stinky garbage for, and welcomed back with great love. He was clothed in clean garments, just as the prodigal son was given a new robe.

The interesting thing about Dave the Dolly is that after his trip diving into rotting potatoes, and subsequent baptism, I could still see his stain. I could still, if I took a deep whiff, detect a faded but evident rotten potato smell. When we know of each other's sins, we often look for the evidence, and sometimes we remind each other of our previous stench. On the other hand, those who don't know which sins we've dabbled in (and then been set free of) don't look for those blemishes in us. When my kids came home that day, they simply saw a prodigal Dave the Dolly returned on the futon. They didn't even ask where he'd been, and they certainly didn't lift him up to smell for potatoes. They just welcomed him back, excited that he hadn't been tossed out and forgotten (well, not for long anyway).

What is perhaps more amazing is that the returned, new Dave still had matted hair and faded paint, but my kids saw him as beautiful. They didn't see what a trip through 10 years of life or a trash can for 18 hours did to him. They saw him in a glorious state because they saw him through love. They saw him as God the Father sees us. He sees us with new bodies, cleansed and set free.[49] Some of the promises in the Bible that remind me of who I am in Christ and how the Father sees me come from the Apostles Paul (2 Corinthians and Colossians) and Peter (1 Peter). They reassure me that I don't smell like rotten potatoes to God. His Son's work on the cross washed me clean, which became a reality the minute He did it but then became a transforming work in me as soon as I accepted it in belief and confessed my sins and need for Him. I love how Paul reinforces what

Christ did for us in letters to both the Corinthians and the Colossians, that as a result, we *might become the righteousness of God* and that *in Christ* we have been *given fullness (filled in Him)*. Without the work of the Son on the cross, it's clear we'd be potato-stained Dave the Dollies without any hope.[50]

2 Corinthians 5:17-21, Apostle Paul speaking

Therefore, if anyone is in Christ, he is a *new creation*. The old has passed away; behold, the new has come. All this is from God, who through Christ reconciled us to himself and gave us the ministry of reconciliation; that is, in Christ God was reconciling the world to himself, *not counting their trespasses against them*, and entrusting to us the message of reconciliation. Therefore, we are ambassadors for Christ, God making his appeal through us. We implore you on behalf of Christ, be reconciled to God. *For our sake he made him to be sin who knew no sin, so that in him we might become the righteousness of God* [emphasis mine].

Colossians 2:9-15, Apostle Paul speaking

For in him the whole fullness of deity dwells bodily, and *you have been filled in him*, who is the head of all rule and authority. *In him also you were circumcised with a circumcision made without hands, by putting off the body of the flesh, by the circumcision of Christ, having been buried with him in baptism, in which you were also raised with him through faith in the powerful working of God*, who raised him from the dead. And you, who were dead in your trespasses and the uncircumcision of your flesh, *God made alive together with him, having forgiven us all our trespasses*, by *canceling the record of debt that stood against us* with its legal demands. *This he set aside, nailing it to the cross*. He disarmed the rulers and authorities and put them to open shame, by triumphing over them in him [emphasis mine].

Peter makes it very clear Who called us out of darkness, implying we did not manage our own way out. We take steps to believe in and accept the hand of forgiveness offered us through Christ by God the Father, but it is the Father reaching into the trash to offer us a way out.

1 Peter 2:9, Apostle Peter speaking

But you are a chosen race, a royal priesthood, a holy nation, a people for his own possession, that you may proclaim the excellencies of him *who called you out of darkness into his marvelous light* [emphasis mine].

And finally, King David. I love pulling this treasure out of the Old Testament because it predates Christ walking this earth as a man, dying for us, and rising again. It lets us know God provides a way out and that Jesus has been there all along. Same God today, yesterday, forever.[51] It reminds us that even if we think we can still see the potato stains on ourselves, that is really a distraction and lie from the enemy of our soul because God no longer sees our confessed sin. He has tossed it far away.

Psalm 103:11-12, King David speaking

For as high as the heavens are above the earth,
　so great is his steadfast love toward those who fear him;

as far as the east is from the west,
　so far does he remove our transgressions from us [emphasis mine].

The challenge is to not be drawn to the trash anymore. To live like we believe this. To know that we are forgiven and justified through Christ and to not let the liar tell us, like the prodigal son during his wayward days, that the pig sty is the better place to eat. I know I'll think about this every time I see Dave the Dolly; I'll be thankful that my kids saw more in him than I did, that my Savior sees me cleaner than I am, because of the cross, and that, like me, Dave the Dolly was worth going after, like the one lost sheep the Good Shepherd went to save.[52]

Thank You, Precious Father. May my children continue to see through Your eyes of grace and unfailing, sacrificial love into their adulthood. Amen.

Life Just Bit a Big Chunk Out of Our Candle: How Do We Keep on Shining?

I have a little journal a dear friend gave to me for my 40th birthday. I carry it around as if it is golden, not only because of my own ideas I jot down in there as they come, but also because my sweet friend wrote an inscription in there that I treasure. As things pop into my mind at the most inopportune times (making dinner, homework fight with a child, phone ringing, coffee intake making its way south), I try to jot down a few words to trigger that thought later on. But as I was looking for the candles to make "13" for my oldest son's party, this one inspired thought grabbed me and would not let me go. It begged to be immediately dumped into these pages. If it still makes it to publication, then I guess it was worth the mad scramble to get it typed after all.

As it turns out, a 13-year-old boy does not always want big chunky number candles on his cake anymore. (Apparently he also does not want everyone to sing to him at his party either.) I am glad I asked, because I never was a 13-year-old boy, and he is, after all, our practice child. I'd probably still hire the clown and get big Mylar balloons if he didn't stop me. I'm simply not caught up to him yet. I see a three-year-old face every time I try to reconcile the teenage one in front of me, at eye level. Major case of denial. Especially when Christian hip-hop songs pump out of the ear buds, and I can only hear Veggie Tales tunes in my mind.

So, when I saw that "3" candle in the "bag of many candle numbers" in the kitchen cabinet, I burst out laughing. You see, the very same son, at three years of age, thought the candle was extra icing, so at his Chuck E. Cheese party, he took a nice big chunk of it between his teeth right in front of all of the guests. He was embarrassed at the time; actually, he still is, but in our crazy-humor way, we have continued to put that bitten "3" on cakes two more times over the years as the younger siblings took their turns at that birthday.

What did that chunk-depleted number "3" candle speak to me from its place in the cabinet? The very sight of it reminded me how very broken we all are, in one way or another. We cover it up as best we can (unless you are a writer and wear everything right on your sleeve without a filter), but when others see us, they still often see the chunk removed. Or alternatively, on occasion, we still declare it as loudly as we possibly can: "See this scar? I'm still wounded! I'm still needy! I'm still hurt! I'm still angry! I'm still a victim." Now, please hear me. I'm not at all aiming this at genuine victims of heinous acts. That pain is valid. I'm more or less directing it toward our "mentality" when we announce our woes to the world, when we are too busy megaphoning our issues to hear God speak at all. It's okay to let people know we are healing, we're in-process, or even that we need help. What I'm talking about is that we have the tendency to point out our missing chunk. Sometimes we want attention, but often, we don't know how to stop looking at ourselves that way. We see it every time we look in the mirror.

As I age and grow in my relationship with Christ, my question is ultimately the same question in everything: Does Christ see me this way? I want to suggest a resounding "No!" He sees us white as snow, purified by what He did for us on the cross, assuming we have professed our need for

Him as our Savior, believe the necessity of His death upon the cross, and declare the truth of His resurrection.

Isaiah 1:18, Isaiah the Prophet narrating

"Come now, let us reason together, says the Lord:
though your sins are like scarlet,
    they shall be as white as snow;
though they are red like crimson,
    they shall become like wool."

Galatians 2:20, Apostle Paul speaking

I have been crucified with Christ. It is no longer I who live, but Christ who lives in me. And the life I now live in the flesh I live by faith in the Son of God, who loved me and gave himself for me.

1 Corinthians 6:11, Apostle Paul speaking

And such were some of you. But you were washed, you were sanctified, you were justified in the name of the Lord Jesus Christ and by the Spirit of our God.

Does He know our hurts, transgressions, brokenness, failures? Yes, He is all-knowing. But does He focus on the missing chunk? No. He sees the candle intact; God sees us as His restored, full candle. So, how can we still give off God's Light even when something has taken a chunk out of us? We may not always feel it, but we are called to believe it if we consider ourselves His children. That part is faith. I'm choosing to see myself as whole under the shed blood of Christ my Savior. I'm not sure we have a choice, do we? If we keep looking at our own missing chunk and declaring it's there, aren't we more or less saying part of the Bible isn't true? That we aren't completely whole in Him? When others want to laugh and point out the missing part of the "3" (and we all know they line up to do this at times), are we to focus on that? In my own life, figuratively speaking of course, I want to live more along these lines:

Yes, thank you. I see you noticed my missing chunk. Yes, that is part of my story, but that's not all of it. Would you like to hear how my candle got restored again? How the wax melted back into perfect shape? It may not be what you see yet, as God is working on me still, but He sees me without the chunk. Isn't that beyond cool? Would you like your chunks restored too?

2 Corinthians 5:17, Apostle Paul speaking

Therefore, if anyone is in Christ, he is a new creation. The old has passed away; behold, the new has come.

If we truly knew who we were in Christ deep down in our hearts, I think we could really cast His Light on and expose the darkness collectively, all of us broken 3 candles lined up together! What does Christ say about us in Matthew 5:14-16?

Matthew 5:14-16, Jesus speaking

"You are the light of the world. A city set on a hill cannot be hidden. Nor do people light a lamp and put it under a basket, but on a stand, and it gives light to all in the house. In the same way, let your light shine before others, so that they may see your good works and give glory to your Father who is in heaven."

He says to put that light out there. But do you know what that assumes?

A) That we're a light in the first place.
B) That we shine.
C) That we are designed to praise our Father in heaven.

If you're at all like me (don't run screaming with this one similarity), you are pretty blown away by that. You are pondering how on earth you could be His Light with your messy divorce, your smart-mouthed kid, your relationship dramas, your out-of-whack financial priorities, that pesky bad habit or addiction, you name it. And should we confess, turn each of those concerns over to Him, and allow Him to do His redeeming work in them? Yes. The Bible tells us to. But when we are in Christ, we have a chance to grab that truth and never look back. How about that one? We can sign up to be His candle and never have to live under the condemnation of the missing chunk?

> Romans 8:1-4, Apostle Paul speaking
>
> There is therefore now no condemnation for those who are in Christ Jesus. For the law of the Spirit of life has set you free in Christ Jesus from the law of sin and death. For God has done what the law, weakened by the flesh, could not do. By sending his own Son in the likeness of sinful flesh and for sin, he condemned sin in the flesh, in order that the righteous requirement of the law might be fulfilled in us, who walk not according to the flesh but according to the Spirit.

I don't know about you, but I'm signing right up for that one! All I have to do is believe and be His candle, His beautiful witness, and He'll take care of the rest? Slap me right on that birthday cake or candlestick or inside that lamp and put me out in front of the masses. We don't ever have to be embarrassed or afraid!

When We Need a Little Help With Our Faith

One of my children surprised me one night with an interesting prayer request: "Mom, will you pray that I believe more in Jesus?" I'm the kind of parent who doesn't get derailed by these questions. I used to, with Child Number One. But I no longer do. This was a fair request, and I genuinely believe my children's faith needs to be their own. I can share the amazing joy and truth that I have found in Christ, but I can't superimpose it onto them. I'm not afraid of questions, doubts, or unbelief. We all struggle with this from time to time, and really our unbelief is the starting zone in our journey toward faith. There are breakdowns along the way where we need someone to change our tires, put gas back in our car, and encourage us. But let's be honest: We're sometimes delayed on the speedway, stuck with our tires all bald.

So, in that moment, I took this child, who is prone to deep reflection, sensitivity, and anxiety in certain places, and I said, "Don't be afraid of your doubts. That's so good you asked me to pray for them. Why do you feel this way?"

The reply squeaked out like this: "Because I like to think about toys and video games a lot and don't always think about Jesus."

Oh, my goodness! Precious! Am I writing about this because my kid is so great? No. I'm writing about this because one of the things I cherish most in raising my kids is coming through: honesty. I am delighted he trusted me with this. Making it up as I went along, I managed to respond: "Oh, Honey, I get distracted too. Thinking about them doesn't mean you don't love Jesus. As you learn to love Him more and more, these things will matter less, but He's not mad at you for liking toys and video games. And you know what else? He gave you an awesome story to remember. He healed you of major food allergies. No doctor could do that, right? But Jesus took them away in one moment of prayer. That may not be someone else's story. They may have a different one. But for you, that is the story He gave you to refer to whenever you wonder if He's *really* there. That is part of the story He is writing for you, and it is beautiful."

I wish I could say that settled the deal and that my child placed his full trust in that declaration, but it actually went more like this: "Okay, Mom, yes, only Jesus could do that, but would you still pray for me anyway?"

My child knew something so fundamental, so simple: Prayer was the place to start. He needed Christ to help him in his unbelief. I have no control over this. Even talking my child through it wouldn't do what only God can do. I know my child knows Jesus. I rest in that. But if there are times he is having a hard time with the fact He is not flesh and blood in front of us, I get that too. I want to be more like my child and like this father who wanted his son free of a demon and cried out to the Savior, "I believe; help my unbelief!" in Mark 9:24.

Mark 9:14-29, Apostle John-Mark narrating

And when they came to the disciples, they saw a great crowd around them, and scribes arguing with them. And immediately all the crowd, when they saw him, were greatly amazed and ran up to him and greeted him. And he asked them, "What are you arguing about with them?" And someone from the crowd answered him, "Teacher, I brought my son to you, for he has a spirit that makes him mute. And whenever it seizes him, it throws him down, and he foams and grinds his teeth and becomes rigid. So I asked your disciples to cast it out, and they were not able." And he answered them, "O faithless generation, how long am I to be with you? How long am I to bear with you? Bring him to me." And they brought the boy to him. And when the spirit saw him, immediately it convulsed the boy, and he fell on the ground and rolled about, foaming at the mouth. And Jesus asked his father, "How long has this been happening to him?" And he said, "From childhood. And it has often cast him into fire and into water, to destroy him. But if you can do anything, have compassion on us and help us." And Jesus said to him, "'If you can'! All things are possible for one who believes." Immediately the father of the child cried out and said, "I believe; help my unbelief!" And when Jesus saw that a crowd came running together, he rebuked the unclean spirit, saying to it, "You mute and deaf spirit, I command you, come out of him and never enter him again." And after crying out and convulsing him terribly, it came out, and the boy was like a corpse, so that most of them said, "He is dead." But Jesus took him by the hand and lifted him up, and he arose. And when he had entered the house, his disciples asked him privately, "Why could we not cast it out?" And he said to them, "This kind cannot be driven out by anything but prayer."

I want to be honest, like David was in the Psalms, crying out to God with everything I am thinking and feeling. I want to admit when I don't have the answers. Part of the reason I find this approach refreshing is not at all for the purposes of displaying false humility. Nobody wants to be around us when we browbeat ourselves. The reasons why I want to live this way are:

1. Because it's honest

2. Because the answer to our unbelief is always Jesus, and like the father of this possessed child in Mark 9, I want to beseech my Savior directly for help

3. Because we all walk around feeling very alone and unapproachable until we admit where we are with our faith

It doesn't matter if you have believed since a confession in your childhood church at eight years old or you just trusted in Christ as your Savior, we all have times when we long for the flesh-and-blood evidence. We need to see others live out their faith, yes, but also their seasons of doubt, until *we know that we know that we know* what is spoken in 2 Corinthians 4:18 (the Apostle Paul speaking):

As we look not to the things that are seen but to the things that are unseen. For the things that are seen are transient, but the things that are unseen are eternal.

Consider also:

> Hebrews 11:1-2, author unknown, but he is recording the words of God
>
> Now faith is the assurance of things hoped for, the conviction of things not seen. For by it the people of old received their commendation.

I expect to have to pray this way, like my child, several more times in my life, and I would happily pray this for anyone who asks me. Let's get real when we need a little help with our faith. No growth happens when we stay stuck and don't call out for help.

A Tribute to Little Man on the Eve of Kindergarten

I promised to include an example of a tribute or blessing spoken over my child. This is simply an exercise in seeing our children with the gifts and beautiful personalities God gave them. I fully realize that some of our kids may be in unpleasant phases of development where we are not currently seeing the "beautiful personality" shining through. That's partly why I write these. I want to remember what I started to see early on because I have a sneaking suspicion some of those attributes will re-emerge after some of the more challenging tween/teen/young adult years.

I chose to include the tribute I wrote to this particular child not out of favoritism but more because my other two are older, and considering this one's personality, I can't picture much of this embarrassing him as he grows older. The other two are at sensitive ages where my tributes are best kept in the house. As I read it, I feel sad, because as he has aged, he has become more serious, more concerned, but I still go back to this happy-go-lucky child I was given and pray and bless based on that, not on what I see now. I know God will do amazing things with this life—with every life—turned over to Him. So, I offer this as my example, and it's now several years out of date age-wise, but may it inspire us all to put to paper, or at least to speak, how big our hearts are for children. Even if you don't have your own, surely we each know a special child in need of our blessing and the Lord's great love.

*****

I just read our traditional *The Night Before Kindergarten* and tucked my fuzzy redhead into bed.[53] Am glad the bassinet is long sold, or I might spend some time tonight staring into it wondering where my solid little infant went. I might wonder what happened to the milky-white-skinned child with the halo of hair who played Baby Jesus his first year on Kwaj, all wrapped in swaddling clothes, carried down the church aisle.

I reflect when remembering that tears fell for my oldest getting on a bus six years ago, for he needed a hand to hold, a reassurance, a cave. But on the eve of Little Man's elementary school beginnings, no tears are there. I've asked myself why all day.

Three short years ago, proud smiles went up for my daughter as she fiercely pedaled off (with me secretly following her) to kindergarten on the island, determined to do this whole thing on her own. But today, that isn't what I see either this time around.

This time, I feel as though Little Man doesn't even need my hand, my reassurance, my following after him. He'll probably make sure the entire bus population recites allergy policies before letting anyone off. He's *that* kid. And there is something so great about the way his confidence eases my mind. He doesn't take the time to overthink like a different child and I do. He doesn't let anxiety build or the challenges of life chew him up. He also doesn't ask a lot of questions; it is what it is, and he'll meet it as it comes, also unlike the hyper-planning of many of the rest of us in our family.

He'll embrace each new experience with vigor and will bounce when he shares a special moment in his day. His exuberance will reach the skies, and if the teacher somehow convinces him he might want to apply himself to academics in between large, endlessly verbal displays of imagination, he'll try it—on his own terms.

He will make friends quickly, and he will feel what they feel because somewhere in the vast gene pool, God answered my prayers and gave him empathy, a quality I long for my children to have. He doesn't have to work at it; he just has it. He might tease and wink now and again, and someone will have to encourage him to settle down, but he won't deliberately be hurtful. He simply gets carried away.

And yes, he will share stories from our family (like farting contests between him and his siblings) at inappropriate times because he sincerely believes everyone stands to benefit from that inside knowledge about the Smith family. He may once in a while sing a song while he thinks, and the lyrics will be adjusted somehow to sneak in the occasional potty word and a loud, proud guffaw to accompany it.

What I will miss during those hours is not the constant conversation (Oh, teacher, you will *not* be lonely, Honey!), but the way he delights in each little thing and the way his soft, candlelit curls bounce when he's happy about something and wants to tell me.

You'll do great, Pirate! You always do.
You have stared food allergies and asthma in the face and have growled right back.

You have conquered toddlerhood in a foreign country, learning to chase small white fish in the lagoon and to love without racial or cultural boundaries.

You came back and grieved the only home you ever knew.

You have developed your own advocacy for health issues in preschool.

And, now, my smallest son, you put those two long Fitzgerald feet on a big yellow bus tomorrow.

Have a super ride, Little Red!

I love you right up to the moon and back!

*****

Psalm 127:3-5, King Solomon speaking

Behold, children are a heritage from the LORD,
    the fruit of the womb a reward.
Like arrows in the hand of a warrior
    are the children of one's youth.
Blessed is the man
    who fills his quiver with them!
He shall not be put to shame
    when he speaks with his enemies in the gate.

Perhaps King Solomon writes a better tribute in Proverbs 3 to his son. I want this for my children, very much. It shouldn't surprise me that the Bible includes this amazing wisdom to speak to the gifts God gives us to carry on Who He is to the generations.

Proverbs 3:1-35

My son, do not forget my teaching,
    but let your heart keep my commandments,
for length of days and years of life
    and peace they will add to you.

Let not steadfast love and faithfulness forsake you;
    bind them around your neck;
    write them on the tablet of your heart.

So you will find favor and good success
    in the sight of God and man.

Trust in the LORD with all your heart,
    and do not lean on your own understanding.
In all your ways acknowledge him,
    and he will make straight your paths.
Be not wise in your own eyes;
    fear the LORD, and turn away from evil.
It will be healing to your flesh
    and refreshment to your bones.

Honor the LORD with your wealth
    and with the firstfruits of all your produce;
then your barns will be filled with plenty,
    and your vats will be bursting with wine.

My son, do not despise the LORD's discipline
    or be weary of his reproof,
for the LORD reproves him whom he loves,
    as a father the son in whom he delights.

Blessed is the one who finds wisdom,
    and the one who gets understanding,
for the gain from her is better than gain from silver
    and her profit better than gold.
She is more precious than jewels,
    and nothing you desire can compare with her.
Long life is in her right hand;
    in her left hand are riches and honor.
Her ways are ways of pleasantness,
    and all her paths are peace.
She is a tree of life to those who lay hold of her;
    those who hold her fast are called blessed.

The LORD by wisdom founded the earth;
    by understanding he established the heavens;
by his knowledge the deeps broke open,
    and the clouds drop down the dew.

My son, do not lose sight of these—
    keep sound wisdom and discretion,
and they will be life for your soul
    and adornment for your neck.
Then you will walk on your way securely,
    and your foot will not stumble.
If you lie down, you will not be afraid;
    when you lie down, your sleep will be sweet.
Do not be afraid of sudden terror
    or of the ruin of the wicked, when it comes,

for the LORD will be your confidence
  and will keep your foot from being caught.
Do not withhold good from those to whom it is due,
  when it is in your power to do it.

Do not say to your neighbor, "Go, and come again,
  tomorrow I will give it"—when you have it with you.
Do not plan evil against your neighbor,
  who dwells trustingly beside you.
Do not contend with a man for no reason,
  when he has done you no harm.
Do not envy a man of violence
  and do not choose any of his ways,
for the devious person is an abomination to the LORD,
  but the upright are in his confidence.
The LORD's curse is on the house of the wicked,
  but he blesses the dwelling of the righteous.
Toward the scorners he is scornful,
  but to the humble he gives favor.
The wise will inherit honor,
  but fools get disgrace.

Part 5
Because I'm Pretty Sure Heaven Has a Jura-Capresso Machine

I sincerely doubt I could write a book that didn't involve coffee references. I've been a coffee freak through and through since my grandmother used to slip it in my bottle with a lot of milk and sugar when I was two years old. I was pretty much homegrown on coffee. I love it in all forms. Knowing there was no Starbucks on the island, my sister made sure she sent me with a hand-tamping espresso machine. That machine and I were good friends; I'd call it "DeLonghi," and it would whir "Bonnie" at me as it went. I had friends who would stop by just for some hand-tamped espresso yumminess on their way back to work (on a bike). I even turned Salad Boy into a coffee snob. Boyfriend takes whole coffee beans in, grinds them in his burr grinder, and french-presses them into perfection almost every day at work.

I love in coffee. Ask my Moms' Prayer friends who have faithfully joined me around my dining room table for going on four years every other Friday morning during the school year. Or other friends who come by to chat. I may not have hot soup waiting for you in the crockpot, but the espresso machine will always be turned on at the sound of the doorbell and a coffee-loving friend walking in the door. My children frequently ask me if they or a latte mug were dangling off a cliff at the same time, which would I save? My answer: "Is the latte mug full or empty?"

When I write, a coffee shop is almost always involved, or at least my own fresh-brewed espresso. As I sat in a café in Rockport, Massachusetts, and prayed, the Lord gave me a poem. As soon as I finished it and completed my prayers, a friend messaged me that a different friend's diagnosis was better than we expected. I love when the Holy Spirit pushes into us with a strong prayer burden. I adore this about Him. This may look different for everyone. For me, at times, I've almost had to pull off on the side of the road, I am so overcome with groans from the Spirit. At other times, I shower-pray, and He brings to mind folks who need prayer in my few moments alone under the steady stream. Figuratively speaking, it helps me to picture the never-ending fountain of relationship with Our Amazing Father Who Art in Heaven.

But coffee is a way of welcome, a door through which some relationships form. I had to include a section on it because I've enjoyed participating in the unique culture that is coffee and the lessons that can be learned from its warm, inviting hospitality. So, put your feet up and pretend you are in the café with me or at home with a warm beverage in hand. I love finding the Lord in the everyday, the ordinary. And I thank Him pretty much every day for making the most magnificent coffee bean.

Romans 12:9-13, Apostle Paul speaking

Let love be genuine. Abhor what is evil; hold fast to what is good. Love one another with brotherly affection. Outdo one another in showing honor. Do not be slothful in zeal, be fervent in spirit, serve the Lord. Rejoice in hope, be patient in tribulation, be constant in prayer. Contribute to the needs of the saints and seek to show hospitality.

Rockport

Foggy day
Feel of clouds weighing down, heaven's weeping heavy in the air—
Either for joy or sadness I do not know.
Briny breeze floats past, gently stroking.
Just the beginning of tourist season
As many dogs as people walk the way.
A man speaking a Slavic tongue on his phone next to me
And a house that sells dark under the guise of wisdom.
I walk past it and pray because I feel the dark try to press in.
I know the feel of dark, the lying whispers it offers.
But I know where real power is, and I'm not afraid.
I pray against it.
I shove light into it.
I quietly tell it it is counterfeit.
And that is that.

And I land on my perch by a faux marble table looking out at the still
marina.
I say: "God, what will you speak to me today in this place? What would
you have me do?"
And I am still.
Because it's then I can hear Him,
And He tells me to pray for several people
Because the praying is more important than the writing in this moment.
He gives me their names.
There is compassion in the dropping from His heart to mine,
Like a deposit of something greater than my own humanness.
And in praying I feel His powerful love for these people.
My heart is fully squeezed tight until I do it
Because He won't let me go.
There are amazing delights and gripping agonies
At the same time
In several lives.
And yet He grabs us as His partner and takes us for a walk,

Arm around us like a close friend,
Sharing this journey,
Offering purpose.
I'm steady now.
I've pushed much into His listening ears.
I think it's an incredible wonder that He tells us whom to talk to Him about,
That He gives them to us to give back to Him.

And the chairs fill in the café,
My kona mocha sitting still,
Temporarily abandoned.
And I'm not sure this is a typical writing day
Because my heart feels stretched beyond what human muscle can contain.
I'm trying to breathe at normal cadence again,
This coffee bar a sanctuary of sorts,
A place of Holy Ground,
A temple of silent prayer,
While all around me the baristas keep grinding the beans,
Whirring the foam,
Tamping the espresso.
There is no visible cross here,
No prayer bench,
No worship-ushering choir.
Just members of His creation,
Both aware and unaware,
Sitting in space that He made.

And I can't go beyond this moment, somehow.
I think I am supposed to drink it in and keep waiting.
And He is across the table from me
Loving me as my head tries to configure.
And I know
deep,
profound
rest.

Bonnie Lyn Smith

A Little Story: Caramel Mochas of Grace

Me: "I think maybe there was a misunderstanding. Is it okay if I have a caramel mocha? That is what I tried to order."

(Me putting on as gracious and humble of a tone as I could muster. But at $4 a pop, I would hope I could have what I had ordered. I'm not at my beloved Starbucks, by the way.)

Them: "I don't understand; you don't want a mocha?" [snotty tone].

Me: "No, I do, but when I ordered it, I asked for caramel and chocolate in it: a caramel mocha. Would that be possible?"

More arguing and attitude.

Me: "I'm sorry this is confusing [thinking to myself: why? this is pretty standard]. This actually used to be on your menu, but that's okay. Just caramel and chocolate syrup, please, if that's okay."

More attitude, but then she made it.

*****

This story isn't about this chick with a rough day, or even, maybe, a rough season of life. It's about the fact that despite our sweetest, most genuine tone and best intentions, sometimes we are just plain misunderstood. Because we're poor communicators? At times, but not necessarily. Because the other person got off the wrong side of the bed that day and takes everything personally? Maybe. Maybe not. There are moments when signals don't get through for whatever reason. Had she not been able to put the caramel and mocha together as a possibility in her head, I would have been polite and accepted that and walked back to my table. She is in the service industry and likely gets a lot of attitude from entitled folks. She really doesn't need mine, and I certainly don't need to have one.

Proverbs 10:11-14, King Solomon speaking

The mouth of the righteous is a fountain of life,
    but the mouth of the wicked conceals violence.
Hatred stirs up strife,
    but love covers all offenses.
On the lips of him who has understanding, wisdom is found,
    but a rod is for the back of him who lacks sense.
The wise lay up knowledge,
    but the mouth of a fool brings ruin near.

I'm more or less finding this line intriguing: *But a rod is for the back of him who lacks sense.* Wow, God doesn't mess around. Solomon has some pretty vivid images going on there. All I know is that I can rage at the people who misunderstand me, or I can see myself as someone capable of similar feelings of running empty. I want my mouth to be a *fountain of life*, my love to *cover all offenses*, and my lips to have *understanding*; I don't want to *bring ruin near*. I want the grumpy clerk at checkout in the convenience store to see someone greater than me: the Holy Spirit. To hear the voice of a gentle, loving Father Who comes in and loves us right where we are.

James 1:19-21, James, brother of Jesus, speaking

Know this, my beloved brothers: let every person be quick to hear, slow to speak, slow to anger; for the anger of man does not produce the righteousness of God. Therefore put away all filthiness and rampant wickedness and receive with meekness the implanted word, which is able to save your souls.

I find it really interesting that James distinguishes "the anger of man" here. The KJV states it as "the wrath of man." Don't we all need to be reminded that he is talking about man's anger and not God's? Ours is often not holy or even warranted. Why are we to be *slow to speak* and *slow to anger*? Because the other person is right? Because we are to be the proverbial doormats that other people can step on with their pain and hostility? No, because *the anger of man does not produce the righteousness of God.* And he doesn't just leave it there, which is nice, since I am always requiring more instruction. He says we can do this by *receiving with meekness the implanted word, which is able to save our souls.* I don't know about you, but unless I have the power of God's Holy Word in my heart, I have a whole slew of other words I'd be more inclined to use when dealing with difficult people. But James doesn't leave us stranded with a command and no resource. He tells us exactly where to go to scoop up those mounds of patience, self-control, and wisdom: God's Word.

Peter takes it a bit further.

1 Peter 4:8-11, Apostle Peter speaking

Above all, keep loving one another earnestly, since love covers a multitude of sins. Show hospitality to one another without grumbling. As each has received a gift, use it to serve one another, as good stewards of God's varied grace: whoever speaks, as one who speaks oracles of God; whoever serves, as one who serves by the strength that God supplies—in order that in everything God may be glorified through Jesus Christ. To him belong glory and dominion forever and ever. Amen.

I adore the word "earnestly." Since I am a melancholic introvert with a penchant for emotional reflection, "earnestly" grabs me in ways so many other adverbs can't. It's almost as good as "deeply." The call to offer hospitality and blessing with our own individual gifts is serious business. I think the key is in the phrase *as each has received.* The word "gift" basically implies that, but that additional emphasis reminds us it was not something we were entitled to. It was given, and just as it was given, so we are to be faithful stewards of it, administering *God's varied grace.* If I were to skip the *without grumbling* section, wouldn't we be a little off the hook? But he puts that in there so we are crystal clear on the expectation of how to represent the Jesus we love. Everything we do, according to Peter, is to be done with (the very words) *oracles of God* and *the strength that God supplies*. I think this verse makes us even more conscious of the fact that we are in His image, and we represent Him as we "wear His Spirit."[54] If we respond to people in any way other than in His character, we misrepresent Him. And that is serious ground.

In this caramel mocha mishap, it's not like someone just punched my kid. That requires a bit of confrontation. But I was sitting here remembering a rather horrible statement made to me about a decade ago. The kind of thing that should stick in your head, should get in the way of your relationship, should inform you with hostility. And I got to thinking that really didn't stick with me past a few weeks or months. It's healed, gone, pretty much forgotten except for a brief flit in my head this morning. That isn't in the way of that relationship when it *should be*. It made me stop and consider that grace is like the caramel and chocolate syrup flowing together. At times, we offer another person only the caramel. Sometimes just the chocolate. But when we can let the whole caramel mocha flow, grace covers. It lets us not walk away angry from being misunderstood. It gives relationship permission to heal. It takes the chip off our shoulder. It loves with a benefit of the doubt.

That's what my Savior offers me, and I want to be His cup of caramel mocha to even the sourest apple in the cart today. Because many days I need that grace myself. And He *always* offers it. He *never* withholds. There is always extra caramel-chocolate sauce at the bottom of the cup when I hang out with Him. I should always have enough to pass on, and shame on me when I don't. Shame on me. He calls me to greater, and He equips me with His amazing Word.

"Ask, and You Shall Receive"

> Matthew 21:18-22, Apostle Matthew narrating
>
> In the morning, as he [Jesus] was returning to the city, he became hungry. And seeing a fig tree by the wayside, he went to it and found nothing on it but only leaves. And he said to it, "May no fruit ever come from you again!" And the fig tree withered at once.
>
> When the disciples saw it, they marveled, saying, "How did the fig tree wither at once?" And Jesus answered them, "Truly, I say to you, if you have faith and do not doubt, you will not only do what has been done to the fig tree, but even if you say to this mountain, 'Be taken up and thrown into the sea,' it will happen. And *whatever you ask in prayer, you will receive, if you have faith* [emphasis mine]."

Okay, true story. I could not make this stuff up. I often bring a few people in my life coffee as a blessing. It's part of my way of sharing friendship. I spent the last of my Starbucks money from Christmas on my Chickie this weekend. So, I literally said to God, just yesterday: "I want to be a good steward of our income. If You want me to keep blessing people with a cup of joe, could You please provide a sign or some Starbucks cards specifically for me?" Again, I was not asking to use them on me. I use them to treat people. Anyway, today in the mail came a Starbucks card from a Christian organization because I won their "Cup of Joy" sweepstakes I entered a while back. Yup. A relationship with Christ is *that* personal. It's not about Starbucks cards, but it does involve a Savior Who listens to the very specific prayers of our hearts. Is every prayer answered that quickly? No. But He knew I needed more Starbucks funds for tomorrow. Awesome! *You are awesome, God!*

The thing about the Matthew 21 verses is that Jesus is speaking and is very clear about wanting to have very intimate dialogue with us. He goes so far as to say we can ask amazing things, and not only is He listening, but we will receive what we pray for! I believe this is an indication of how very personal He wants to be with us, how closely we can walk with Him. I realize on the grand spectrum of life, there are greater things to ask for than Starbucks cards. But it's all about the heart behind it. I didn't want those cards so I could suck down a few extra lattes this week. I wanted them to bless His children, whether they knew Him or not. He sent some, so clearly He was good with that. I understand the greater context of these verses and that this was a demonstration of His power. But it was also a view into what He expects of us, not just the disciples. He wants us to partner with Him. Do we pray in great faith that He cares on all levels? I've prayed that prayer for other needs in my life, and when it was what He wanted for me, He provided. The hard part is letting Him lead. I'm not good at that. It requires significant amounts of trust. That's where it more or less breaks down. We need to be able to accept the answer, His leading, His yes, as well as His no.

In an earlier section of the Gospel of Matthew, as part of His well-known "Sermon on the Mount," Jesus talks about how He is found. Granted, this isn't about Starbucks cards here. It's about finding Him when we seek Him. His grace is free and available for the one who approaches Him and asks. Always an invitation. He follows it up with how much the Father in heaven *gives good things to those who ask Him.*

Matthew 7:7-12, Jesus speaking

"Ask, and it will be given to you; seek, and you will find; knock, and it will be opened to you. For everyone who asks receives, and the one who seeks finds, and to the one who knocks it will be opened. Or which one of you, if his son asks him for bread, will give him a stone? Or if he asks for a fish, will give him a serpent? If you then, who are evil, know how to give good gifts to your children, how much more will your Father who is in heaven give good things to those who ask him!

"So whatever you wish that others would do to you, do also to them, for this is the Law and the Prophets."

It is here that we see consistently, in Jesus's own words, that He's not messin' with us. He wants us to ask, to seek the good gifts of His Father, our Father, because of the complete work on the cross. If we're doing His work with what we ask, He will keep pouring out. And what about this one?

Psalm 37:3-6, King David speaking

Trust in the LORD, and do good;
   dwell in the land and befriend faithfulness.
Delight yourself in the LORD,
   and *he will give you the desires of your heart.*

Commit your way to the LORD;
   trust in him, and he will act.
He will bring forth your righteousness as the light,
   the your justice as the noonday [emphasis mine].

As I grow to better comprehend this incredibly intimate God, my prayers lately have sounded like this:

Lord, should we continue to take this many dance classes? If this is something that will glorify You in the way You created her, please help us find room in the budget.

Lord, do you want us to shrink a 30-year mortgage to a 15-year? Will You have our backs in that? Will You show us somehow what direction to take?

Lord, is this relationship one that needs to sit for a while, or would You have me act? Does it need to heal? If I need to act, please burn it on my heart.

Lord, I really want to be able to bless this person, but this fundraiser is way bigger than anything I have the skills for. Will You take the helm and lead?

Lord, should I fight this battle of my child's at school or trust the staff? What lesson should I be teaching her? Is it time to let her have her own wings here? To fall if she has to, and then get back up again?

And I find myself comforted in the waiting places where His answer isn't yet clear, by Jeremiah 33:1-3:

> The word of the LORD came to Jeremiah a second time, while he was still shut up in the court of the guard: "Thus says the LORD who made the earth, the LORD who formed it to establish it—the LORD is his name: Call to me and I will answer you, and will tell you great and hidden things that you have not known."

I want to know these things. I want to ask greater. I want to partner with

God, the only One Who can give me eyes to fully see.

Parenting in a Coffee Shop

I enjoy being in a coffee shop for various reasons: to write, read, observe people, talk to a friend, treat someone, etc. Of course, I can come up with almost any excuse to sit in one for a few hours. Really, just smelling the coffee alone calls me in like a beacon. I feel like I've finally made it to the mother ship when I smell fresh beans grinding or brewing. But some of my very best parenting moments also happen there. When a child has a particular issue to talk out, we can focus on each other better, away from home, in a different setting. If one of them has a challenging project, I will take that child for a muffin or decaf iced latte to help him focus and break down the task into smaller pieces. Several years ago, I took Chickie to a local coffeehouse to plan out her report on fairy tales. On other occasions, we have come just to de-stress and play some Skip-Bo®. During those times, the kids tend to share more of their lives with us.

When asked what she wanted for her upcoming birthday, Chickie's reply was: "A Starbucks gift card." I think my smile hit a world record. Girl after my own heart! Because the gift card doesn't only mean coffee. It means coffee in a coffee shop with Mom or Dad. It means face-to-face time. It means much more than that, really. To me, to our family, it signifies: "Mom, I want to do one of your favorite things with you. I want to be in *your* hangout. I want to come into *your* cave. I want to share that with you, not just in consuming coffee but the experience. I want to be together." Are there any better statements made to us relationally than when we find that connection with someone? That safe place?

At coffee time with Chickie, she stated: "Mom, this was very nice. I'm so glad we got to catch up with each other. We don't always have time to go into all of this at home." Aw, two coffees later, and she opened up about so much, topics that don't get covered between homework battles and activities. I love it when kids feel heard. It makes all of the difference in a childhood, no matter what issues they face along the way. It heals my heart when she can reflect back like that. In those moments, I feel like I've made a deliberate choice to hear my kids and not let my own defenses shut them down, re-parenting the little Bonnie along the way as well. I love how God does that. He makes all things new.

2 Corinthians 5:17, Apostle Paul speaking

Therefore, if anyone is in Christ, he is a new creation. The old has passed away; behold, the new has come.

This is a short verse and yet says so much. This one verse promises, that *in Christ*, we are a new creation. I love the part about *the old has passed away*! I don't know about you, but I need this every single day. I want to start fresh, feet hitting the floor each morning, knowing I can start over. And when I meet my children with a clean slate, with ears open to hear their hearts in our coffeehouse moments, I get to be new and fresh—if I choose to approach it *in Christ*. Now, this verse means that, overall, once we know and trust Christ, that is true for us, going forward, but it's also an invitation for the everyday, moment by moment. Even if I or my children somehow messed up yesterday with each other, we get to try again. I can call on Jesus to help me really do it well this time. *The new has come!* And *He* is the new that has come to us.

I truly believe these café moments are what it would look like if we pulled up a chair to His table. He invites us to be new in relationship with Him, just as we hope our children and other dear ones give us that opportunity to start fresh with them, and they with us. I think He would want to talk to us whether we are playing Skip-Bo® or working on a project or just relaxing with a chai tea latte (a new passion of mine). He loves the conversation and hearing from us, just as we cherish those moments with our own children and loved ones. Maybe we would open up more if we fully grasped that we might not have gotten yesterday right, but He still saves that seat for us. We can always be His guest at the table, when we are *in Christ* and ready to be made *a new creation*. I want my kids, and people in general, to feel that way about me, don't you? I want them to see me reflect the unconditional love of the Father. If I continue to do some of my best parenting in a coffee shop with them, I want them to see that I, too, seek the very best Parent there is and that I cherish the moments I spend actively engaged with Him, always wanting more, never wanting to leave the table or our time together.

The Latte Lady

A few years ago, while living in the tropics, I had to move across the island to a different house right around the time we were trying to decide if we were going to stay a third year. While being closer to school and town and having a great view of the ocean waves from our patio were huge pluses, the small move was almost too much on top of the stress of trying to make such a major decision. I kept asking: "God, is this Your answer? Is this Your provision for me to stay another year? Or is this simply a beautiful gift to enjoy, seeing the ocean from all of the front windows, for a few months left here?" I didn't have an automatic answer, but I knew He would answer me. I just didn't know when.

Then along came the "latte lady." She was someone with whom I did volunteer work and whom I had gotten to know a little throughout the year. She also shared my passion for top-notch espresso drinks, which were hard to come by on our tiny island. What's more, she had a super-automatic espresso machine, something I was saving up to buy by selling all of our no-longer-used goods at home. When I inquired about how it worked, I expected a brief lesson. I enjoyed a morning sitting on her beach, drinking lattes with a third friend and watching Little Man and my latte friend loading hermit crabs into his little, plastic pick-up truck. I did not expect a phone call three times a week with a made-to-order espresso drink brought across the street to my house as the kids were off to school and before my eyes fully opened to start my morning.

It seems simple enough, but her friendship in this way was so much more to me. It was a gift and a hug from the Father. It was an "It's okay to enjoy what I bless you with today. You don't always have to know about tomorrow. Enjoy today." It kept me stable during a tough time before, during, and after a major life-changing decision to return home. It was a shared interest that was allowed to blossom and bless in my last few months there. It was a smiling friend at my door with a warm mocha or caramel macchiato in the morning, which is a tough time for me anyway. Even my three year old learned to greet her, and if my older two were busy eating breakfast when the latte wagon arrived, they knew her as my latte lady. She'd come in, and we'd exchange an empty, clean cup from a few days before with a new one, filled with whatever magical concoction she created in her kitchen that morning. In my world, it was a *good and perfect gift from above*, and her hands were the ones to deliver it to me at a time I needed it most.

James 1:16-17, James, brother of Jesus, speaking

Do not be deceived, my beloved brothers. Every good gift and every perfect gift is from above, coming down from the Father of lights with whom there is no variation or shadow due to change.

It seems true that we mostly make our friendships based on common interests. One friend of mine on the island and I shared political frustrations as well as lengthy discussions about serial episodes of Lost and the older X-Files series. We could drink coffee and talk about that for hours, almost forgetting the little preschoolers playing at our feet. Another friend and I laughed about so many of the same things and enjoyed analyzing people dynamics on the island and how different people function in this tiny island world. But my latte friend brought a gift she was likely somewhat unaware of: a reminder that the Father desires to delight us and love us in *all* circumstances. I was sad to be there only a few more months to enjoy this new friendship, but I also know she came into my life at a very specific time and in a very specific way. It helped me see I can accept some things in the present and not stress about the future.

If you are a coffee or tea enthusiast, you know that a shared cup is a meeting of the minds and hearts. People bond over java like they bond over dance or a joy of music. My engineer husband bonds with his friends over tweaking existing programs to offer more. I am so grateful for my latte friend. What she brought me went beyond the caramel sauce drizzled on top or the amazing consistency of the foam. It calmed me and made me stop and smell the brew, to wonder at His creation. To be still.

Psalm 37:7a, King David speaking

Be still before the LORD and wait patiently for him.

Psalm 46:10, author unknown, but he is recording the words of God

"Be still, and know that I am God.
   I will be exalted among the nations,
   I will be exalted in the earth!"

When Our Latte Foam Just Isn't High Enough

I just overheard a very dysfunctional conversation in the public writing space I am in. Not placing judgment. It was textbook dysfunctional. So am I some days, so I get it, but here was the scene: Woman walks in and discusses, at great length, how the Lexington store gets her latte foam "yay tall" and that she is expecting the same consistency and height on the latte she is currently ordering. (I love me my perfect foam too, but I hope to be a respecter of persons first.) She then proceeds to tell a man next to her, where she chose to sit, that she expects him to turn down the app he is on. (It is notably noisy, but her way of talking to him is pretty dishonoring. He has a hearing issue, by the way.) Then she sits down with a friend and proceeds to tell her how she expects the next playdate with their kids to go. I tuned out at that point but heard something about boundaries from the other woman (good for you!).

In moments like this one, I have an overwhelming desire to walk over and hug the woman being demanding. To wash her feet as Jesus would. To hold her, rock her, and say: "It's okay. Somebody somewhere trained you to feel like you have to hold all of the balls up in the air and that if one drops a little, it's your fault. It's not your fault. Jesus wants you to relax, to know His great rest, to be peaceful, to trust Him and other people. Other people will disappoint you, but He will restore you in the places where you hurt." This time I didn't feel like that was the right approach. I have spoken at other times when I have felt God leading me. So, I quietly offered this up: *Lord, please help this woman to chillax in*

You, and if it's not me, then please bring someone else into her life to give
Your ministering touch and bring peace. Amen.

Let's look at this a little more closely. When we demand things of
others or express high levels of disapproval, what are we really saying?
Are we saying we set the bar higher than others (um, arrogance much?)?
Are we meaning to simply communicate uber-clearly (um, control
much?)? Is our intention to help that person be a better person (um, lack of
humility much?)? I think we are saying we don't trust. We don't trust
anyone but ourselves to get it all right. We don't trust that the planet will
keep spinning around the sun correctly without our input and help. What
does King David say in Psalm 8?:

> O LORD, our Lord,
>   how majestic is your name in all the earth!
> You have set your glory above the heavens.
>   Out of the mouth of babies and infants,
> you have established strength because of your foes,
>   to still the enemy and the avenger.
>
> When I look at your heavens, the work of your fingers,
>   the moon and the stars, which you have set in place,
> what is man that you are mindful of him,
>   and the son of man that you care for him?
>
> Yet you have made him a little lower than the heavenly beings
>   and crowned him with glory and honor.
> You have given him dominion over the works of your hands;
>   you have put all things under his feet,
> all sheep and oxen,
>   and also the beasts of the field,
> the birds of the heavens, and the fish of the sea,
>   whatever passes along the paths of the seas.
>
> O LORD, our Lord,
>   how majestic is your name in all the earth!

Let's go deeper still. If the height of our latte foam is one of the
many things we micro-manage, aren't we actually saying that we don't feel

that we are good enough? What about the man whose app was too loud? Yes, that has been me. I've been disgruntled with the guy next to me on an airplane who won't stop guffawing to the movie he is plugged into. But really, whether that person is clueless or not sensitive to the world around him or not, our reactions are what need to be examined. Are there gentle ways to ask someone to lower the volume? We define ourselves, sometimes very wrongly, by the dynamics that set us off. What about defining ourselves by how we can grace people? This woman was even trying to plan every possible behavior (on the part of the other woman's child, of course) on the future playdate. Why is it so important that we tell others what to do, how to act, etc.? We are afraid to be disappointed, yes. We are afraid to be hurt or have our loved ones be hurt, maybe. We are afraid if the day doesn't go a certain way, everything we measure ourselves by will fail.

But what does Jesus say? He says He will take care of us, He's got it covered, *to seek His kingdom*. I don't see anything in these verses about twitching over our coffee or what the person next to us is doing. He calls us *little flock* and tells us *not* to be afraid, that He has been pleased to give us the kingdom.

Luke 12:22-34, Luke the Physician narrating

And he said to his disciples, "Therefore I tell you, do not be anxious about your life, what you will eat, nor about your body, what you will put on. For life is more than food, and the body more than clothing. Consider the ravens: they neither sow nor reap, they have neither storehouse nor barn, and yet God feeds them. Of how much more value are you than the birds! And which of you by being anxious can add a single hour to his span of life? If then you are not able to do as small a thing as that, why are you anxious about the rest? Consider the lilies, how they grow: they neither toil nor spin, yet I tell you, even Solomon in all his glory was not arrayed like one of these. But if God so clothes the grass, which is alive in the field today, and tomorrow is thrown into the oven, how much more will he clothe you, O you of little faith! And do not seek what you are to eat and what you are to drink, nor be worried. For all the nations of the world seek after these things, and your Father knows that you need them. Instead, seek his kingdom, and these things will be added to you.

"Fear not, little flock, for it is your Father's good pleasure to give you the kingdom. Sell your possessions, and give to the needy. Provide yourselves with moneybags that do not grow old, with a treasure in the heavens that does not fail, where no thief approaches and no moth destroys. For where your treasure is, there will your heart be also."

"Good Espresso? I Certainly Wasn't Expecting That From Here"

I'm sitting at an establishment that is known for its bagels more than its coffee. I'm trying to get some work caught up. A dressed-to-the-nines man orders a bagel but starts off his comments with: "That must be a new espresso machine. I haven't seen that before." Naturally, that conversation stands my ears at attention. The kind person behind the counter offers: "Actually, we've had it the whole time I've worked here, a year and a half." (I personally happen to know that espresso has always been part of their gig, at least in recent years.) Wall Street Dude (WSD) replies: "Well, I know it's new because I've not seen it before." (Because in his world, he's always right, smarter, and never corrected. Know anyone like WSD?) She graciously blows past it. At some point, WSD starts to leave and makes a point to let her know, with Gucci on, in a loud, booming, condescending voice that echoes off the windows: "Outstanding espresso, by the way. *I certainly wasn't expecting that from here.*"

To be fair, in WSD's world, he may think he has paid the Little People a compliment they should savor for days. But for the rest of us sitting here, we are left wanting to wash his entitled, looking-down-from-on-high words out of the air and cleanse the place from top to bottom. For him, they may just seem like "the help"; he may think he should ease his conscience by throwing them a little bone once in a while. Maybe he was genuine but insensitive? I guess that's entirely possible.

Only a few minutes before WSD came in, I offered to help a staff member clean a significant spill someone made in front of me—not because I'm so awesome, but because we are the same: the one behind the counter and I. In my world, the exchange of money and service doesn't change who we are. They go home to problems and joys just like I do. It made me stop and think: Are we raising WSD attitudes or servants of our community? I'm going to share this story with my kids at the dinner table and see what they think.

But, more importantly, I'd like to consider what God thinks. In so doing, I'm not trying to draw a judgment on the servant being "poor" or WSD being "rich," only that he seemed to interact with her in a way that separated them along socioeconomic lines, or at the very least: those who serve and those who are served. After looking at Proverb 22:2 from the Old Testament, I'll end with a favorite passage of mine about Jesus. It speaks for itself about our attitudes toward one another. The Son of God washed the feet of His disciples. Nothing about His example beckons forth the put-down attitude of WSD. Jesus met His disciples right where they were: tax collectors, fishermen, etc. If only we could take on that attitude the next time we don't like the way we are served or think we have something coming simply because we are the ones paying and standing on the outside of the counter.

Proverbs 22:2, King Solomon speaking

The rich and the poor meet together; the LORD is the maker of them all.

John 13:1-17, Apostle John narrating

Now before the Feast of the Passover, when Jesus knew that his hour had come to depart out of this world to the Father, having loved his own who were in the world, he loved them to the end. During supper, when the devil had already put it into the heart of Judas Iscariot, Simon's son, to betray him, Jesus, knowing that the Father had given all things into his hands, and that he had come from God and was going back to God, rose from supper. He laid aside his outer garments, and taking a towel, tied it around his waist. Then he poured water into a basin and began to wash the disciples' feet and to wipe them with the towel that was wrapped around him. He came to Simon Peter, who said to him, "Lord, do you wash my feet?" Jesus answered him, "What I am doing you do not understand now, but afterward you will understand." Peter said to him, "You shall never wash my feet." Jesus answered him, "If I do not wash you, you have no share with me." Simon Peter said to him, "Lord, not my feet only but also my hands and my head!" Jesus said to him, "The one who has bathed does not need to wash, except for his feet, but is completely clean. And you are clean, but not every one of you." For he knew who was to betray him; that was why he said, "Not all of you are clean."

When he had washed their feet and put on his outer garments and resumed his place, he said to them, "Do you understand what I have done to you? You call me Teacher and Lord, and you are right, for so I am. If I then, your Lord and Teacher, have washed your feet, you also ought to wash one another's feet. For I have given you an example, that you also should do just as I have done to you. Truly, truly, I say to you, a servant is not greater than his master, nor is a messenger greater than the one who sent him. If you know these things, blessed are you if you do them."

Laptops and Lattes

From the ADHD section of this book:

> Like so many mornings lately, I didn't want to get out of my bed and face the heaviness in our house. I didn't want to look at dragons lashing about in the spiritual world, the devil trying to dance on my back and the backs of others. But then the author of Nehemiah spoke from the depths somewhere in my mind and heart: "Do not be grieved, for the joy of the LORD is your strength" (Nehemiah 8:10), and King Solomon declared: "The name of the LORD is a strong tower; the righteous man runs into it and is safe" (Proverbs 18:10). *I want to live in that tower right now, Lord. Thank You for fortifying it for me. Crawling in...leaving laptops and lattes behind. Just. Need. You. Amen.*

*****

If this is you at this moment, I want to encourage you. Better days are ahead. Circumstances can stay the same for a while. Sometimes change is on its way but takes some time. Please be reassured that if you are consulting God, the one true God Who sent His Son Jesus to die on the cross for all of us (and Who rose again), He is working on it. I hope you will read the appendices I have included in the back of the book. The first appendix is to acknowledge folks walking through really hard stuff and getting out to the other side—or at least being able to see Him working in their lives as they wait out a difficult season. The second appendix is to show a real example of what talking to God looks like. If you know Him, most awesome. Keep engaging in the conversation. But if you don't, start talking to Him. What can it hurt? If you're not sure He's there, what will it change? I guarantee that if you are looking for Him with your whole heart, you will find Him. Check out these promises. As surely as He gives them to me, He offers them to you, if you seek Him.

Matthew 7:7-12, Jesus speaking

"Ask, and it will be given to you; seek, and you will find; knock, and it will be opened to you. For everyone who asks receives, and the one who seeks finds, and to the one who knocks it will be opened. Or which one of you, if his son asks him for bread, will give him a stone? Or if he asks for a fish, will give him a serpent? If you then, who are evil, know how to give good gifts to your children, how much more will your Father who is in heaven give good things to those who ask him!

"So whatever you wish that others would do to you, do also to them, for this is the Law and the Prophets."

Revelation 3:20, Jesus speaking through the Apostle John

"Behold, I stand at the door and knock. If anyone hears my voice and opens the door, I will come in to him and eat with him, and he with me."

Jeremiah 33:1-3, Jeremiah the Prophet narrating

The word of the LORD came to Jeremiah a second time, while he was still shut up in the court of the guard: "Thus says the LORD who made the earth, the LORD who formed it to establish it—the LORD is his name: Call to me and I will answer you, and will tell you great and hidden things that you have not known."

Whether or not you are going through a hard time right now, it is good for all of us to stop our crazy-busy lives from time to time and put down laptops and lattes. I love them like the next gal, but we can't hear God speaking to us when we are frenzied. I hope this book was a healthy pause for you, that you found in it something that resonated with your spirit. God gave you that spirit to respond to Him. I'm so glad I responded 33 years ago. I honestly don't know how to do life without Him. I haven't done it perfectly, but His grace has me in its grasp and never lets me go. Once you believe in Him, this promise is secure for you too.

Romans 8:38-39, Apostle Paul speaking

For I am sure that neither death nor life, nor angels nor rulers, nor things present nor things to come, nor powers, nor height nor depth, nor anything else in all creation, will be able to separate us from the love of God in Christ Jesus our Lord.

Won't you check out the appendices? Hopefully they are useful tools to either encourage your walk of faith or get you started. Don't let another day go by without giving Jesus a chance. He already knows who *you* are; you just need to catch up and get to know *Him*.

Appendix 1
Heroes of My Faith

Heroes. We all have them. Sometimes they are people who have done amazing things or have overcome significant challenges. Often they are people getting through, waking up and relying on Christ afresh, waiting on answers, praying for patience. When I think of heroes, I think of the verses of Hebrews 11, where the author lists heroes of the faith, from Abraham[55] to Rahab[56] to Samson and King David. So many interesting choices in there. You know why? Because they had their own moments of failure. That's right, like you and me, they weren't perfect, not even close. When I think of heroes, I think of so many people in my life, friends and family, who are:

- Trying to raise children alone as a single parent while frequently battling with the other parent living elsewhere, or sometimes when there isn't another parent in the picture at all
- Dealing with broken marriage covenant relationships, or attempting repair before the marriage dissolves
- Battling breast cancer
- Watching a child suffer
- Braving childhood diabetes
- Working full-time jobs and also trying to care for others (children, spouses, or parents in seasons of great need)
- Facing long-term job loss and desperately seeking provision
- Caring for mentally ill family members
- Climbing out of depression
- Facing bullies, or watching their children face them
- Attempting to raise teenagers to love God and become responsible citizens of the planet
- Scaling walls to get beyond their addiction

- Learning to recognize unhealthy emotional/relational patterns in their lives and then replace them with healthy ones
- Longing to meet a future spouse
- Waiting on news of a viable pregnancy
- Wading through great, tragic loss
- Dealing with an IEP that seems to place limits on a child's future, or struggling to get the right IEP and best possible aid for a child
- Praying for healing for a family member
- Going through several iterations of a career until they find the one they are at peace with
- Hoping for justice from a system that at times fails to offer it
- Anticipating leaving the limbo they are currently in to begin the next chapter

And these are only some of the stories in my social circle. We all have them. We can all make a list a mile long. That was by no means an exhaustive list. While that focuses on friends and family walking through difficult seasons, they are just as much my heroes as the following friends and family who are:

- Accomplishing a degree
- Celebrating 30 years of marriage and still going strong
- Writing that book
- Getting an award for a beautiful piece of architecture they designed
- Heading on that missions trip
- Feeding the hungry
- Taking Operation Christmas Child boxes to the drop-off centers, or even the country!
- Marrying that person they waited for, honored God with
- Embracing parenthood for the first time
- Completing that marathon or half-marathon
- Championing a cause for social justice or a cure
- Politicking with grace
- Taking disappointments, offering them to God to change into blessings, and watching Him delight not only them, but the world, with their offering

- Getting a business off the ground, or reviving one already in existence

Whatever they do, when they do it wearing grace and humility, putting themselves second behind our amazing God Who makes it all possible, I see evidence of my beautiful Savior. And I want to emulate how they represent Him.

While much of this list has been drawn from my adult life, some of my biggest heroes are the students in our junior high Sunday School class who have honest, open conversations; wrestle well with questions of faith; admit when they don't know something; and choose to try to honor God more and more every day through their actions and attitudes at school, home, the workplace, the sports arena, etc. Last summer we worked through a fabulous book written by teens at the time of authorship, Alex and Brett Harris: *Do Hard Things: A Teenage Rebellion Against Low Expectations*.[57] These kids do hard things in great faith.

My husband and children are my heroes. They hold me to a standard, one that God designed for me to keep me safe. They try to live it out themselves, most days, and they know that prayer is the answer. Really, Jesus is. Every time.

Which brings me to my ultimate hero, a Holy Father in heaven Who thought so much of me and you and all of us (not because we earned it or are awesome on our own but because He loved us that deeply) that He offered His only Son to die for us so that we could have eternal life and relationship with Him.

John 3:16-17, Apostle John narrating

"For God so loved the world, that he gave his only Son, that whoever believes in him should not perish but have eternal life. For God did not send his Son into the world to condemn the world, but in order that the world might be saved through him."

He gave me breath, and His amazing grace is the very reason I can look up and take each new day as its own. His Son is my everything. His Holy Spirit is my Comforter and Counselor. I must seek the entire trinity of a Holy Father, Christ the Savior, and Holy Spirit to find God's purpose in each new day, and every day that I do, I experience a little piece of glory; I'm a little more excited about eternity with this God I cannot yet see. I am so incredibly grateful to hold His precious hand as I walk through this life. If you don't know Him, please consider meeting Him in both the Old and New Testaments. The Gospels of Matthew, Mark, Luke, or John can be a good place to meet Jesus in the flesh. He can hold your hand too. He can show you what you were created for, the plans and purposes He wove into YOU.

Jeremiah 33:3, the Lord speaking through Jeremiah the Prophet

"Call to me and I will answer you, and will tell you great and hidden things that you have not known."

Jeremiah 29:11-13, Jeremiah the Prophet narrating

"For I know the plans I have for you," declares the Lord, "plans for wholeness and not for evil, to give you a future and a hope. Then you will call upon me and come and pray to me, and I will hear you. You will seek me and find me, when you seek me with all your heart."

Appendix 2
How on Earth Do We Enter a Conversation With the Savior of the World?

A dear friend of mine was recently asking me how to talk to God. She doesn't have a faith background; she doesn't go to church; she doesn't (until recently) read her Bible. She wanted to start at Point A, her personal Point A. What I mean by that is that we sometimes come from traditions or organizations or denominations that say: You must do A, then B, then C, and yeah, then D, in order. I am Type A. I totally dig order. But the more I grow in Christ, the more I realize it's about simply coming to Him, period. Reading the Bible is awesome and life-giving; growth can't happen without it. The same is true of being in the fellowship of other believers in church.

But how do we help a generation of people, many of whom haven't grown up with any Jesus knowledge or context? Maybe they don't even have a Bible. One of my daughter's little friends asked one day: "Well, what is a Bible anyway?" So, yes, we have a generation coming up (I'm referring to those in their twenties, even early thirties) that has no full context. Are we seriously going to insist they come to church to meet God? Or that they read the chapter of John and then get back to us? Dear heavens, I surely hope not. My personal mission is to show them Jesus through my life, have them *taste and see* the only thing that could possibly satisfy their soul's hunger, and most importantly, start the dialogue between them and God. As I'm fond of saying: "He already knows you intimately. He's waiting for you to catch up in the relationship."

Psalm 34:8, David (not yet king) speaking

Oh, taste and see that the LORD is good! Blessed is the man who takes refuge in him!

Bible reading will hopefully come from longing for more of Him, but it can wait. So can coming to church, if that is an area of woundedness or fear for them. This generation needs to meet Jesus right where they are. We need to shake off the church burden. And that's exactly what it is. It hangs around our necks like evangelical Bible tracts. They are wonderful things in and of themselves, but the minute they become *first*, we lovers of Jesus get all squeamish and nervous and stress that our role is to get people into church. I absolutely encourage every person I introduce to Christ to come to church, whether or not he or she initially accepts Him as Savior. But I stop there. Getting someone to desire fellowship and the Lord's Word is the Holy Spirit's job. My job is to tell people about my beautiful Savior and show them His book, the Bible, that can teach them more. I do, however, ask them if they would like relevant Scripture to encourage them in the place of life circumstance that they are in. He always has a word for us. Always. This gets them interested in the Bible, a book so incredibly applicable to our lives, and it shows them I am not the source of wisdom, but rather, He is.

So, when this sweet friend asked me how to start this faith journey, I said: "Talk to Him. Tell Him stuff. You don't have to be completely sure yet. Just see if He answers." By answer, I am clear that I mean: Look for where God could be working in your life after you have had a conversation with Him, not necessarily an audible voice. I encourage the person to get the conversation started on his or her end. God is already talking; we simply need to start listening.

Sometimes I feel the very best way to have people understand what we mean by praying is to model it.[58] So, we started meeting, and she started listening to me pray. I also sent her a walkthrough of my day of what prayer can look like. Yes, there are moments when Christians spend time in prayer for a while, beseeching the Kingdom of God for this person or that person, in intercessory prayer. Sometimes we pray in groups together, adding on to each other's prayers as the Spirit leads. But to someone just starting to check Him out, the most important thing is to get her talking to God. We need to know how to be alone with God because at the end of the day, we can't piggyback our faith. It has to be ours. With the hope that it may be helpful, I include my advice here.

Okay. First, I completely understand that you've never wanted anything more in your life than _____. I know how agonizing the wait must be. I also understand you don't want to come off as bargaining with God. I encourage you to talk aloud or in your head or whatever and tell Him your honest feelings. He knows them anyway. God sent Jesus to earth to save us, but Jesus coming to earth as a man also makes it possible to have relationship with us more directly. So we wouldn't feel so alone. So we would know He too walked this earth. His Son was a living, breathing, walking man just like us but also part of God himself. He knows how we feel. He took all of that anguish on Himself on the cross. I realize not all of this is maybe absorbed yet by you or feels real. That's okay. Talking to God is like any relationship; it grows over time. I think even if you feel right now that you are talking to yourself, that's okay. Even if you don't feel that He's there or listening, your intention is to talk to Him. What I'm trying to say is don't get hung up on feeling it. Faith is a step toward something you can't see or experience directly always, but it will grow. You only need a tiny amount right now. And whether you feel it or not, He is totally tuned into you. He delights in each step you take toward knowing Him better. He already knows and loves you. He is waiting for you to catch up and know and love Him back.

I used to ask God for things all of the time. That is fine, but it seemed to be all I did. But now I thank Him when I see Him act in my life or remember how He has been faithful, and I praise/worship Him when I see Him reveal Himself—and even when I don't. My prayer life falls into several categories, but each prayer is directed at conversing openly with Him. I still ask for things, because the Bible says:

Matthew 7:7-11, Jesus speaking

"Ask, and it will be given to you; seek, and you will find; knock, and it will be opened to you. For everyone who asks receives, and the one who seeks finds, and to the one who knocks it will be opened. Or which one of you, if his son asks him for bread, will give him a stone? Or if he asks for a fish, will give him a serpent? If you then, who are evil, know how to give good gifts to your children, how much more will your Father who is in heaven give good things to those who ask him!"

If you are seeking Him, I promise you will find Him. He doesn't tease us. He promises to open the door to you. The part about evil/sinful refers to the fact we are not without sin. Christ was the only human walking the earth without sin. His point is even though we ourselves are not God and are therefore not perfectly holy in all that we do, we know how to give good gifts to our children. Even more so does God! It is an illustration of His point. He said this while walking on the earth. He wants to lavish us; we don't always get what we want exactly when we want it, but He does want to delight us and give us our heart's desire.

You can pour out your heart to Him. He wants to hear from you. He wants honesty. You can tell Him your frustrations, disappointments, struggles, anger, hopes, dreams, unmet desires, etc. He wants to know it all. I often talk to Him either out loud or in my head in the car driving somewhere, in the shower, even on the toilet. I talk to Him as if I'm not alone all day, as if He is Mark sitting right there next to me, except He's God. When I lived in Japan, it really made an impression on my host family that I don't have to go to church to talk to God. Or a shrine. They couldn't believe He'd listen to me anywhere...even in the bath! I kind of tell Him things as they come into my head. Here are some examples, and it literally goes like this. My prayers are in italics. Normal font is my daily life.

Lord, Little Man went onto the bus angry at me this morning. Please bring peace to his day. Help him to know You are with him and to look to You when he needs help.

I listen to a friend's message on voice mail.

Lord, please bless _____. Oh, God, please show Yourself real to her in every area she needs You, Lord, and help _____ to get back on track. Help me to get to _____ in Your timing and not forget to check in. Help her to see You through my friendship with her.

Clean kitchen, write an email, see a friend's prayer need. I stop and ask for that friend's need.

Insecure thought pops into my head.

Holy Spirit, I need You to flood me with peace. I block those thoughts in the name of Jesus. Speak truth into me, and block lies. I am a child of Christ.

Wash dishes.

Oh, Lord, _____ popped into my mind. You must have put her there. Please let her know how real You are. Help her to see You when You reveal Your beautiful self. Give her eyes to see You and know Your deep love for her. And a baby, Lord, that is also on my list for her still...please open that womb and create healthy life, a blessing from You. And the house, Lord, and the business, Lord...please bless her. Help my daughter's faith to grow, too, through answered prayer for _____.

Later driving on the way somewhere....Oops, almost hit that squirrel! Oh, an ambulance!

Lord, please bring healing to whoever is in that ambulance and wisdom to medical personnel and comfort to fearful family members and friends.

Oh, and friends, Lord....please help _____ to heal of that awful lung infection...thank You, Lord.

Driving along, I see beautiful leaves.

Oh, Lord, thank You for those gorgeous leaves! You painted those! It reminds me of Little Man's hair, which I love, by the way.

On my way into one of my kid's activities...

Lord, help me to be kind and always have a loving word for ____. If _____ shows up, help me to have Your words to bring her peace. Oh, and ____, Lord, she needs You still, so much. Help her to grab hold of how real You are during this storm in her life.

Overcome with a grateful heart at hearing news of answered prayer in someone's life (which happens to me several times daily):

Oh, Lord, You are so faithful and true. You defeated sickness! You breathe life! You are the great comforter and lover of my soul.

> Okay, so you get the idea. I don't pray volumes all day long, just through situations as they come up. When I pray over or with someone, it might be longer and more focused on that person (my moms' group prays together out loud for an hour every other Friday), or if I'm confessing my wrongdoings and nasty attitudes to God, then that might go on a bit, but overall most of my prayer is a thought shouted up to Him or quietly in my heart here and there between dropping the soap and shaving my legs, literally. I sometimes will find Bible verses (Psalms are great for this) that express my anguish, and I cry out to Him in moments of pain by reading His Word to Him. Sometimes I will speak His promises to Him, like I did when I asked the Lord to restore what the locusts had eaten in your life. That is from the Bible.
>
> By the way, you don't have to choose which of the three persons of God to talk to. I've learned to be specific over time, but essentially, that part doesn't matter. If your heart is aiming a prayer at God, all of Him (Father, Son, and Spirit) hear you.

*****

Starting the conversation with God is as easy as that. If you want to have a relationship with Jesus and the gift of eternal salvation, it is only a matter of telling Him that, of accepting His invitation, of confessing your need for Him and your desire to make Him Lord of your life. It's saying, essentially:

Yes, I'm a sinner in need of a Savior. Yes, I believe You, Jesus, the Son of God, died on the cross for my sins and rose again. Yes, I declare that You are sovereign Lord, my Creator, the one and only true God. Yes, I want relationship with You and the eternal salvation You bought with the price of the cross. Yes, I want to know You and follow You. Change my heart and life, oh God!

Romans 10:9-13, Apostle Paul speaking

Because, if you confess with your mouth that Jesus is Lord and believe in your heart that God raised him from the dead, you will be saved. For with the heart one believes and is justified, and with the mouth one confesses and is saved. For the Scripture says, "Everyone who believes in him will not be put to shame." For there is no distinction between Jew and Greek; for the same Lord is Lord of all, bestowing his riches on all who call on him. For "everyone who calls on the name of the Lord will be saved."

If you have done this sincerely, you belong to Him and He to you. The Holy Spirit now indwells you; you will likely start to recognize that feeling of peace, that comforting presence, that wisdom and guidance. Tell someone, get in a Bible-preaching church with other believers, and start reading His Word. You will never look back! And you will delight in the purposes He has preordained for you each and every day as you enjoy His sweet presence and company. May the Lord bless you and keep you. You're on a fabulous journey of faith! I'm so glad to have you join me there.

Book Club Discussion Questions

Part 1 Reflecting the Little Ones

1. In "What Preschool Bonnie Learned Today in Sunday School," the author states: "We made clocks with a cross that went around marking the time, reminding us that He is with us each hour of the day. There is no time when He is too busy for us." Do you think you really believe this, not just on a head level but also on a heart level? How would it change you if you greeted each day knowing that God was with you in the small and seemingly insignificant moments, as well as the bigger challenges of life?

2. The author discusses, in "Lessons From Frogger-oggy," how her child still saw his stuffed frog as "broken" even after she had made some repairs. She then connects this to how we sometimes see each other, or even ourselves, and contrasts that with how a Holy God sees us once we trust in His saving grace. If you saw yourself as He sees you, would that change how you interact with others? How would realizing how deeply known you are, by a Father Who so greatly loves you, bring you peace?

3. In "Keeping the Dreads Because That's Just How I Roll," the author talks a lot about what it means to live genuine lives by not putting on pretenses and instead unmasking ourselves so we are real and approachable to others. It's a fine balance between keeping some things private (healthy boundaries) and being someone people can relate to, a person who can offer friendship and a listening ear. Do you tend to be more private or open? In what ways do you feel challenged to adjust your relationships with others and how you share your life?

4. In "Dave, Jr.: I Once Was Lost but Now Am Found," the author recovers a lost toy and relates that to the story of the Parable of the Prodigal Son in Luke 15:11-32. She talks about what it was like to welcome him back, blemishes and all, and why her life feels lost in areas where she does not trust God. Perhaps you do not presently feel lost, but has there been a season in your life or even a current area that makes you feel like you are drifting about without an anchor? What would it look like to trust Him fully in that place? Do you believe you can be found, as Dave, Jr., and the prodigal son were?

5. In "Ninja Marshmallow and Other Brave Warriors," the author makes this statement about an art project her son was really into: "That's how I think of God: infinitely creative and imaginative, waiting to place us in some truly awesome scenarios." Do you consciously think about which scenarios could bring purpose to your life each day? Do you believe you are an active participant in most scenarios in your day? If you knew that you could effect change in your everyday world, how would that build hope and promise in your life? She talks about being willing to be "the marshmallow in His hand."

Is that something that you could easily do, or would it be a huge challenge? Why?

6. The author refers to battling evil in "Swimming With Sharks." In your own life, can you relate to feeling as though you are swimming with sharks? Do you believe in the concept of spiritual warfare? If you are a Christian believer, do you feel you are conscious of the "armor of God" and how to wear it on a daily basis? Which pieces fit more naturally, and which ones do you perhaps forget to wear?

7. Do you believe there really is a Room 9, as the author suggests in "There Are No Problems That Can't Be Solved in Room 9"? Why, or why not? How would hope be more prevalent in all areas of your life if you grasped the promises of God to live in the "shadow of His wings," as King David sang in Psalm 63? What would that even look like in the everyday?

Part 2 Dysfunction Junction, What's Your Function?

1. Judgment of others is a topic in both "Reflections on Judgment: What Side of the Whirlpool Are We Actually On?" and "Same Goal, Same God: Looking Past Differences in Parenting Styles, Even Within the Church Community." Do you know anyone, including yourself, swirling around in the whirlpool, needing some grace and help to get out? How does judgment keep them/you there, and alternatively, how does grace help them/you escape? If you are a church attendee, what would more grace in the church look like? What would the absence of grace look like? How is grace different from condoning wrong choices?

2. In "Abandonment: At Times, People Walk Away From Us, but Are We Ever Called to Do the Same?" the author discusses a passage in Matthew 10:1-15 that she feels is often misunderstood. Do you agree with her understanding of those verses? Why, or why not? What lessons can we glean from biblical promises and accounts, and Jesus Himself, about how to handle abandonment? Do you believe that relationships can be redeemed, even after much time and space? If you learned how and when to let a problem sit and ask God to create something amazing with it, could that bring more peace into your life?

3. The author discusses, in "When Our Expectations Leave No Room for Him to Bless," how setting appropriate expectations can make a difference in our viewpoint and relationships. She says that if we don't let God adjust our expectations, that can lead to disappointments and unfair assessments of others. This can set them up to fail us and place limits on what we think God can do or is already doing in our lives and relationships. Where do you struggle with expectations? What would change if you invited Him to show you the blessings He is pouring out from both expected and unexpected sources?

4. The author opens up the discussion of anxiety and fear as chains in "Free in Him: Clearing Our Attic of Anxieties and Realizing Our 'Chains' Are Just Phantoms and Lies" and then shares personal examples in her life with "Cage" and "ADHD: An Unwanted Intruder That Offered Another Opportunity for My Savior to Guide Me." Can you relate to any part of her journey? Do anxieties weigh on you, or loved ones, as if they are chains? Where can you claim more victory through trust in the powerful name of Christ? Where is it a struggle to do so? Can understanding what anxieties are really thieving from us—knowing Jesus is bigger than those anxieties—help us to walk in greater peace, even when major life tremors are still happening, and all the answers have not come in yet?

5. In the section "Feeding the Heart of the King," do you agree with the Esther principle? Why, or why not? Have you ever tried it? What changes if you take a posture of servanthood and humility when you confront something difficult? How is this different from being passive and allowing toxic behaviors to run amok? This is illustrated slightly differently in "Sweep the Floor"; what would servanthood and trusting God in the midst of tension look like in one of your everyday scenarios?

6. What did you think of the author's statement that we are all like the biblical Samson and Delilah in some way in "Samson and Delilah, the Shih Tzu Variety"? Do you relate to one of those biblical characters more than the other? Why, or why not? The author uses the analogy of a well. Is it hard not to draw from wells other than the ones God told you to draw from? What happens when you do?

7. What did you think of the author's discussion of Advent in "Dear Advent: Where Are You?" If you celebrate Advent, was this a picture of your own Advent season some years? The discussion was about more than Christmastime. Do you feel it is important to have a way of life that reflects Advent all year? Where could more peace and rest perhaps be found if you took this approach?

Part 3 When Love Stops at My Door, and His Name Is Jesus

1. In "Bus Driver Angel," "Wal-Mart Marcy," and "His Kenyan Rose," the author discusses how people are put in our path to bless and encourage us and that we, too, can do the same for someone else. Where have you seen this play out in your own life recently (either you receiving or giving a blessing)? Has anyone spoken directly into your life in a way that seems as if God placed that person there? Does that bring you comfort each day to see Him working through you and others?

2. The author mentions dead fruit being pulled off of her branches in "When the Gardener Comes: What I Want to 'Perch in My Branches'—And What I

Don't." Do you see this in your own life? What usually follows a season of pruning? Do you agree with the author that it is usually preparation for something bigger and better ahead? How does seeing the Father as the Gardener of your heart and soul change the way you think about your daily life?

3. In "God Is Dancing in the Dance Studio, and He Dances Better Than I Do," the author suggests that God doesn't just stay in a church building; He can be honored and worshipped in other places (such as a dance studio) by those who believe in Him. Do you agree? Why, or why not? What would it mean for our sense of carrying Him with us into the everyday if we didn't limit Him to Sundays or church services? It says in Leviticus 26:11-13, "I will walk among you and will be your God." Do you believe Him? In what way is that hard to grasp?

4. In "What's Your Good News?" the author mentions scenarios where people she admires still proclaim good news despite devastating loss and circumstances. Do you know people like this? How does being around that person encourage you in your faith and remind you how real God is in your daily life? How does it strengthen your understanding of Who He is when you have this perspective in the face of adversity and significant loss, or in the wake of things that simply cannot be "undone," as the author states? (The author later gives a specific example in "When Horror Comes to Town: The Boston Marathon.")

5. What do you think of coming into each situation with an open heart to serve instead of receive, as discussed in "Do We Come to Serve or to Be Served?" How does the author's initial assumption about what was going on vary from what she was able to see by the end of that observation? How would adjusted perspective and expectations give us more of a sense of purpose and awareness of blessing others? Does this mean we are always to give and never to receive? Why, or why not?

6. What picture of marriage is the author offering in "Suddenly You Find Yourself Marrying Him All Over Again" and her tribute "To Mark on the Occasion of Our 20th Wedding Anniversary"? What does the author mean when she talks about the things that war against marriages? Do you agree with this? In what ways can you better protect your marriage (if you are married) or encourage someone else in his or hers? Not everyone is married to someone who shares their faith. How could your own faith help you ward off attacks on your marriage, even when your spouse does not share that same perspective?

Part 4 Words That Bless Our Children and Knowing Who We/They Really Are

1. As mentioned in "How Do You Parent an Extrovert If You're an Introvert, and Vice Versa?" where do you see God's amazing creativity in the many

shades of introvert and extrovert that we find in our families, workplaces, churches, communities, events, etc.? Can you delight in the unique gifts that blend from one end of the spectrum to the other? How does knowing God's purpose in each unique personality help us to be more loving, honoring, and appreciative of those qualities playing a role in His plans? How does this tie in to the subject matter in "What's Really Behind the Things That Drive Us Nuts?"

2. Do you believe God is there waiting with us, as suggested in "I'm Just Going to Curl Up With You Until You're Ready"? When have you needed this the most? How would it have changed your perspective to know He was there to hear you cry out for help or talk to Him? How could you perhaps pray Psalm 23 in brand-new ways, or for the very first time? What does it mean to "take every thought captive," as in 2 Corinthians 10:5?

3. In "I'm His Bon. Oh, Yes, I Am!" the author talks about the importance of seeing ourselves as God's children, if we place our faith in Christ. If you believe in Christ, how important do you feel it is to truly understand this before trying to convey it to others? What nickname would God affectionately bestow on you? How is this intimacy with God vital to a correct understanding of who you are and how He can relate to you on all levels throughout the day?

4. How do you compare your life with that of Dave the Dolly in "Dolly in a Stinky Sack of Potatoes"? Are there places where you still believe people see your stains, or even look for them? Do you struggle not to do the same with others? How does understanding the way in which God views us prodigal children, assuming our genuine repentance, redirect us from walking in shame to walking in victory?

5. In "Life Just Bit a Big Chunk Out of Our Candle: How Do We Keep on Shining?" do you agree that we still have more than a flicker of light in us even when life has taken a "bite" out of us? Where do we go to get that source of light? Does our brokenness (imperfections, sin) have to define us? Why, or why not?

6. How does being honest about struggles with faith ultimately help us as well as others, as mentioned in "When We Need a Little Help With Our Faith"? Do you agree that no growth can happen when we don't get honest about these struggles? How can we grow stronger and learn more about God when we cry out in these moments to Him and to others walking in faith alongside us?

Part 5 Because I'm Pretty Sure Heaven Has a Jura-Capresso Machine

1. In "A Little Story: Caramel Mochas of Grace," the author offers Proverbs 10:11-14, James 1:19-21, and 1 Peter 4:8-11 as biblical examples of how to deal with difficult miscommunications and misunderstandings. She suggests we find ways to edify and bring grace to each situation based on these verses from the Bible. How could we walk in greater peace with others, even in the most unpleasant or negative of scenarios, despite their reaction, if we lived out the truth of these verses?

2. How does the discussion in "Ask, and You Shall Receive" encourage you to walk in greater faith, knowing you have a Father in heaven Who loves you and wants what is best for you? Would you ask more, talk to Him more, and dare to hope for greater things if you truly believed He was listening and wanted to bless you with good gifts? How is this different from looking at God as a supernatural "vending machine?" Under what conditions does He want to give good gifts to His children? How do we pray to that effect?

3. In "The Latte Lady," the author recounts a time in her life when God's provision, in the form of a temporary friend loving her through coffee, sustained her. How has provision come when you've needed it the most? When can we see that He loves to meet us right where we are and delight us in ways that are unique to us and that He created us to love and appreciate? How does having eyes open to appreciate and be thankful for these moments carry us through difficult times or rough days?

4. The author examines issues of trust and control in "When Our Latte Foam Just Isn't High Enough." She looks at demanding attitudes and compares them with what the Bible says. What does a demanding attitude tend to reveal about the heart? How would a biblical response, one informed by God's advice, be the remedy to this way of thinking, as evidenced by Luke 12:22-34?

5. In "Good Espresso? I Certainly Wasn't Expecting That From Here," the issue of people looking down on others, posturing themselves as superior in some way, is the author's topic. How is the biblical example of Jesus washing the feet of His disciples in complete contrast to a condescending attitude or acting as if you're better than others? How is the believer in Christ to emulate this in everyday life? How does this challenge you to be more honoring with those you find hard to respect? How would you feel if others were to treat you from a level plane instead of from a posture of "better than?"

6. In "Laptops and Lattes," the author challenges us to put down the "busy" and either begin or continue a conversation with God.[59] After sharing a moment of her own anguish, she quotes Proverbs 18:10, which describes God as a "strong tower" that the "righteous run to" and "are safe." Do you feel He is a strong tower in your life? How would life change for you, right now, in this

moment, if you knew that whatever life circumstance you face, you could run to Him, trust Him with it, and seek refuge? If you don't desire this, what is stopping you? How could life be vastly different if you could count on this forever truth?

Bibliography

Chapman, Gary D. *The 5 Love Languages: The Secret to Love that Lasts.* Chicago, IL: Northfield Publishing, 1992.

DeYoung, Kevin. *Crazy Busy: A (Mercifully) Short Book About a (Really) Big Problem.* Wheaton, IL: Crossway, 2013.

Eldredge, John, and Stasi Eldredge. *Captivating: Unveiling the Mystery of a Woman's Soul.* Nashville, TN: Thomas Nelson, 2005.

Evans, Tony. *Victory in Spiritual Warfare: Outfitting Yourself for the Battle.* Eugene, OR: Harvest House, 2011.

Fitzpatrick, Elyse M., and Dennis E. Johnson. *Counsel from the Cross: Connecting Broken People to the Love of Christ.* Wheaton, IL: Crossway, 2009.

Hallowell, Edward M., and John J. Ratey. *Driven to Distraction: Recognizing and Coping with Attention Deficit Disorder from Childhood through Adulthood.* New York, NY: Pantheon Books, 1994.

Harris, Alex, and Brett Harris. *Do Hard Things: A Teenage Rebellion Against Low Expectations.* Colorado Springs, CO: Multnomah Books, 2008.

Johnson, Bill. *Hosting the Presence: Unveiling Heaven's Agenda.* Shippensburg, PA: Destiny Image, 2012.

Keller, Timothy J. *The Prodigal God: Recovering the Heart of the Christian Faith.* New York, NY: Dutton, 2008.

McHugh, Adam S. *Introverts in the Church: Finding Our Place in an Extroverted Culture.* Downers Grove, IL: InterVarsity Press, 2009.

Miller, Paul E. *A Praying Life: Connecting with God in a Distracting World.* Colorado Springs, CO: NavPress, 2009.

Swanberg, Dennis, Diane Passno, and Walter L. Larimore. *Why A.D.H.D. Doesn't Mean Disaster.* Wheaton, IL: Tyndale House, 2003.

Voskamp, Ann. *One Thousand Gifts: A Dare to Live Fully Right Where You Are.* Grand Rapids, MI: Zondervan, 2010.

Wilkinson, Bruce. *The Dream Giver: Following Your God-Given Destiny.* Colorado Springs, CO: Multnomah, 2003.

Wing, Natasha, and Julie Durrell. *The Night Before Kindergarten*. New York, NY: Grosset & Dunlap, 2001.

Ytreeide, Arnold. *Jotham's Journey: A Storybook for Advent*. Grand Rapids, MI: Kregel Publications, 2008.

Ytreeide, Arnold. *Bartholomew's Passage: A Family Story for Advent*. Grand Rapids, MI: Kregel Publications, 2009.

Notes

[1] The term "apostle" is used to describe those in the New Testament who testified to faith in the risen Christ to spread the Good News to others. In the first century Christian church, some of these apostles had met and walked with Jesus during His years as a man on earth.

[2] We resided on Kwajalein Island (affectionately referred to as "Kwaj"), Kwajalein Atoll, Republic of the Marshall Islands. The island housed a U.S. Army installation in the South Pacific. It was approximately 3.5 miles by 0.5 mile in size, with a population of about 1,600 people on that particular island at the time.

[3] "Jacob's well was there; so Jesus, wearied as he was from his journey, was sitting beside the well. It was about the sixth hour."

[4] Eldredge, John, and Stasi Eldredge. *Captivating: Unveiling the Mystery of a Woman's Soul*. Nashville, TN: Thomas Nelson, 2005.

[5] A wonderful allegorical story about recognizing the dreams God gives us to pursue and function in our giftings and talents from Him can be found in this very fast read:

Wilkinson, Bruce. *The Dream Giver: Following Your God-Given Destiny*. Colorado Springs, CO: Multnomah, 2003.

[6] John the Baptist can be found in Matthew 3:1-6, Apostle Matthew narrating

In those days John the Baptist came preaching in the wilderness of Judea, "Repent, for the kingdom of heaven is at hand." For this is he who was spoken of by the prophet Isaiah when he said,

"The voice of one crying in the wilderness:
'Prepare the way of the Lord;
make his paths straight.'"

Now John wore a garment of camel's hair and a leather belt around his waist, and his food was locusts and wild honey. Then Jerusalem and all Judea and all the region about the Jordan were going out to him, and they were baptized by him in the river Jordan, confessing their sins.

[7] The term "prophet" is often, but not always, associated with the Old Testament writers who were given positions of authority to speak the truth of God to leaders and people during key times in biblical history, pointing to the coming Messiah (Jesus Christ) in what they recorded. They were God's messengers to communicate to the people about forthcoming judgment or deliverance. God continued to use prophets in New Testament history.

[8] This story was inspired by the Parable of the Prodigal Son in Luke 15:11-32.

And he said, "There was a man who had two sons. And the younger of them said to his father, 'Father, give me the share of property that is coming to me.' And he divided his property between them. Not many days later, the younger son gathered all he had and took a journey into a far country, and there he squandered his property in reckless living. And when he had spent everything, a severe famine arose in that country, and he began to be in need. So he went and hired himself out to one of the citizens of that country, who sent him into his fields to feed pigs. And he was longing to be fed with the pods that the pigs ate, and no one gave him anything.

"But when he came to himself, he said, 'How many of my father's hired servants have more than enough bread, but I perish here with hunger! I will arise and go to my father, and I will say to him, "Father, I have sinned against heaven and before you. I am no longer worthy to be called your son. Treat me as one of your hired servants."' And he arose and came to his father. But while he was still a long way off, his father saw him and felt compassion, and ran and embraced him and kissed him. And the son said to him, 'Father, I have sinned against heaven and before you. I am no longer worthy to be called your son.' But the father said to his servants, 'Bring quickly the best robe, and put it on him, and put a ring on his hand, and shoes on his feet. And bring the fattened calf and kill it, and let us eat and celebrate. For this my son was dead, and is alive again; he was lost, and is found.' And they began to celebrate.

"Now his older son was in the field, and as he came and drew near to the house, he heard music and dancing. And he called one of the servants and asked what these things meant. And he said to him, 'Your brother has come, and your father has killed the fattened calf, because he has received him back safe and sound.' But he was angry and refused to go in. His father came out and entreated him, but he answered his father, 'Look, these many years I have served you, and I never disobeyed your command, yet you never gave me a young goat, that I might celebrate with my friends. But when this son of yours came, who has devoured your property with prostitutes, you killed the fattened calf for him!' And he said to him, 'Son, you are always with me, and all that is mine is yours. It was fitting to celebrate and be glad, for this your brother was dead, and is alive; he was lost, and is found.'"

[9] An oversimplified definition would be the battle between good and evil that Christians can engage in with Christ's power through prayer in the name of Jesus to battle back evil. The book mentioned below is one of the best resources on spiritual warfare. It is an in-depth discussion on the subject as well as a great tutorial on how to wear each piece of the "armor of God" Scripture found in Ephesians 6.

Evans, Tony. *Victory in Spiritual Warfare: Outfitting Yourself for the Battle.* Eugene, OR: Harvest House, 2011.

[10] "My Armor Still Fits and Works in Bizarro World" offers a more thorough investigation and explanation of the armor of God of Ephesians 6.

[11] This book is a wonderful treatment of where to find God in the really raw, ugly stuff of life, especially if you're not sure you truly know Him yet. The Gospels are the best way to meet Jesus, but Voskamp's book helps expand on how to live in a place of trust and thankfulness once you've met Christ and have received His redemptive work on the cross for us.

Voskamp, Ann. *One Thousand Gifts: A Dare to Live Fully Right Where You Are.* Grand Rapids, MI: Zondervan, 2010.

[12] The authorship of Psalm 91 is not known. Some think it may have been Moses because Psalm 90 claims his authorship.

[13] A psalm of King David after he had committed adultery with another man's wife, Bathsheba (2 Samuel 11)

[14] When He responds to our prayers, He may use different people or a different approach, but what He speaks to us will never contradict the Bible. He will always remain true to Who He is. This is why it is very important to develop a prayer life that coincides with reading His Word.

[15] Tax collectors during this time were known to be very corrupt, adding fees and taking money off the top, which is why they are associated as a certain brand of sinner in the Bible.

[16] Matthew 18:1-5, Apostle Matthew narrating

At that time the disciples came to Jesus, saying, "Who is the greatest in the kingdom of heaven?" And calling to him a child, he put him in the midst of them and said, "Truly, I say to you, unless you turn and become like children, you will never enter the kingdom of heaven. Whoever humbles himself like this child is the greatest in the kingdom of heaven.

"Whoever receives one such child in my name receives me."

Matthew 19:13-15, Apostle Matthew narrating

Then children were brought to him that he might lay his hands on them and pray. The disciples rebuked the people, but Jesus said, "Let the little children come to me and do not hinder them, for to such belongs the kingdom of heaven." And he laid his hands on them and went away.

Mark 10:13-16, Apostle John-Mark narrating

And they were bringing children to him that he might touch them, and the disciples rebuked them. But when Jesus saw it, he was indignant and said to them, "Let the children come to me; do not hinder them, for to such belongs the kingdom of God. Truly, I say to you, whoever does not receive the kingdom of God like a child shall not enter it." And he took them in his arms and blessed them, laying his hands on them.

[17] Hebrews 11:1-2, author unknown, but he is recording the words of God

Now faith is the assurance of things hoped for, the conviction of things not seen. For by it the people of old received their commendation.

[18] Based on the old song "Conjunction Junction" from Schoolhouse Rock!

[19]"Nothing but the Blood," *Words and music:* Robert Lowry in *Gospel Music*, by William Doane and Robert Lowry (New York: Biglow & Main, 1876).

[20] Proverbs 1-29 are most commonly thought to be attributed to King Solomon, son of King David.

[21] Again, this is not referring to cases of abuse and harm or toxic influence. This discussion is about relational conflict without those factors.

[22] This account in the Old Testament is covered more in the "Samson and Delilah, the Shih Tzu Variety" section of this book.

23 Judges is believed to have been written by Samuel the Prophet, but it is not clear from the text.

24 The Lord warned Cain, son of Adam, in Genesis 4:6-7:

The LORD said to Cain, "Why are you angry, and why has your face fallen? If you do well, will you not be accepted? And if you do not do well, sin is crouching at the door. Its desire is for you, but you must rule over it."

And after Cain murdered Abel, his brother, the Lord punished Cain but also offered him this protection in Genesis 4:15-16:

Then the LORD said to him, "Not so! If anyone kills Cain, vengeance shall be taken on him sevenfold." And the LORD put a mark on Cain, lest any who found him should attack him. Then Cain went away from the presence of the LORD and settled in the land of Nod, east of Eden.

25 Chapman, Gary D. *The 5 Love Languages: The Secret to Love that Lasts.* Chicago, IL: Northfield Publishing, 1992.

26 When Jesus had received the sour wine, he said, "It is finished," and he bowed his head and gave up his spirit.

27 Matthew 6:10

28 Matthew 10:29-31, Jesus speaking

"Are not two sparrows sold for a penny? And not one of them will fall to the ground apart from your Father. But even the hairs of your head are all numbered. Fear not, therefore; you are of more value than many sparrows."

29 Two amazing books I have read on this subject, both with slightly different intentions:

Swanberg, Dennis, Diane Passno, and Walter L. Larimore. *Why A.D.H.D. Doesn't Mean Disaster.* Wheaton, IL: Tyndale House, 2003.

Hallowell, Edward M., and John J. Ratey. *Driven to Distraction: Recognizing and Coping with Attention Deficit Disorder from Childhood through Adulthood.* New York, NY: Pantheon Books, 1994.

[30] Luke 10:38-42, Luke the Physician narrating

Now as they went on their way, Jesus entered a village. And a woman named Martha welcomed him into her house. And she had a sister called Mary, who sat at the Lord's feet and listened to his teaching. But Martha was distracted with much serving. And she went up to him and said, "Lord, do you not care that my sister has left me to serve alone? Tell her then to help me." But the Lord answered her, "Martha, Martha, you are anxious and troubled about many things, but one thing is necessary. Mary has chosen the good portion, which will not be taken away from her."

[31] Jesus washed the feet of His disciples in a posture of servanthood. See John 13:1-17.

[32] This story can be found in Genesis 37:12-36.

[33] The Ark of the Covenant: a sacred chest containing two stone tablets inscribed with the Ten Commandments, kept in the biblical tabernacle and later in the Temple in Jerusalem. It was carried by the Hebrews during their desert wanderings. http://www.thefreedictionary.com/ark

[34] In the context of this particular biblical account, God removed the blessing of children from Michal because of her spiteful attitude. This is an example of God's punishment in the life of one person, and the reason it was so important as a consequence for Michal was because of her continued allegiance to her father's line and bitterness toward her husband David's line, which was God's choice for Israel at that time. She was unable to bear an heir to God's chosen throne. God offers different consequences to people according to His purposes and the nature of their sin, but I feel it is very important to clarify that there is no connection to infertility issues always equating to punishment from God. This was a specific situation and context.

[35] KJV. The ESV actually says: "Yet you are holy, enthroned on the praises of Israel."

[36] Refer to the section of this book entitled "Feeding the Heart of the King."

[37] For the biblical reference for the parable of the prodigal son (discussed in the sections: "Dave, Jr.: I Once Was Lost but Now Am Found" and also "Dolly in a Stinky Sack of Potatoes"), see note 8.

Below is an awesome book shedding light on this parable. It has helped me so much to understand dynamics in and perspectives of both the prodigal son and his older brother.

Keller, Timothy J. *The Prodigal God: Recovering the Heart of the Christian Faith*. New York, NY: Dutton, 2008.

[38] First discussed in "Whose Court Is the Ball in Anyway?"

[39] I am not referring to the size of a church or number of people who attend. I'm referring to personal growth only here.

[40] Judges 16:23-30, author unknown, possibly Samuel

Now the lords of the Philistines gathered to offer a great sacrifice to Dagon their god and to rejoice, and they said, "Our god has given Samson our enemy into our hand." And when the people saw him, they praised their god. For they said, "Our god has given our enemy into our hand, the ravager of our country, who has killed many of us." And when their hearts were merry, they said, "Call Samson, that he may entertain us." So they called Samson out of the prison, and he entertained them. They made him stand between the pillars. And Samson said to the young man who held him by the hand, "Let me feel the pillars on which the house rests, that I may lean against them." Now the house was full of men and women. All the lords of the Philistines were there, and on the roof there were about 3,000 men and women, who looked on while Samson entertained.

Then Samson called to the LORD and said, "O Lord GOD, please remember me and please strengthen me only this once, O God, that I may be avenged on the Philistines for my two eyes." And Samson grasped the two middle pillars on which the house rested, and he leaned his weight against them, his right hand on the one and his left hand on the other. And Samson said, "Let me die with the Philistines." Then he bowed with all his strength, and the house fell upon the lords and upon all the people who were in it. So the dead whom he killed at his death were more than those whom he had killed during his life.

[41] Ytreeide, Arnold. *Jotham's Journey: A Storybook for Advent.* Grand Rapids, MI: Kregel Publications, 2008.

Ytreeide, Arnold. *Bartholomew's Passage: A Family Story for Advent.* Grand Rapids, MI: Kregel Publications, 2009.

[42] Kevin DeYoung writes a great book on this subject.

DeYoung, Kevin. *Crazy Busy: A (Mercifully) Short Book About a (Really) Big Problem.* Wheaton, IL: Crossway, 2013.

[43] The relevant section of 1 Kings 18 can be found here in verses 41-46; this occurred right after an incident staged by Elijah where Ahab's Baal was proven to be a false god and Elijah's God (the God of Israel) proved Himself mighty and real:

And Elijah said to Ahab, "Go up, eat and drink, for there is a sound of the rushing of rain." So Ahab went up to eat and to drink. And Elijah went up to the top of Mount Carmel. And he bowed himself down on the earth and put his face between his knees. And he said to his servant, "Go up now, look toward the sea." And he went up and looked and said, "There is nothing." And he said, "Go again," seven times. And at the seventh time he said, "Behold, a little cloud like a man's hand is rising from the sea." And he said, "Go up, say to Ahab, 'Prepare your chariot and go down, lest the rain stop you.'" And in a little while the heavens grew black with clouds and wind, and there was a great rain. And Ahab rode and went to Jezreel. And the hand of the LORD was on Elijah, and he gathered up his garment and ran before Ahab to the entrance of Jezreel.

[44] Luke 23:39-43, Luke the Physician narrating

One of the criminals who were hanged railed at him, saying, "Are you not the Christ? Save yourself and us!" But the other rebuked him, saying, "Do you not fear God, since you are under the same sentence of condemnation? And we indeed justly, for we are receiving the due reward of our deeds; but this man has done nothing wrong." And he said, "Jesus, remember me when you come into your kingdom." And he said to him, "Truly, I say to you, today you will be with me in Paradise."

[45] I credit many people in my life for this idea, but Chris and Jolene DelSanto brought this idea to me tangibly during one of their visits to our home group, now His Presence Christian Fellowship, in Boston.

[46] An interesting look at the introvert/extrovert dynamic inside the church can be found in this book:

McHugh, Adam S. *Introverts in the Church: Finding Our Place in an Extroverted Culture.* Downers Grove, IL: InterVarsity Press, 2009.

[47] Exodus 4:10-17, Moses narrating

But Moses said to the LORD, "Oh, my Lord, I am not eloquent, either in the past or since you have spoken to your servant, but I am slow of speech and of tongue." Then the LORD said to him, "Who has made man's mouth? Who makes him mute, or deaf, or seeing, or blind? Is it not I, the LORD? Now therefore go, and I will be with your mouth and teach you what you shall speak." But he said, "Oh, my Lord, please send someone else." Then the anger of the LORD was kindled against Moses and he said, "Is there not Aaron, your brother, the Levite? I know that he can speak well. Behold, he is coming out to meet you, and when he sees you, he will be glad in his heart. You shall speak to him and put the words in his mouth, and I will be with your mouth and with his mouth and will teach you both what to do. He shall speak for you to the people, and he shall be your mouth, and you shall be as God to him. And take in your hand this staff, with which you shall do the signs."

[48] Refer to note 8.

[49] For further exploration of how to get people to grasp this concept, as well as many others about how God the Father sees us, consult:

Fitzpatrick, Elyse M., and Dennis E. Johnson. *Counsel from the Cross: Connecting Broken People to the Love of Christ.* Wheaton, IL: Crossway, 2009.

[50] Colossians 1:27, Apostle Paul speaking

To them God chose to make known how great among the Gentiles are the riches of the glory of this mystery, which is Christ in you, the hope of glory.

[51] Malachi 3:6, the Lord speaking through Malachi the Prophet

"For I the LORD do not change; therefore you, O children of Jacob, are not consumed."

Hebrews 13:8, author unknown, but he is recording the words of God

Jesus Christ is the same yesterday and today and forever.

James 1:17, James, brother of Jesus, speaking

Every good gift and every perfect gift is from above, coming down from the Father of lights with whom there is no variation or shadow due to change.

[52] Luke 15:3-7, Luke the Physician narrating

So he told them this parable: "What man of you, having a hundred sheep, if he has lost one of them, does not leave the ninety-nine in the open country, and go after the one that is lost, until he finds it? And when he has found it, he lays it on his shoulders, rejoicing. And when he comes home, he calls together his friends and his neighbors, saying to them, 'Rejoice with me, for I have found my sheep that was lost.' Just so, I tell you, there will be more joy in heaven over one sinner who repents than over ninety-nine righteous persons who need no repentance."

[53] Wing, Natasha, and Julie Durrell. *The Night Before Kindergarten*. New York, NY: Grosset & Dunlap, 2001.

[54] This concept was first introduced to me in similar terms in this book:

Johnson, Bill. *Hosting the Presence: Unveiling Heaven's Agenda*. Shippensburg, PA: Destiny Image, 2012.

[55] Father of many nations, as promised by God in Genesis 17

[56] The prostitute who welcomed and helped the Israelite spies in Joshua 2

[57] Harris, Alex, and Brett Harris. *Do Hard Things: A Teenage Rebellion Against Low Expectations*. Colorado Springs, CO: Multnomah Books, 2008.

[58] This book is one of the best treatments of the subject I have ever read. It explores what the Bible says about prayer and puts it in terms that are easily relatable and applicable to our lives. It breaks down common hang-ups about approaching a Holy God in conversation.

Miller, Paul E. *A Praying Life: Connecting with God in a Distracting World*. Colorado Springs, CO: NavPress, 2009.

[59] Further information on this topic can be found in the appendices.

Updates on future publications can be found in the following ways:

Twitter: @BonnieLynSmith

Facebook: http://www.facebook.com/bonnielynsmith

Espressos of Faith blog site: www.bonnielynsmith.com

Email: njos@bonnielynsmith.com

GROUND TRUTH PRESS
P.O. Box 7313
Nashua, NH 03060-7313